The Lawyer Who
Blew Up His Desk

The Lawyer Who Blew Up His Desk

and Other Tales of Legal Madness

Joseph Matthews

Ten Speed Press
Berkeley, California

"For As Long As We've Worn Our Bodies" by Flora Durham, from *Sola* (Santa Cruz, CA: Alcatraz Editions, 1980), with permission of the publisher.

"Some Days retired from the rest" by Emily Dickinson, from *The Single Hound* (Boston: Little, Brown & Co., 1914).

Ten Speed Press
Post Office Box 7123
Berkeley, California 94707
www.tenspeed.com

Distributed in Australia by Simon & Schuster Australia, in Canada by Ten Speed Press Canada, in New Zealand by Tandem Press, in South Africa by Real Books, in the United Kingdom and Europe by Airlift Books, and in Malaysia, Singapore, and Indonesia by Berkeley Books.

Cover design by Cale Burr
Text design by Jeff Brandenburg/ImageComp

Library of Congress Cataloging-in-Publication Data:

Matthews, Joseph L.
        The lawyer who blew up his desk : and other tales of legal madness
/ by Joseph Matthews.
        p.   cm.
        ISBN 0-89815-974-1 (alk. paper)
        1. Law—United States—Anecdotes.   I. Title.
K184.M38   1998
349.73—dc21   97-47373
                                                                                  CIP

First printing, 1998

Printed in Canada

2 3 4 5 6 7 8 9 10 — 02 01 00 99

For Dot

Contents

*"Tell me thy company,
and I'll tell thee what thou art."*

—CERVANTES, *Don Quixote*

*"If a man studies all his life and
then discovers he is an idiot, is he right? . . .
A man must cultivate his own nonsense,
not somebody else's."*

—HENRY MILLER, *Nexus*

Introduction

Queens, NY

A young lawyer was arrested yesterday and charged with the torture and dismembering of more than a hundred cats he had adopted over the past year through newspaper ads offering free kittens to good homes. Police were alerted by a legal secretary to whom Ronald Arbuthnot allegedly confessed his kitten murders during an attempt to enlist her help in getting him a job.

After his arrest, Arbuthnot told police he had begun his cat killings soon after being fired—for not being aggressive enough—from his first job as an apprentice trial lawyer, and that since then he had been unable to find work as a litigator.

A police search of Arbuthnot's room turned up notebooks which meticulously documented his year's development in being able to torture the kittens with diminishing hesitation or remorse. According to police, the notebooks' last entry read: "Three in one sitting today. Ronald Arbuthnot, . . . Esquire!"

Recognize Ronald?

Known a lawyer or two with something of the Arbuthnot in him?

Your spouse, perhaps? Or rather, your ex? Or maybe that old friend you just don't feel like calling anymore? And, of course, if you've ever been a client . . . .

Or is it that Ronald seems disturbingly familiar because on occasion you have glimpsed him . . . in the mirror? Having finally made it home from another head-pounding day at the Bar? Or seen him in your partners, associates—the ones you used to admire?

And even if you're not acquainted with such extremes as Ronald, you may well recognize some of the other members of the profession who inhabit these pages: the courtroom warrior who snorts ginseng to help himself "come down"; the lawyer who drops all his clients to run away with a phantom motorcycle gang; the barrister who flees in skullcap and beard to the shadow of the Wailing Wall; the lawyer who blows up his desk.

I can say with clean conscience that personally I never quite reached Ronald's state—animal abuse has never been my style. I must admit, though, that during my twenty-odd years as a trial lawyer I did on occasion tear off an arm or a leg of my own. And beat colleagues, friends, and loved ones over the head with it. Not a pretty picture. But a large part of the problem is that you don't see the picture, don't see what you're doing to yourself—to your other, better selves—and to everyone around you. No, people deep in the fractious world of courtroom law just can't see it.

But they feel it. The humans inside the lawyers. Slowly but inexorably twisted by the adversarial life, parched by the barren legal landscape, drained by failed expectations all around. Carrying on, but carrying with them a dull, relentless ache. So many on the verge of sitting down, curling up, and collapsing in on themselves.

My own odyssey through the trial lawyer life began in San Francisco at the end of the 1960s. An impressionable young man, I was emerging into adulthood neither unmoved nor unscathed by those tumultuous times, emboldened to act but deeply uncertain how or where. Then I glimpsed a small cadre of courtroom lawyers who were speaking unpleasant truths on behalf of those who most often went unheard. Performing at the point of the era's surging politics, supported by the crowd's weight yet seemingly unconstrained by its bulk. Articulating and demanding fundamental fairness. Many times besting the forces of "justice" on their own terms, and when unable, at least amplifying the voices of those the Law was taking down.

Heady stuff, these courtroom battles. And what seemed a perfect fit for someone like me, someone so thoroughly, if romantically, enraged. So, without any sense of its cost to the shape of my life, I plunged into the criminal defender ranks in the then-roiling streets around San Francisco Bay.

All too soon, though, it was the 1980s and courtrooms were being reshaped to fit the nation's new culture of vengeance. Ronald Reagan and Ed Meese. Star Wars and war on the poor. Demolishing mental health care and building prisons. The glorification of market brutality and the institution of a social determinism, which declared that whatever the less fortunate got, they deserved. The criminal law reduced to a grinding machine that both reflected and implemented the new barbarism, utterly refusing to recognize the humanity of those caught in its jaws—unless, of course, you had enough money or celebrity to grease its gears—and no longer even pretending to heed rights or rules it found inconvenient. And civil actions faring no better: legal battles becoming less and less efficacious in righting the wrongs of an increasingly venal and fractured society.

Yet despite its resurrected medievalism, criminal law still seemed to offer something apart: a continuing engagement with all classes and races, a stepping-over-lines I was unable to see anywhere else. And the criminal courtroom still a place of tremendous energy and passion: intense comradeship with the few who fought alongside; and during trial, a rush of adrenaline unmatched by any other. Where else but a criminal trial must you play each moment simultaneously to so many different audiences: witness, jury, judge; your client, his family and friends; supporting counsel and opposing D.A.; and your own buried griffins of conscience? All without a script? And with someone's life on the line?

Moreover, trial work continued to offer a place for what I still imagined to be skills of honor: quick wits and tongue; the ability to spring trip wires of emotion from the hedgerows of reasoned disputation; the capacity to call up, as needed, cunning, bluster, or charm.

For more than two decades, then, I was a courtroom lawyer. And when giving it full attention, from all reports quite a fine one. But even in the intoxicating early days I found myself unabatedly vexed, restless. I moved on, and on again, from one sort of practice to another: public defending; then a high-profile private practice with fat fee cases and headline crimes; a two-year teaching hiatus; and finally into and out of a series of small offices where I tempered the intensity of criminal work with a mix of civil litigation. With each change hoping that if I did things a bit differently, I might just find a way to get it right.

The pieces that follow form a mosaic—not just of courtroom law, but of its world and of lives within it. A world that stunts and corrodes its men and women; that feeds exactly those traits that in most of its practitioners least need to grow. A world, finally, that does so many of its denizens—and those they are close to—more harm than the good they are able to do others.

These tales, then, of what I found in that world . . . and of what, at last, I left behind.

———※◦◈———

The events described in these tales are true. However, many names, dates, places, and descriptions have been changed, identities disguised. Although truth is a defense to libel, you have to remember that many of these people are lawyers . . . .

Beside the Call of Duty

It wasn't until I had quit practicing law that I was able to begin sorting out just how and why it had been such an unhappy, unhealthy existence for me. Yet while still fully in harness I knew that things were seriously amiss, not least because the help I rendered people that felt the most certain and true seemed to involve labors to which my professional training and official duties were either irrelevant or directly opposed. The more innocent moments of extramural service ranged across such things as simply sitting in a courthouse holding cell for the longest time—repeatedly lying to the judge that I was still "conferring"—while my client who wasn't supposed to do such things did his best to stop sobbing. Or driving a thousand miles inside thirty-six hours with a prisoner's mother so she could visit him for twenty minutes before his trial and still make it back on time to her job, because the company's family emergency policy couldn't seem to make room for a son in jail.

I must admit, though, that my tramontane doings at times went considerably further, clearly crossing the line into illegality—intentional if mostly minor transgressions against the very system in which I was an "officer of the court." Disclosure of the more extreme instances will have to wait until an old man's memoirs, but my efforts for one particular client can at least serve up some examples of what I mean.

I had been vaguely aware of Augie for some time before I actually met him. For several months I'd been hearing snippets about this European mystery man who was part owner of some hip club or restaurant in London or Berlin—I wasn't sure exactly what or where. Every mention of Augie seemed to involve him flying in from somewhere or flying out to somewhere else, often taking my former girlfriend and still near–family member Susan with him. I finally met Augie, sort of, at Susan's brother's wedding when he and a squad of similarly cool international types showed up late, slouched in a corner, and left early. Over the next year or so I got to know him a bit better, though we were still far short of what could be called friends. I learned that he had sold what in fact had been only a small interest in the music club in Germany, was no longer flying off hither and yon, had taken a low-pay, long-hours job as an assistant chef, and had settled in and down with Susan. During our occasional visits, I also realized that what I had once taken for a severe case of European "attitude" was actually just a combination of natural taciturnity and a slight discomfort with English.

After a year of quiet living, Augie and Susan had saved some money and borrowed some more and with two other friends were searching for an affordable spot in which to open a little restaurant. At six o'clock on a Sunday morning, agents from Interpol and the Drug Enforcement Administration surrounded their apartment and ended the restaurant plans. Augie went quickly from not quite a friend to very much a client.

He had been arrested on a rare international warrant, issued by the German federal prosecutor's office and charging that through his former nightclub Augie had been tangentially connected to a hashish smuggling scheme. The German authorities knew that the amounts of hashish moving through the club had been small, that

Augie had long since sold his interest in the place, that since then he had barely spoken to the other people involved, and that he had not even visited Germany in over a year. Also, by then Germany was far more concerned with harder drugs than with the comparatively benign marijuana and hashish. Nonetheless, the B.K.A.—the German equivalent of a combined F.B.I. and Drug Enforcement Administration—had pressed ahead with the cumbersome process of international extradition. It seems that the smuggling scheme had included a German customs cop who was sliding the hashish through the airport right under his B.K.A. cohorts' noses. And that little wrinkle had made the B.K.A. *very* angry.

Halfway up the special elevator that goes only to the jail, the stench has already hit you: equal parts urine, disinfectant, and fear. So when the elevator finally opens, it is the wall of noise that overwhelms: heavy iron doors slamming heavy iron frames; inmates deep in the labyrinth of cells, bellowing up and down the row or howling to a deputy for another blanket or to see the medic or to have them check if they got it right that he has to wait so long to go back to court; all set against the riotous full-volume roar of the televisions, the sixteen-hour-per-day flicker and blare that helps keep the all-day-all-night-in-the-cages men at a constant manic pitch.

Cold, damp, green-walled county jail, top floor, criminal courts building, San Francisco. The Seventh Floor, as the jail is known by courthouse regulars, does not house temporary arrestees—drunk drivers, petty thieves, drug users—who are bailed out or released within a few hours or days of their arrests: those people are processed at the city jail on another floor. Nor is the Seventh Floor bothered with the middling miscreants who have been sentenced to jail terms of up to one year: a separate facility—also miserable, but at least with occasional fresh air, recreation, school programs, and face-to-face family visits—on the outskirts of the city houses them. No, the Seventh Floor is reserved for heavies and crazies: people arrested for serious crimes who, while awaiting trial, have bail so high they cannot post it or have been denied bail altogether; inmates who have been convicted and sentenced to county jail terms but are extremely violent or pose some other security risk too great to do time in the "general population" jail on the city outskirts; prisoners who are on their way to state or federal prison but who await administrative formalities; and convicts already serving prison terms who have been sent back to be tried for crimes they committed in San Francisco before having been nabbed somewhere else. Oh, yes, and a few miscellaneous federal detainees, which on this occasion included a certain German held for international extradition.

Waiting to flash my attorney card through two barred doors to the deputy who would eventually get around to answering the buzzer, I wondered how to explain the situation to Augie, as far as I understood it myself. I knew as much about the law of international extradition as the next experienced criminal lawyer, which is to say, almost nothing—the cases just rarely happened. It turned out there wasn't much to know. Since Augie was not charged with violating American law and the U.S. government was merely holding him for transfer to his country of citizenship, he had almost none of the legal protections that would apply to a U.S. citizen being extradited abroad, or to anyone charged with a crime in a U.S. court. International extradition is more a matter of state than of law; if a nonpolitical crime is covered by an extradition treaty with the nation involved—and drug offenses always are—there is virtually nothing a lawyer can do to stop it.

Through the main iron entry door and into a series of antechambers and holding cells. Then that always difficult first moment facing humans behind bars: trying not to stare at the men in the holding tank directly opposite the front desk, but refusing to look also an affront. And the deputies who know how to leave you twisting: five or six of them talking or shuffling papers, ignoring you, letting you stew—part of the ritual. Can't allow yourself to seem impatient; only makes them move slower. Long used to all this, yet once again I'm inflamed by their deep and unremitting antipathy toward anyone they view as "on the Other Side."

At last checked in, briefcase searched again (metal detector and bag inspection already at building's entrance), led to another barred door, wait . . . . Where to look? How to look? . . . and wait, until a deputy from the other side comes to unlock. Now finally, but oh-so-slowly . . . wait, he stops to check something, speaks to another guard, wait . . . until . . . at last . . . I'm through the bars and onto the interview row.

Twice a week, family and friends of Seventh Floor prisoners are allowed visits on a phone through a thick Plexiglas shield, for fifteen minutes—or less, at the whim or ire or understaffing of guards. However, prisoners have a constitutional right to the "effective" assistance of a lawyer. And so jails provide some sort of semi-private face-to-face attorney access—limited by discomfort, discourtesy, disorganization, and downright intimidation, but not quite as restricted by time or physical barrier as for non-lawyer visitors. I give Augie's name to the guard, who relays it into the bowels of the cells, then I retreat to the row of interview cubicles.

Most local criminal lawyers do their jail interviews just before or after they make a courtroom appearance downstairs for another client. This not only saves an extra trip to the building but also tends to fit better inside the jail's narrow logistic barriers. In particular, no one is allowed in during "feeding," which eliminates lunchtime visits and also makes a stop on the way home impractical, since jail dinner—serving, eating, collecting, cleaning—is 4:30 to 6:30 P.M., and visits continue to be off-limits during the hour-long prisoner "count" that follows the day's last meal. Public defenders, who do much of the interviewing, have their offices in the building and so get to the Seventh Floor during daytime hours. The interview rooms are also used during the day by parole and probation officers, as well as by local cops, the F.B.I., D.E.A., and any other agency that wants a word with a prisoner. The result of all these people squeezing into a few morning and afternoon visiting hours is that daytime interviewing is always crowded and chaotic and often either rushed or delayed. It had long been my custom, then, to see clients in the quieter evening. And as usual, on this night I was the only visitor. In order to be out of the guard's direct line of sight, I passed the first cubicle and put my briefcase in the second. Old habit. Then I stepped back into the corridor, lit the obligatory cigarette and waited some more.

Obligatory? I didn't even smoke. But the cigarette is the universal pacifier and unit of exchange in every jail and prison in the world. Even those who have never smoked are likely to become two-packers: cigarettes are the simplest and one of the only officially permitted props for coping with the infernal boredom of incarceration. And also the main objects of barter for the few other things that can improve jail's version of daily life—extra food, smuggled drugs, protection. Even the empty packets are useful: imagine how much time can be killed turning two dozen Camel packs into the interlocking folded mini-squares of a homemade, which is to say cell-made, photo frame. So, one of the first lessons a criminal lawyer learns is that even if there is little other comfort to bring a prisoner, at least come up with a pack of smokes.

The interview cubicles themselves are each about five feet by seven, just enough for a small metal table and two chairs. The door can be closed, but a small window in it allows monitoring by the guards. Claimed to be for the visitor's protection—true, not all relations between prisoners and their lawyers are wondrously harmonious—the window also allows the guards to enforce a law the encapsulated version of which is emblazoned on a large red wall sign above each interview table: "NOTICE: DO NOT GIVE *ANYTHING* TO INMATES."

Which leads to why my own cigarette was obligatory. A new pack on the table could serve as an excuse for hassles from a guard, but less so an open pack with a lawyer who was smoking. So, as a practical matter, in the interview cubicle a prisoner can smoke as many gift cigarettes as he can stand—the deputies don't stand around watching whose pack they come from. And if the lawyer brings a brand that is sold from the jail commissary cart, the prisoner can take a whole pack back to his cell and still pass muster if searched. Jail guards know well this ritual cigarette exchange and don't often expend energy trying to stop it. Nonetheless, prudence suggests observing the niceties—showing your own smoking to the guard—since just one ornery deputy can cause much more trouble than the precautions cost: harassment of the prisoner; extra searches or other barriers to the lawyer's visits; or in cases of a lawyer whom the jailers particularly detest, or of items other than cigarettes, barring the lawyer entirely from the jail, and even immediate arrest.

Augie was grateful for the smokes. We didn't say much that first visit. In general terms I told him about extradition and he quickly understood that there would be little chance to stop it. He asked me to pass some messages to Susan, including the name of a lawyer to contact in Germany who could begin the process of defending him there. Since he hadn't gone to court yet here, neither of us knew exactly how or when the extradition would proceed. And because he hadn't yet been presented with any formal papers, we didn't know any details of what he was charged with in Germany. So, there was no point in our discussing what had gone on there years before. After a few minutes I put away my notepad and got ready to go.

"Maybe I have one more cigarette," Augie said, even though he had already slipped the pack into his jail-orange jumpsuit to take back to his cell. But not going back yet to his eight-man cell was precisely the point. Although I'd given no legal help and held out little hope for any, the visit had been a great relief to him—the first time in the two days since his arrest that he had been out of the pressurized madness of the cage.

For Augie, the cell was particularly rough. Reflecting the city's diverse population, there was considerable ethnic variety in the jail. But as in all U.S. cities, the proportions widely disfavored racial minorities. Augie happened to be housed in a cell with seven black men in their teens and twenties, part of a police pogrom of the time against ghetto crack users, whose bails were too high for them to be released pending trial.

Augie's life in the cell consisted of vigilantly maintaining a front that he was a major international player. The message to his cellmates was that he had access on the outside to a lot of money—not inconsistent with still being inside; the jail grapevine informed quickly that there was no right to bail on international extradition—and to extremely dangerous people. Thus, through hope of reward or fear of retaliation on the outside, the image was intended to persuade his cellmates not to mess with this strange white guy with the funny accent. Of course, this image was also implicitly a challenge, and so from time to time Augie had to defend himself. The result was a crowded pit of raw nerves, tense as a nightmare, cold, fetid, and except for the dead of night, unbearably loud.

During the next several visits there was a bit of work to be done, helping Augie help his German lawyer with the upcoming case there. Since I wouldn't be taking any active role in that defense, though, there was no purpose in going over the fine points of potential legal strategies in Germany. So, conversation was soon reduced to the mundane—which is how things eventually got interesting.

Although I could do nothing to stop the extradition, Augie's German lawyer wanted the proceedings here to be as protracted as possible in order to give him time to prepare Augie's defense. As a consequence, I made the German prosecutor and his liaisons in the U.S. consulate in Berlin and in the local U.S. Attorney's office dot every "i" and cross every "t" in a procedure nobody knew much about, the transoceanic back-and-forth of which took up considerable time. Time Augie spent locked up on the Seventh Floor, a place not intended for long-term confinement—most prisoners are only there a matter of days or weeks before being transferred to more permanent quarters.

There was no longer anything about which I needed to consult with Augie, but since I was his only way out of the cell, I decided to visit him once in awhile. What began as an onerous, occasional good deed for a client, though, soon became a twice-weekly act of friendship, and over his four months on the Seventh Floor I wound up spending scores of hours with Augie in the tiny interview cubicles. Initially, we passed the time speaking of Susan and how she was doing, of mutual friends and mutual places (in particular Greece, where we both had traveled), of the lawyers and judges who drove me crazy, and of the cellmates who on quite another level drove him mad.

One evening Augie appeared in the interview area looking more than usually wan and pale. He told me that lately he hadn't been able to stomach the horrid jail meals and hadn't eaten at all the past few days. After a cigarette and news of Susan, we began to talk about food. It was a commonplace for prisoners to rhapsodize about the foods they missed, but rarely had they the breadth of imagination and experience of this chef, this man who had eaten well all over the world and who had professionally prepared many of the dishes he had tasted on his travels. That evening the visit passed quickly and by the time I left, Augie seemed somewhat heartened.

A few evenings later we spent a listless half-hour together, in part because Augie was still not eating much, but also because I simply wasn't able to keep up a good front every time I walked into that miserable place with nothing to offer him but my company. As we were about to part, though, I remembered that this night I had brought him a little something extra. I got up and looked out the cubicle window to make sure the guard was nowhere near, went back to the table, and told Augie to close his eyes. Taking my hand from a pocket, I twisted my fingers under his nose.

"*Knoblauch!*" he exclaimed the German word for my gift of a garlic clove.

"*Skorda,*" I beamed back the word in Greek.

From that night on, my descent down smuggling's slippery slope was a fast and perilous one. It started, as those school drug pamphlets warn, with the soft stuff: a regular supply of garlic plus a few other "pocket" spices to make Augie's food more palatable. Of course, Augie had to be careful on the way back to and in the cell. But prisoners are expert at concealing small items. And the spices created little of the inmate interest and its attendant dangers that drugs do, particularly since Augie's young cellmates had little experience of or taste for cardamom, cumin, or turmeric.

As those pamphlets say, though, it was just a matter of time until we graduated to the hard stuff. I soon realized that it would be no cause for alarm or confiscation if a search turned up a sandwich in a lawyer's briefcase; everyone knows how pressured criminal lawyers are, how often they simply don't get to eat their lunch . . . . Initially it was just simple things, but quality: Westphalia ham on Bavarian black bread; or Camembert, baguette, and fine French mustard. I would stand by the closed door to watch for an approaching guard, my open briefcase on the table strategically placed between Augie and the door while Augie chewed with back half-turned, in one hand a pen poised dissemblingly over a legal pad, sandwich in the other and ready in a flash to be dropped into a paper sack in the briefcase.

It was a visit with Susan that gave me an idea for the next stage down the road to perfidy. Sitting on their kitchen table was Augie's Walkman. This was a time before they had hit the U.S. market, and few people here even knew what they were. Augie, though, was a lover of both music and technics and had splurged at a recent audio show where the new Walkman had been displayed. On my next visit to the jail, the guard who searched my briefcase was curious about this device, but I explained it as a portable recorder I had brought to play my client some witness statements. Not so unusual, and since the guards had no right to hear our evidence, they passed through the machine and its little headphones without further ado.

I think the first tape I brought Augie was late Mozart, though it could have been early Rolling Stones, both favorites of his. Our cubicle evenings now became sensual reveries for Augie. Eyes closed, wired to the Walkman (Haydn, Charlie Parker, Van Morrison—I aimed not only for Augie's tastes but also for antidotes to the cells' noxious noise), Augie would slowly roll the sandwich of the day round his mouth, flavors linking with sounds to take him, for a time, far away. It was about then that I began to bring him visual feasts as well: color prints of Hundterwasser and Hockney; photo spreads of favorite Greek islands; glossy cookbooks; snapshots of family and friends.

The cookbooks soon began to plant bigger ideas. But progress into more complex culinary adventures would not be without its difficulties. As I became more bold, I had also to become more cunning—prosciutto and melon, you see, cannot easily be made to look like a neglected tuna sandwich. Some food I tried to deliver still warm, so now smells, too, had to be hidden, wrappings to serve as olfactory as well as visual concealment. Added courses required new and varied hiding places. Soon, though, I was able to manage quite a selection of meals, including one in particular of which I'm quite proud: fresh-cooked fettuccine with pesto kept warm and moist in two thermoses until a block from the jail, then put into sealed baggies and carefully pressed within a large stack of papers held together firmly with criss-crossed rubber bands, the top sheet of which was an official German government document stamped "Confidential—United States Department of State."

The time finally arrived when all my legal stalling tactics had been exhausted and a date was fixed for Augie's extradition to Germany. When I visited him the evening after the last court hearing, I expected to find him really down. But he wasn't. Quiet. Thoughtful. But not down. I began to apologize about not being able somehow to stop the extradition, but Augie cut me off with a smile. We had both known all along there was no way to stop it, he reminded me. But in the meantime his German lawyer had been given a chance to get Augie's defense together. Also, Augie had been able to ready himself for the pressures of the trial and for the prison time that might follow. And he had been able to talk daily on the phone with Susan so that she, too, was more prepared for the ordeal to come. Besides, Augie said, without this time on the Seventh Floor, how would he and I have become friends?

There were still three days before Augie would be picked up by the German authorities. Time for a last supper. Susan came by my place and we planned a meal from the would-be menu of the restaurant she and Augie had been about to open. The next day we did the shopping, and on the following evening carefully precut and mixed, then prepared, portioned, wrapped—no aluminum foil; it sets off the metal detector—and concealed the goods so they would still be warm when I got to the jail.

This time it was Augie who stood guard at the window while I unpacked our dinner. "Our" dinner because I thought at least on this final night we should be able to have a meal together.

The napkins and paper plates had been easy, simply pressed between documents. The tableware, though, I had to be extra careful with; until now Augie had eaten even steaks and schnitzel with his hands because getting caught bringing in even a plastic knife would be looked upon with serious disfavor. The guards were now so used to my evening visits that I didn't bother to wear lawyer clothes anymore, and an old corduroy jacket served the purpose well: the lining opened easily, and I lightly stitched two settings of plastic picnic ware along the inside seam of each sleeve.

New potatoes roasted in olive oil, rosemary, and garlic presented the next problem. If you're thinking hollowed-out books, forget it; the guards at the building entrance often did a quick flip through the pages of any books they encountered, either because the trick had appeared in too many old movies or because it was an easy way for them to seem like they were doing something. No, books were out. But while all through my youth my skinny calves had led to frequent teasing ("Hey, Wednesday legs! When's dey gonna break?"), they now did exemplary service in a pair of oversized motorcycle boots: from ankle to knee there was enough room to fit—and to walk with remarkably well—eight individually wrapped little gems of potato. Per boot.

Now came the real test. It is a long-held culinary truth that salmon poached in lemon and dill, plus asparagus tips in hollandaise, simply will not take the same beating as roast potatoes. So the boots just wouldn't do. But, among other things, trial lawyers learn how to improvise . . . .

Augie kept turning to watch me with amazement—I had to scold him several times to keep an eye on the corridor—as I stripped off jacket and sweater to reach under my shirt for the precisely-cut pieces of rubber that I had taped tightly across my upper torso. I had ransacked my house and combed the hardware stores for something firm enough to keep the salmon and asparagus from being crushed yet flexible enough not to look unnatural under my bulky clothes as I walked in and ever so carefully raised my arm to the lawyers' sign-in sheet. And as was confirmed when we slid out the goodies, not only did my choice of a cut-up hot water bottle keep the food whole, it also kept it warm. Three hollowed-out old fountain pens held just enough extra lemon-dill sauce to rechristen the salmon. And two decorative parsley stalks had stood up bravely under my lapels.

That night we left the Walkman headphones on the table so we both could listen, and though it might not normally be considered dinner music, Augie appreciated my choice of *Beggars Banquet,* even at considerably less than appropriate volume.

We had to eat quickly, of course, taking turns guarding the window. And we were both a little shaky by the time we had gulped it all down, so to calm things a bit I switched tapes to Bach's *Coffee Cantata.* Augie sat back with full stomach, grinning, and was about to light a cigarette when I told him the meal wasn't quite finished. Nothing complicated—no more room on my body—but it seemed that German chocolate cake was an appropriate dessert for this going-away party, and two pieces came through only slightly flattened in a compartment of my briefcase.

When we had swallowed the last bites and finally could relax, I brought out my camera and set it by the door, engaging the automatic timer. The photo shows two men on metal chairs, one in a frayed corduroy jacket and the other in a bright orange jumpsuit, a postprandial blush coloring slightly the weary pallor on their faces, "NOTICE: DO NOT GIVE *ANYTHING* TO INMATES" just above their heads.

Horns
and a
Tail

Flaubert might have described her as being in the August of her life. Of course, things were a little different back then. So, let's say late June, early July. At any rate, someone who had turned several folds in life's fabric. And with character fortified by the journey. I noticed her across the room, watched her during the party. I thought I saw her watching me.

From a friend I got a thumbnail sketch: former public health administrator in the Northwest; now back to school in some sort of social science; divorced, but not too recently. Being unattached myself—as I seem to have been for much of my time in practice— I prevailed on the friend to give me a casual introduction.

"You two don't know each other? This is Ellie Tolbert. New in town."

"Well, relatively. I'm only relatively new at most things."

The remark came out unaffectedly direct rather than artfully vague. And a warm smile came with it.

I didn't do a very good job suppressing a grin, but she seemed to enjoy my rather foolish expression.

"I must admit, I've been, well, noticing you."

"So I've noticed," she laughed. "Of course, it is a small party."

"So, looks like you didn't need me after all," my friend put in. "Still, it's a nice formality, an introduction. Sort of like being sworn in when you take the stand, eh, counsel?"

"Ah, yeah," I mumbled quickly. "I suppose so."

Ellie's mouth twitched but steadied. Her eyes, though, dimmed and darted for cover. However long she paused, it seemed much longer to me.

"He's a lawyer," my friend added, as if stating the now-obvious would somehow resolve Ellie's silence.

"Oh," she finally managed. "That's . . . nice."

Don't

It was the beginning of my second year in law school. Wanting to stretch my life as far beyond those walls as possible and trusting my ability to hustle up something when the time came, I took my entire semester's scholarship check and bought a car. The time came quickly: a part-time teaching assistant job barely covered my rent plus overpriced law school textbooks, but with a metabolism somewhere to the left of a barracuda, my body's demands for monstrous amounts of food remained a seriously pressing problem.

I was saved from starvation by a law professor for whom I had worked the previous summer, helping turn his tape-recorded mumbles into the minimal level of coherence required for legal academic papers. Regrettably, nothing in his current research grant required him to spend any of it on outside expenses, so he now managed to write his papers all by himself. As I lingered in his office one morning hoping at least for an invitation to lunch, the phone rang: a high-powered trial lawyer acquaintance, asking the professor if he knew a student who could help with an Italian translating project. Literal translations had already been done, the professor related after the call, but by an Italian whose English renderings the lawyer thought required considerable tightening.

My Italian proficiency reached only the menus of restaurants I couldn't afford to eat in, a point that brought me back sharply to the reason I was now in the professor's office. Well, I reported, my Italian's a little old—(two years of high school Latin, to be precise)—but I'm sure I can bring it up to date. The professor clearly wanted to do this lawyer a favor but just as clearly didn't want to be bothered with details: I'm sure you can, he said.

That afternoon I phoned the lawyer's office. After first going through a receptionist, a paralegal, a case manager, and an "associate," none of whom had any idea what I was talking about because I couldn't provide a client name or case number, I was transferred to the lawyer's personal secretary. Yes, she could set up an appointment, and asked for my "available dates." Reaching a quick compromise between a voice that reminded that you never get a job if they think you need it and a far louder cry from my stomach, I provided her with a wide range of possibilities beginning that very afternoon when, I informed her, I had had a last-minute cancellation (property law class, my almost daily personal cancellation).

Two days later, I arrived not at the office building I had anticipated but at a mammoth sort-of-Georgian residence. To my relief, I was expected: with eyes both curious and averted, a straw-haired, moon-faced young woman in designer coveralls invited me in. The vaulted entryway was dominated by an enormous tapestry the central image of which was an empty throne carried aloft by tethered birds of prey flying in futile pursuit of a lamb floating above. Whatever its provenance and aesthetic qualities, the tapestry immediately informed of a value many times my entire net worth, newly purchased car included. The young woman led me into a living room—although I felt that was probably not the word the inhabitants used—the high-fashion black and white furnishings of which distinctly spoke the word Italian.

"One moment, please," the young woman said with an accent from somewhere with long, dark winters, somewhere definitely not Italy. As she left the room, she gave me a quick and obviously disapproving once-over.

I wasn't certain which piece of furniture I was meant to sit on, so I remained standing. Fortunately, the door soon opened and Mariangela Moratti curved into the room. Smiling graciously, she introduced herself and, noting my lack of response, explained that she was the wife of Jordan Haller, the lawyer who had recruited me to translate. My confusion, however, was not entirely over her identity. Her presence had instantly heated the room, transformed it from cool Italian fashion to warm Italian style. She indicated two facing sofas: I sank clumsily into thick white cushions; she settled on the couch opposite.

It was not her husband who needed the editor, but Mariangela. "Bassani. You know Bassani?"

"Which . . . ah, one of the Bassanis?"

She sensed my stall but passed right over it: "Giorgio Bassani. The 'lost heart of Ferrara.'"

Mariangela had been born in Ferrara, she told me in an English that displayed both the thoughtfulness of a received language and the lilting inflections of her mother tongue. When she was still a small child, her family had fled the tightening fist of fascism, first to Portugal, then on to Argentina. The Ferrara of her childhood was now gone forever, she said. Not only from the passage of time but from the empty space left by those who had been torn away and had never returned. Gone forever, she repeated with softening eyes, except in the pages of Bassani.

"Oh, yes, Giorgio Bassani," I mimicked. "But . . . I don't really know his work . . . all that well."

Rather than casting a shadow, my unfamiliarity with Bassani seemed to brighten Mariangela. She rose and, begging my indulgence—"*Mi scusi, momento*"—flowed out the door.

When Mariangela had gone, I realized that I hadn't fully exhaled once since she'd entered the room. I breathed deeply now, savoring the feeling that had overwhelmed me and trying to sort out what the feeling was. Mariangela wasn't beautiful in any way I had ever responded to beauty, which is to say she was a woman—late thirties, early forties—and I was a boy who had known only girls. She also presented a number of concurrent impressions which seemed, to that particular boy, antithetical: she was rich yet genuinely friendly; grown-up yet unabashedly enthusiastic; married but undeniably sensual; neither writer nor academic yet consumed by the literary word.

And her voice. Later I was to become enchanted by Mariangela's face, the contours and movements of which revealed both the life she had lived and the life she still sought. But in this first meeting, it was her sounds that transported me. Never had I known such a voice, beginning in the belly and rolling with slight vibrato directly out from the throat. "Giorgio Bassani," she pronounced, and I was enamored of the name. "Lost heart of Ferrara," she breathed, and I too was heartsick. I had just turned twenty-three.

Mariangela returned with a book and a sheaf of papers. She pressed the copy of Bassani's *Le storie ferraresi* into my hands but could not quite let go of it, turning the pages for me and overflowing with sighs and Italian noises interspersed with sentences read out loud. Such bittersweet prose, Mariangela said, such a tragedy that it had not been translated. I understood none of the Italian, but I was certain that Bassani's words were as moving as Mariangela was moved.

In the doorway appeared a lean man of about fifty, dressed in a finely tailored gray suit, white shirt, and somber blue silk tie. He remained on the threshold, seeming not to want any of what the room had to offer. Close-cropped sandy curls had receded far back on the man's head, exaggerating the length of his angular face and giving it a look of unremitting severity. Mariangela was delighted to see him but he responded by reminding her a bit impatiently that he was home early only to take "the boys" to a basketball game. Some of Mariangela's pleasure slipped away, but she held her smile and introduced me: her husband, Jordan Haller. To this point, he had evinced no interest in my presence, but when Mariangela said I was the law student hired to help with her translations, he said, "Good, some firming up is what they need." He shook my hand, once up, once down, told Mariangela that when they got home from the game he'd have Inga put the boys to bed, and was gone.

The sheaf of papers in Mariangela's hand seemed to her suddenly to offend, dirty linen to be taken away and washed. She quickly sifted through them and handed me a portion. "Lida Mantovani," Mariangela pronounced a name I would find among the pages. "I am afraid I have not given her justice."

Two fair-haired little boys clattered into the room, nestled against Mariangela's legs and gleefully exclaimed that it was time to leave for the basketball game. The smaller boy suddenly became thoughtful and asked, "Marigi, aren't you coming with us?" but Mariangela said laughingly that this night was only for the men. She hugged the little one and he beamed again, then the two ran off toward Jordan Haller's call. Mariangela gazed after them for a moment. "My husband's," she said. "I do not have my own."

That night I looked over Mariangela's translation of the story "Lida Mantovani." Of course I wasn't able to compare it meaningfully with the Italian, but Mariangela's prose was much finer than I had been led to expect. The grammar and syntax were nearly flawless, the sentences undulating in a rhythm at the same time elegant and slightly alien, much like Mariangela's speech. With a phrase turned here and there they could be easily honed into smoother, if perhaps no longer as lyrical, English.

Whether Mariangela's version accurately reflected the tone of Bassani's original, however, was another matter. I went to the university library to find out if anything else of Bassani's had been translated, and if so, to see how his voice had been rendered in English. Mariangela had embarked on the project because Bassani in general was little known in the U.S., and this favorite book of stories in particular had not been published here. What she did not realize, though, was that under a different title—*A Prospect of Ferrara*—the stories had been translated into English and published in Britain several years before. Like a student who has found a copy of tomorrow's exam sitting unguarded on the teacher's desk, I checked out the book along with a couple of Italian-English dictionaries, slipped them under my arm, and hurried home.

After a suitable several days' delay, I phoned Mariangela and told her I had completed the first part of "Lida Mantovani." In fact all I

had done was check the literal accuracy of her version against—
and borrow here and there from—the British translation and pol-
ish up a few of the rougher Mariangelisms. She was anxious to see
the pages and asked if I could come over that evening.

When I read to Mariangela my version of the story's beginning,
she was enthralled. She could hear not only the more natural
English, she said, but also my pleasure at Bassani's work. It was my
shared enthusiasm, it seemed, that pleased her most. And her pleasure was infectious—without knowing why, I asked if she would
read the original Italian to me. To sense the story's true emotions, I
ad-libbed, and she said, "Yes, yes, absolutely, we must." She left the
room and returned with an open bottle of wine and two glasses,
then asked if I had eaten. I answered truthfully that I'd had a little
something—peanut butter and crackers, probably. Mariangela put
down the wine, grasped my hand, and said, "Come, come on,"
drawing me through the entry hall into a large, formal dining
room. Her hand was very warm.

The dining table was set for two; although it was nearing ten
o'clock, the dishes had not been used. Mariangela glanced at the
table, hesitated, then led me into the kitchen. She sat me down,
nodded in agreement with some private thought, then opened the
oven: a dizzying redolence of herbed meat and garlic surged
through the room. She took from the oven a serving platter with
four individually tied pillows of veal covered in a thick brown
sauce. "Osso buco," she named the dish, and filled a plate with two
of the veal shanks and a heap of pale yellow risotto. She led me
back to the black-and-white sitting room where she set the plate on
a polished ebony table for which food was clearly not intended,
and poured us each a glass of wine.

I ate the thick savory food, drank the heavy red wine, and
Mariangela read to me from the heart of Ferrara. As that mesmeriz-
ing voice coursed through the hills and streams of Bassani's
Italian—"*Magra, affilata, limata dall'ansia e dalle privazioni . . .*"—
I closed my eyes and was a small child again, just emerged from a
hot bath and wrapped with loving arms in a vast soft towel. When
finally I opened my eyes, I realized she had stopped reading some

time before. She was sitting quietly, looking far beyond me and relishing the spell she and Bassani had cast over the room.

Inga took care of that. From the open doorway the au pair asked whether the boys should stay up until their father got home. Mariangela wondered about the time and Inga said it was eleven. Mariangela's eyes darted around several different thoughts, then she said No, she imagined Jordan would work very late, she would be right up herself to put the boys to bed.

Back in my room, I found myself still in such a fever that I tried to read "Lida Mantovani" again in the Italian. The wine and food had been too much, though, and I fell asleep with the book on my chest. Next morning I immediately set to work transposing more of the story. It was a moody, wistful tale of a young woman escaping poverty through a grudging marriage to an upright older man. "All he need do to make his point," the British translation described the husband's tack at controlling Lida, "was occasionally to mention her restless past, and the need to redeem it by behaving better as she grew older, by living worthily, serenely." I compared it with Mariangela's version: "He had only to mention her past now and then, her restless carefree days, and how she must forever and again do penance by passing a quiet and proper existence, by becoming someone else."

I was getting paid now, the minimal hourly rate having been dictated by the husband but the number of hours reported abundantly by Mariangela. And I was getting fed: Mariangela gave me a sumptuous meal whenever we worked together and sent me off with ample provisions to keep me until our next meeting.

Not all my hours with Mariangela were spent eating and translating. We spoke of anything and everything: her sense of America and her double expatriateness as an Italian who had come of age in Argentina; the East Coast of my childhood; the world of literature; and, from Mariangela, the seasons of love. On occasion we would work on a Sunday morning when her house was empty, finishing up with a stroll through the quiet, leafy streets. More often, though, I came in the evening, after she had fed the boys and Inga had taken them upstairs. I never saw the husband.

Our work consisted of reading aloud my "translation" and discussing the changes I had made from Mariangela's version. She objected only rarely to my alterations, gently explaining why a particular word I had chosen—often one lifted from the British translation—missed the sense of Bassani's original. She never asked where I had learned my Italian and seemed to avoid putting me in the position of having to pronounce more than one word at a time. Each evening ended with Mariangela reading to me the text I was to translate next, as if I would be able to render the phrases worthily into English only if Mariangela first rolled the Italian across my neck and shoulders. On the nights we worked I would head home and get right into bed, falling asleep with the sound of Mariangela's voice still in my head.

After "Lida Mantovani" we moved on to "The Stroll before Supper." It, too, was a painful tale of mismatched marriage, of a brilliant physician whose profession was his life, wedded to a younger woman but remaining a stranger to her: "Bent over a book even while he ate, deaf to all that went on around him . . ."

The Sunday morning I arrived to begin work on the new story, Mariangela's husband was just going out. His polite hello failed to mask his choler. I went into the sitting room while he and Mariangela remained by the front door. I could make out none of their agitated words until the husband raised his voice: "For God's sake, I've got a trial! You know what it's like when I've got a trial!" There was silence, a few mumbled words, the front door opened and closed. After a few moments a visibly upset Mariangela came into the room. It was obvious that I had heard. "I am sorry," she said. "He is not like that . . . . Not truly."

We tried to work on "The Stroll before Supper" but Mariangela could not concentrate, and over certain passages she faltered: "The house never failed to remind her that those who lived in it or passed through it could not know one another, were alien to one another"; "Nothing could escape his gaze! And yet, at the same time, it almost seemed he saw nothing at all." After a short while Mariangela said she simply could not work anymore that morning.

I was relieved to escape the unhappiness in her eyes and left without setting a next meeting.

I didn't see Mariangela for a while. I had recently become apprenticed to a big-time criminal lawyer and had begun work on a high-profile homicide case. I was spending all my time doing research, interviewing witnesses, and in every way possible immersing myself in the electric world of the murder trial and its lawyers. Law school, literature, everything else paled. After several weeks, though, I found myself thinking about Mariangela more often, and more insistently. I called and apologized that my legal work had kept me from finishing the next story. Mariangela was as gracious as I had expected, though not as disappointed as I had hoped. We made an appointment, but I had to break it and it was two more weeks before we got together again. Mariangela was pleased to see me but seemed to have only slight interest in the work. I, too, easily fell off the track and instead spoke of the lawyers with whom I was working, of how drawn I was to the flame of their courtroom skills. Mariangela nodded at my breathless descriptions but said little. The following couple of meetings were more of the same: dispassionately we went over the work, Mariangela feeding me and sending in hyperbolic reports of my hours, but we took no leisurely walks, had no conversations about literature or matters of the heart.

Over the next several months I worked only sporadically on the other three stories. I would "translate" a portion of a story and mail it or drop it off at her house. We would discuss the changes only perfunctorily, sometimes just on the phone. Mariangela did not read to me: she no longer seemed to have the impulse; I no longer thought I had the time. When I had finished the final story in the collection, I called and left a message with Inga that I would put the pages in the mail. Mariangela called back and asked whether, since it was the last piece, I wouldn't bring it in person sometime and have a glass of wine. I was leaving the next day to search for a witness in another state and might be gone for a week, and by then Mariangela would have left for a month in Italy, so I agreed to come over that evening.

Mercedes and Porsches were lined up in front of the house. Inga in evening wear was surprised to see me and showed me into the black and white sitting room. The voices of a cocktail party came across the entryway from a living room I had never been in. After several minutes an elegantly dressed Mariangela came in and greeted me with lingering kisses on both cheeks. She apologized for keeping me waiting, indicating vaguely the gathering across the way, then fumbled to explain why she had not told me they were having a party: she wanted to see the work and knew I had little time and many other things to attend to; she wanted to thank me quietly, personally, for all I had done; and these were her husband's associates, not anyone I would be interested in. Yes, of course, I agreed, you're right.

On a side table she had set out a bottle of wine. She poured us each a glass and offered a toast: "To Bassani."

"*Il cuore perduto di Ferrara* [The lost heart of Ferrara]," I replied.

My bumpy Italian made us both smile and we relaxed a bit. I sat on the thick white couch; she sat opposite.

Mariangela took the final pages from me and pretended to read them but after a few moments looked up. "It starts when you are very small," she said without preface. "I can remember all those nights, lying in bed, seeing through the dark an enormous white-haired man rocking a tiny little me against his wide, wide chest . . . . You see, small girls were told that somewhere there is someone who will love her 'no matter what.'" Mariangela's gaze drifted around the room. "But the difficult part is knowing which is the 'love' . . . and which is the 'no matter what.'" Voices floated across the hall, then the doorbell rang. I could hear Inga answer it. I finished my wine.

Mariangela took my arm and we headed for the front door, pausing to peer in at the party: men in blue and gray suits, women in black dresses and pearls, all of them drinking and talking but standing quite still.

"They are nice people. Most of them very nice," Mariangela said. "This man, he helps to build a new hospital; he and my husband, they fight in court against the problems for it . . . . And that man, by the table, he has spent two years going to court against that bank. For the people who invest."

I nodded: "Yes, I'm sure."

Mariangela studied my face, then her eyes lifted over my shoulder. She stared at the tapestry with the rising lamb and throne, then slowly lowered her gaze to my face once again.

"Don't," she said quietly. "Don't do it."

I didn't give much thought to what Mariangela might have meant that night: I wasn't anything like those people, I was certain, was in no danger of becoming like them. I would practice a much different law, and for different reasons. Years later, though, after I had stopped practicing but had not yet sorted out why, I thought again of Mariangela Moratti and of that moment in the tapestried hallway. It finally occurred to me that it wasn't the aims or subjects of the law those people did that Mariangela had meant, but what the doing of it did to them, made of them. Suddenly I wanted to speak to her, to hear that voice again, so I dug out an old address book and called. A teenage boy answered the phone. When I asked for Mariangela, there was a silence. After a few moments the boy said, with difficulty, "Mariangela. She . . . doesn't live here anymore."

Natural Selection

Two men in tuxedos, leaning against the bar in an enormous ballroom, watching the antics of a formal-attire, high society scavenger hunt.

First Man: "This place is like an insane asylum."

Second Man: "Well, all you need to start an asylum is an empty room and the right kind of people."

—Morrie Ryskind, *My Man Godfrey*

Of course, I'd seen these faces before. But never so strained, so bereft of pretense, so naked in their doggedness and fear. And never so many of them. Over my last two years of law school I had attended classes with diminishing frequency and large lectures not at all, so I had almost forgotten what the species of inchoate lawyer looked like when assembled in its curious if limited varieties. And now it was 8:00 A.M. on a misty summer morning and there were hundreds of them, my peers, the men and women with whom I was to spend my days once we had passed into the hallowed profession.

That is, half of them were. For it was preordained that the other half would not pass these initiation rites, this grueling three-day marathon known as the bar exam.

In a stroke of diabolical genius, the bar examiners had chosen the cavernous marble basement of the Masonic temple as the site for this test of inculcation and will. Diabolical in that gathered here were all of the region's candidates who had elected to type, rather than handwrite, the exam: three hundred machines on wobbly metal tables set on the bare floor of a windowless marble sarcophagus. Ten rows of these narrow tables crossed the basement hall, with chairs placed close together along both sides of the tables such that examinees were forced to stare directly into the frightened eyes of their competitors.

I saw no friendly faces as I joined the crowd shuffling toward the basement entry: many from my graduating class were taking the exam nearer their homes in other cities; many more were handwriting the exam at another site; and still others were here but I had seen so little of them over the past three years that even if we might once have been casually acquainted, we were now at most vaguely familiar. Some candidates did arrive at the hall in groups: law school friends, or people who had met in an exam preparation course and had studied together daily. But as these knots of compatriots neared the exam room, their bonds began to loosen. And once inside, they looked at each other not only with a clammy recognition that all were now utterly on their own, but also with a surge of disheartening comprehension that, given the odds, the success of one might mean the failure of another.

I lugged my typewriter toward the back of the hall but found that those obsessed with having no one behind them, plus those who wished to face the rear wall and thus see as few of their fellows as possible, had already claimed all the last row seats. I settled for a forward-facing position in the penultimate row and set down my machine. Under the tables was a jerry-rigged extension cord network that criss-crossed the floor of the great hall to connect the typewriters with some power source outside. I bent down to plug in my machine, and when I rose again someone was gingerly approaching the seat across from and slightly to the left of me. He was older than the straight-through-college-into-law-school graduate, forehead furrows pushing back thin, irresolute hair to expose a broad expanse of loose skin the color and consistency of uncooked poultry. Watery, half-lidded eyes simultaneously sought and avoided mine while he hesitated behind the chair as if awaiting my permission. When I went back to my own business, he began to settle in.

It was no simple process. The typewriter he put on the table was only one of two; a manual backup machine he placed on the floor. After setting up his first machine and connecting it to the power cord, he put an attaché case on the table, turned its combination lock, and snapped it open. Despite considerable trembling, his bony half-nailed fingers managed to withdraw from the case a fistful of pens, enough typing paper for the first draft of a Russian novel, and a large stack of the standardized booklets used by those who handwrote the exam, apparently in the event that the majority of his typing fingers should somehow suddenly turn rigid and useless. I watched as he arranged paper and booklets in perfect piles, put one sheet of paper into each machine, tested both, replaced the test paper with fresh pages, put the manual machine back on the floor, tried out half of the dozen or so pens, took off his watch and placed it on the table, drew from his pocket a plastic case out of which he shook a pair of earplugs, and with still-jumping fingers laid the plugs on top of the typing paper. Then he closed his eyes, took a deep breath, sat back, opened his eyes and stared, perfectly still, at the wall behind me. I turned to see that he was fixed on a large clock: there were still thirty minutes before the exam was to begin.

I continued with my own more modest preparations and watched the hall fill with people in various states of emotional and physical readiness. In the row immediately ahead was a barrel-chested guy who appeared to be preparing for a jump from his Marine paratroop plane: snappily checking and rechecking his machine and matériel, his chair and his clothes, and ending each bit with a solid slap to the thigh. Next to him, a man who looked as if he had spent the past week on a bender—haggard, unshaven, eyes pinched and darting suspiciously, neck muscles not fully in control of his head—was searching his slept-in clothes for a pen, or for more of whatever chemical he had taken to get himself to and through this first exam morning. Two seats away sat a woman dressed more for a board meeting than for an all-day subterranean exam: tailored suit, heels, hair-knot clasped tightly by the talons of a heavy silver bird, nails neither too long for typing nor too short for success and freshly painted the same confidence-building red as her lips. Next to her, an ascetic-faced man in his forties stood behind his chair with the look of an old hand at this game (though being an old hand could only mean that his previous experiences had been failures), doing stretching exercises with annoying rhythmic grunts. And next to him, an enormous young man with a crew cut and a blank look, knees curled to his chest, head on crossed arms, massive shoulders slowly rising with breath then suddenly dropping as if in defeat.

Idling at the front of the hall were two monitors who had announced as we entered that whatever seat we took would remain the same for all three exam days—two three-hour sessions each day—and that we could therefore leave our typewriters in place at each day's end. Near the monitors was a small table with bins for our finished exam papers, and in front of the table a tall pole microphone with an oversize head, like those at which 1930s crooners were often pictured. Shortly before 9:00 A.M., three more monitors entered the hall carrying stacks of examination questions; they and the other monitors fanned out and took up positions at the midpoint of each row. Shuffling and nervous small-talk dropped to a murmur. When the monitors had set themselves and looked back expectantly at the doorway, the chief proctor made his entrance by taking two steps in and stopping. Amazing how quiet three hundred people can be.

The proctor—very short and mostly bald—waited several beats, then strode to the microphone with the posture of a man unused to having people pay attention to him and determined to make the most of it. He waited for the silence to become painful, then drew from his pocket a large stopwatch on a chain. He let it dangle, beholding it as if it contained immense and unfathomable powers, then slipped it back into his pocket. Stepping behind the microphone, he looked down at his feet, then very slowly raised his head to the waiting throng.

I can see now that all this might have worked as a melodramatic but nonetheless effective choreography intended to heighten the solemnity of the moment and to emphasize the proctor's power. Unfortunately, the mike stand had been adjusted by someone considerably taller than the proctor, so that when he raised his head toward the breathless examinees, it appeared to those sitting directly opposite that his face had been replaced in its entirety by the oversized microphone. The few of us who were still able to emit any sound at all managed a nervous giggle or two.

His voice did not improve matters. It was squealy and squawky, emerging from vintage speakers and bouncing off the marble walls in truncated high-pitched bursts as if passing through a psychedelic sound wheel. If we had difficulty listening, however, we had no trouble understanding: the exam questions were now to be handed out but no one was to break the seal until the proctor pronounced the word "Go!" There would be three compound legal problems to be addressed in separate essays during the three-hour period, each problem to receive roughly an hour's attention, though the exact division of labor was up to each examinee. We would not be hearing again from the proctor until noon when he would pronounce the word "Stop!" upon which sound we would be permitted to finish the sentence we were typing and no more; violators would be subject to "extreme" penalties. Then a final warning: though the clock on the wall might be "reasonably functional," we were not to rely on its accuracy. "This," the proctor said gravely, holding up the stopwatch again, "is the only time that matters."

The morning's questions were passed out and soon we heard "Go!" followed by the surprisingly salacious sound of three hundred paper flaps being ripped. Just as I dove into the first question, I was distracted by a twitching across the table: my well-armed but tremble-fingered neighbor couldn't get an earplug in and dropped it onto the marble floor where it bounced into the maze of chair legs and extension cords. I caught a glimpse of panic as he fell to his knees in search, but already someone across the room had struck the first keys in anger, then two and ten and twenty more joined in and I was driven back to the task at hand.

The exam was to test us in those areas the State Bar considered fundamental to the lawyer's calling: contracts; real estate; corporations; trusts; lawsuit procedure; torts; plus a token bit of constitutional and criminal law. I had just begun to sort out the first question—something about an exchange of land for oil drilling rights complicated by someone inconveniently dying (thereby making lots of well-paid work for lawyers)—when the trickle of typewriters became a rushing cascade and then a thunderous river of steel slamming onto mammoth marble boulders.

It was overwhelming. The noise not just of three hundred typewriters on wobbly metal tables but of three hundred machines on metal tables multiplied by each reverberation off the marble floor, marble walls and low marble ceiling. I couldn't focus, couldn't hear myself think. All around me were pained expressions and heads turning in desperation as if looking for escape. I glanced at my chicken-skinned neighbor: earplugs finally in place, he was straining over his exam and rapidly losing the last tinge of color from his face.

Once I began hitting my keyboard, however, I no longer heard the noise. It became simply one more ingredient in an already boiling cauldron, joining the clock, the fear of missing altogether a significant legal issue or of discussing for page after page an issue that did not exist, and the pressure of three hundred other people racing and grasping and floundering, not with you, but in a desperate struggle to put you behind them.

Every once in awhile I would raise my head to think, and in those moments the noise again became deafening, though by now I heard it as if from a listening booth—remarkable but no longer fearsome. Each time I looked up I would notice the people around me. Probably just a matter of timing, but no one else ever seemed to take a break. Not once did my pallid neighbor look up, though on the other hand I rarely saw him actually hitting the keys on his machine.

Noon, and the end of the first session, came quickly. I finished a few minutes before the hour and, unable to summon the energy for any editing, walked up and turned in my answers. Several others had already finished and lingered at the front, watching all those who continued frenetically working. There was an odd look on the faces of those who had finished early, a satisfaction in having done with it and in managing to say all they had to say within the allotted time, but stained by resentment toward those still grunting and pushing to the very last, and creased by the worry that perhaps they, too, should be typing that one thing more.

The proctor strode in and put an end to the struggle: "Stop!" he squawked into the microphone, and the speakers blared it over the tops of the still-straining heads. Most of the typewriters quieted within moments but a few tripped on for an extra sentence or two. Those who had already turned in their answers craned their necks and glared at the offending parties. The proctor barked "Now!" and the last tick-tacking trickled away.

Outside in the painful and extraneous sunlight I spotted an erstwhile law school friend I had not seen much of the past two years. He was standing with several other exam takers, a couple of whom I recognized from law school. Hungry for human contact after the morning's battering, I went over and joined them.

We were all foaming with adrenaline and doubt. Each wanted to be assured by the others that we had analyzed the questions in the same way, had spotted all the same legal issues. On the other hand, no one wanted to volunteer that one issue or another had been crucial, only to have the others look incredulous and shake their heads. So, over lunch at a nearby café we didn't so much dissect the morning's exam questions as circle round them, nipping at their heels until by acclamation we came to agreement on the legal problems each question had raised. After each such agreement, however, at least one of the group would pale and stop talking until finally, like a cageful of zoo animals who had waited too long to be fed, we all chewed our sandwiches in somber, self-absorbed, and somewhat hostile silence.

Apparently a lot of others had the same lunchtime experience, for at the convocation of the afternoon session the glaze over people's eyes had qualitatively changed: fear of the impending unknown had been replaced by anguish over the recently regretted. Thinking of the morning's legal issues they had muddled, muffed, or missed completely, and certain that few others had made the same mistakes, people took their seats determined not to be outdone again.

The second session began much like the first, except that this time my total immersion occurred within moments of opening the exam. Time and the throb of a wicked headache sailed unnoticed above me as I ground through the first two questions. I had just plotted my answer to the third when I felt, as much as heard, a new and different pounding. I raised my head and there was the paratrooper banging his fist on the next table, soon joined in the banging by the woman executive and two other people along the row. To the paratrooper's other side, the haggard, chemically-enhanced examinee jerked his head spasmodically while the battle-tested exam veteran stared straight ahead, motionless, eyes wide. The huge young guy next along the row hugged his pulled-up knees again.

Further down the row someone was on the floor, poking at the extension cords. Still banging on the table, the paratrooper began calling out, "Power! Power!" and several others joined in. Even through his earplugs my pallid tablemate now heard something amiss and turned to find the entire row behind him standing and banging and shouting. Probably not what he expected—he turned back quickly and hunched down with terrified eyes. Most people around the hall, though, could hear nothing of the commotion over the typewriter roar, and the few who noticed immediately went back to work, immensely relieved that it wasn't their row's electricity that had failed.

The executive with red nails stopped pounding and began calling out for someone "in charge." Two monitors finally headed over, but just as they reached the row, the power mysteriously returned. Happy not to have to deal with the problem, the monitors shrugged and turned away. Red-nails started after them, demanding a more satisfying response, but noticed that her row-mates were already back at their machines. Even the paratrooper, her most vociferous ally in outrage, had immediately returned to his work. She stood over him, staring down his neck, but he remained fixed on his machine and refused to look up. Lipstick chewed off in anger, the executive straightened the silver bird in her hair and grimly retook her seat.

The rest of the afternoon was uneventful. At session's end I noticed the paratrooper, the exam veteran, and several others from the troubled row seeking some sort of redress for lost time, but the proctor was unmoved. The woman with red nails approached, but instead of joining in, sneered at the group as she passed and left the hall.

Though utterly exhausted that night, I couldn't resist going over my review materials, hoping that from what had been asked the first day I could deduce what would be covered the next two. Instead, I wound up replaying my answers over and over again in my head, searching memory for colossal blunders and crucial omissions until the heat behind my eyes became unbearable and I had to close them and lie down.

I slept badly. And from the look of my fellow candidates the next morning, so had everyone else. There was even less small talk than the day before; tight-lipped and narrow-eyed, people made straight for their waiting typewriters. When I got to my seat, my pale and tremulous neighbor was already staring at the clock on the wall, paper loaded into both machines, earplugs at the ready beside a squadron of perfectly aligned pens. Behind him, the wild-eyed scruffy one, apparently having upped his dosage overnight, was squinting painfully and blinking despite the cool indirect light in the basement. Again slapping through his checklist, jaw set, the paratrooper readied for the next jump. The woman executive wore a different but equally tailored suit, nails a more courageous red than the day before and once again matched by her lips, the same heavy silver bird tightly clutching her gathered hair. And the exam veteran was again doing his stretching exercises, but perfunctorily now and without the previous day's confident grunts. As I settled in, I glanced over the rest of the hall. There was something different about the forces arrayed against the exam this morning, something weaker, thinner, but I couldn't put my finger on it. Then the exams were being passed out, I had no more time to consider, and off we went.

About an hour into the morning session it happened again. The thudding began immediately in front of me, the paratrooper, the executive, and several others pounding the table and calling out, "Power! Power!" The few other exam takers close enough to notice barely looked up, then went back at their work with increased vigor, braced by the knowledge that someone else was falling behind. "Power! We want power!" the row called out, and from down the next row came a shouted reply—"Power to the People!" A bearded guy in a T-shirt was standing with his fist raised high—"Power to the People!" he bellowed again and looked around with a fierce expression. Unable to hold it, though, after a moment he broke into a grin and sat back down to work.

The monitors fiddled with the extension cords and soon the electric flow was restored, but the red-nailed executive and two others continued to sputter and fume, demanding dispensation, reparation—I even heard the word "justice." The paratrooper, on the other hand, went right back to work, though keeping an eye out lest the monitors decide to grant concessions. The executive caught the trooper in this visual lurking, and as she stepped toward him, pointing a red-tipped finger, the monitors took the opportunity to walk away. The other aggrieved exam takers went back to their seats, leaving the older exam veteran standing by himself between the rows, unsure of what to do next. Grasping the situation quickly, red-nails waved to the exam vet to give up the fight, pointed him to his seat and returned to her own. He stared after her, but once at her typewriter she did not look up again. The old hand looked around for someone else to tell him it was all right, and when there was no one, groped to his seat. The whole thing had taken no more than a minute and a half.

Later in the morning another electrical break occurred on the opposite end of the hall, but our area made it through without further incident. Despite their loss of test time, the executive and the paratrooper each finished three or four minutes before noon. Without looking at one another but with similar self-satisfied gazes at the still-toiling masses, they took separate routes to the front table and turned in their exams. I finished a minute later and also went up front.

The proctor strode in just before the hour. He stepped to the mike, drew timepiece from pocket and let it swing ominously. At the stroke of noon, the proctor lifted his brows and opened his mouth to the enormous microphone. Only nothing happened. His eyes went wide, then he tried again, throat muscles pushing and mouth forming the word "Stop!" Standing just a few feet away, I could make out a faint croak instantly lost in the marble-echoed thunder; but those still typing couldn't hear a thing. The proctor banged on the mike, kicked the stand, and jiggled the cord, all the while mouthing, "Stop! Stop!" But nothing. Most of the three hundred had not yet finished their answers and raced on headlong, heads down, squeezing out that one more argument, those final few phrases, banging on their typewriters until that very last moment when the word would come down that they must go no further. Except, the word didn't come.

Now the proctor was frantic, again and again shouting, "Stop!" into the dead microphone, then suddenly bolting away to shout directly at the examinees in the front row. Although a few people raised their heads at this unexpected acoustic alarm, it was obvious that the proctor and the one monitor—the other had run out to find help—couldn't stop the whole hall this way, and the proctor returned, distraught, to his microphone. As soon as he had moved away, the front-row test takers took a quick look around and went back to work.

The one remaining monitor scurried around madly, on hands and knees checking the microphone lines, then following the cord outside. The proctor pinballed between shouts into the dead microphone and equally futile attempts to get the hall's attention by coming out from behind the mike and wildly waving his arms. Disney's *Fantasia*, I thought: Mickey Mouse as the sorcerer's apprentice, desperately trying to stop the unheeding animated brooms from pouring bucket after bucket of water onto the floor of the sorcerer's laboratory.

More people staggered to the front and turned in their papers, forming a now sizable audience standing and watching the comedy. But not all of them saw the humor. The paratrooper and red-nails stood a few feet apart, snarling at the front rows of examinees who continued to work. Grumbles could also be seen, if not heard, from others who had finished. Small affinity groups formed to voice complaint about all those who were getting more than the allotted time, but there was nowhere to direct their protests: the second monitor, too, had now disappeared and the proctor was nearly apoplectic.

As the extra seconds became minutes, several of those who had finished burst out of their passive frustration and began to replicate the proctor, frenetically bouncing to and fro between shouts into the dead mike and wild pinwheeling of arms. This new ring in the circus caused several other spectators to chuckle openly . . . which didn't help matters. One of the complainers turned and shouted that we had to *do* something, and when no one responded, he screamed, "But they're getting ahead of us!"

The number of complainers continued to grow, vigilantes now ready to take the law into their own hands. Several advanced on the front row and shouted into the faces of those still typing that their time was up. Other posses fanned out through the rows, screaming at people to stop and snatching papers out of typewriter rolls. Up front, red-nails was retrenching; she had grabbed the stack of papers already turned in and was feverishly searching them for her own, a task made more difficult because the papers had no names, only code numbers. Someone else noticed what she was up to, yanked part of the stack out of her hands and began his own search. Back among the rows, someone was now shaking the tables to interfere with as many typists as possible; a couple of others adopted this tactic and soon several people were running up and down the rows screaming and slamming and shaking. More test takers brought their papers to the front, though whether from completion, exhaustion, or intimidation it was impossible to tell. The exam veteran was among them, but as he neared the front table he was confronted by the paratrooper, who with several others was trying to force latecomers to put their papers into a separate, unofficial pile. His path blocked, the old hand neither tried to force his way to the official exam bin nor made any move toward the unofficial pile; this perhaps his third or fourth attempt at the Bar, he stood stock still, staring down at the papers in his hand as if he knew that turning them in or not really didn't matter.

Near my seat at the back of the hall, a confrontation was turning nasty. An early finisher had tried to grab the paper out of a still-working typewriter and the typist had sent him sprawling onto the table behind, right next to my jittery earplug neighbor. A monitor had just returned and rushed toward the combatants. The other monitor also came back in, spotted the executive and several others arguing over the stack of completed papers, and scrambled over to rescue the exams.

Suddenly a screech pierced the typewriters' roar: ". . . gonna sue you people!" A guy shaking his fist at the proctor heard his words career around the room and jumped away from the mike. The proctor realized the power was back on and started shrieking, "Stop! Stop!" The typewriters began to die out and the commotion in the rows quickly subsided. Soon all the machines had stopped but one, which ticked on feverishly near the back of the hall. But none of the recent complainers seemed bothered now, and a monitor unhurriedly made his way over and put a gentle hand on the offender—the haggard guy with the drug-narrowed eyes. When he stopped, there was a moment's collective hush as intense as had been the three hours of noise. The tailored executive ran red nails through her hair disheveled in battle, dislodging the great silver bird and sending it clanging onto the marble floor.

During the lunch hour I found a sandwich shop where there was no sign of anyone from the exam. I went to a little park nearby where I sat on and felt with my hands a patch of grass, ate my sandwich, then headed back for the afternoon session.

Ears still ringing and eyes glazed, I once again took my seat. To my relief, the trembly pale one wasn't back yet, and I didn't look up at anyone else. Extra monitors came in and took up positions, then the proctor entered, visibly shaken by the morning's madness. He gestured to the monitors to pass out the exams. I looked around: the lines of battle seemed thinner; there were gaps in rows I had thought were full. I panned across the row in front of me and saw that the huge young guy who clutched his knees wasn't there; his typewriter, too, was gone and I realized that he hadn't been there for the morning session either. A monitor reached my pallid neighbor's typewriter and paused, wondering whether to leave a copy of the exam. I nodded and the monitor put down a copy. But by then I knew that, earplugs notwithstanding, he wasn't coming back.

Coin of the Realm

Deputy District Attorney Warlow and I are in Judge Barrington's chambers before the afternoon criminal "calendar"—the schedule of court hearings—begins. Afternoons are always a gamble with Barrington, but it seems I'm lucky today: his lunchtime bourbons have masked rather than inflamed his irascible prelubricated self.

"No guarantees," Warlow says. "Plead him to one count, that's the best I can do for you."

"For me? It's not *for* me, Warlow. Somebody else involved, remember? And you know I won't plead him to the joint."

"Hey, guy's a sleazebag. Anyway, I didn't say plead him to the joint. I said plead him open. Maybe he gets county time."

The "joint" is state prison, and for my slight 19-year-old client whose only criminality is repeat drug use, it would be a dehumanizing pit of violence and sexual abuse. "County time" is up to a year in a local jail, a miserable enough experience but not necessarily a permanently crippling one. "Pleading open" means pleading guilty to a charge without knowing in advance from the judge whether the sentence will be state prison or county time. In this particular case, if I can't manage a plea bargain for my client and he goes to trial instead, he will certainly be convicted and—under the new draconian laws for "two-time losers"—is likely not only to go to prison but to get an even longer sentence there. So, I have to work out some kind of plea for him. Or else I will have done nothing at all. And the joint would probably destroy him.

"I mean," Warlow goes on, "if the presentence report comes back that he's a real sweetheart like you say, judge'll probably give him county time. Right, judge?"

Judge Barrington says nothing, keeps a straight face behind steepled fingers, but I would swear there is a smile lurking.

I look back at Warlow: "My guy just can't take that risk, can he?"

"Come on," Warlow says. "You've got to take some chances. There's no game you can play without taking chances."

"For God's sake, Warlow, what game do you . . . ?"

"Listen," the judge interrupts, speaking in a measured tone from his large leather swivel chair. "If you don't like the odds with me, how about a sure fifty-fifty?" He pulls a coin from his pocket and moves it around his fleshy fingers. "Heads, the joint; tails, county jail. Now, you can't get any fairer than that, can you?"

Mouthpiece

Dinners in the Seventh Floor jail turned out not to be the last sort-of-lawyer services I performed for my friend Augie. Eventually, the authorities in Germany recognized that he had been only peripherally involved in the hashish scheme there and released him on probation. But not before he had languished for several months on the Seventh Floor and then in German jail for another half-year. While he was held in Germany, we carried on an international postcard correspondence, the best of which was his last card to me: "Change of Address" printed across the photo of a large brick building caught in dynamited mid-collapse, with nothing more than Augie's release date handwritten on the back.

When he returned to the States to pick up the pieces of his life, we renewed our occasional dinners together, though Augie now did the cooking. By this time I had progressed from recalcitrant lawyering to none at all. But when a year later the German prosecutor's office called Augie to tell him that a magistrate would be coming to the U.S. to obtain Augie's testimony about someone else in the former smuggling scheme, it was lawyer time again.

The night before he was to testify, Augie stayed at my apartment; I pretended to counsel him that there was nothing to worry about and he pretended not to worry. Augie had been in touch with friends and lawyers in Germany who had filled him in on the situation regarding the person whom the German authorities were now pursuing, as well as on several others who might have been prosecuted but so far had not. As a condition of his probation, and before being allowed to leave Germany, Augie had already been required to give testimony. It had been an immensely delicate and stressful business, trying to implicate only himself, the customs officer, and two other defendants who had already been sentenced, without compromising anyone else. Augie had been most concerned about his boyhood friend, Bert, who had gone to jail in the U.S. for bringing a small amount of hashish into this country but who had not been tied to the nightclub scheme in Germany; if Bert were drawn into the German legal net, his punishment there as a two-time offender might be considerably more harsh than was Augie's. But Bert had not been mentioned during Augie's questioning in Germany. And Augie had managed to give evidence there that had been truthful—and accepted as such—without having implicated anyone but himself and the three others who had already been convicted and thus could no longer be damaged by it.

Now he was going to have to repeat the performance, telling the truth if not the whole truth, trying to avoid compromising this new defendant or anyone else as yet uncharged, and without contradicting his testimony of over a year before. He was still on probation in Germany, and if his new testimony was disbelieved or inconsistent with his earlier evidence, he feared the consequences. Would they revoke his probation? Even extradite him again and put him back in jail? Or when he next visited Germany, would they arrest him and hold him until he said what they wanted? Whatever the precise risks, one thing was clear: he couldn't afford to incur the German authorities' wrath by refusing to testify at all.

In the morning, we joked about my heavy-duty international lawyer outfit: double-breasted designer suit from a secondhand store, lining a bit worn but the outside still wickedly sharp; a thrift store Savile Row dress shirt (someone else's monogram hidden under the suit); and cool Italian shoes from the rummage sale at Sts. Peter & Paul Church—all recently gathered to replace the entire lawyer wardrobe I had precipitously given away the year before to punctuate my retreat from active practice. By the time we got into the car to head for the German consulate, though, the joking had stopped. In fact, we weren't saying anything at all. In addition to my worries about Augie's performance, I was grappling with anxieties of my own. Lawyers always have butterflies before important confrontations: Will the failure to spot or to understand something cause grief to the client? Will saying or doing the wrong thing spell disaster? And this time I was on my way not to court but to the German consulate—technically, not even U.S. territory—to do battle with a German judge and lawyers over events in Germany and points of German law in a legal proceeding I knew virtually nothing about, representing someone who, because he had already served his time, had few or no rights. Oh, yes—and I don't speak German.

As we approached the high-walled compound with the black and gold Deutschebund eagle perched imposingly over the courtyard, I was wondering what kind of attitude to strike. Lawyers put great stock in the first impression they make—or think they make —on other lawyers and judges. This is in great measure simple vanity, of course, but it can also be a matter of some import. If a judge or adversary perceives you as strong-willed, in command of the case's facts and applicable law, in control of your client and interested enough to give the case your full attention, you are far more likely to be given credence for your assertions and room for your maneuvering, and less likely to be hit with badgering, deceit, and undue pressure. In other words, if the lawyers and judges think you can "take it," you won't have to. Yet here was Augie walking into the maw with a lawyer who didn't know the rules and didn't even speak the language.

We intended that the prosecutor surmise from Augie's failure to have a German lawyer fly over to represent him that he could not afford to do so, which was certainly the case, confirming by this penury that Augie was well out of the smuggling business. Unfortunately, the prosecutor, the magistrate, and the defense lawyer for the new suspect would also see that without a German lawyer—or even a German-speaking one—present, Augie would be vulnerable to intimidation and manipulation. The prosecutor knew that I was the lawyer who had caused them so much trouble trying to extradite Augie two years before, but since Augie ultimately had been returned to Germany, what badge of honor was that? And the defense lawyers might know through the German grapevine that I had been the U.S. lawyer for Bert, Augie's boyhood chum, when he'd been arrested in this country bringing in a briefcase lined with hashish. I had gotten Bert quite a light sentence, better than many others might have done given the complete unavailability of any defense, but the fact was he had been convicted and sent to jail. Two skirmishes, two clients gone to jail: hardly a legal scorecard to inspire awe. Well, at least I was wearing this suit . . . .

Through high iron gates—after passing muster on the intercom—then a heavy bulletproof electric door, credentials to a guard in a bulletproof booth, two more thick electric doors, and into a large reception room. We were soon joined by some sort of underling who introduced himself to Augie politely if coolly in German, and to me with equal politesse but less cool, in part, it seemed to me, because of hesitant English. Without having premeditated doing so, I responded in an artificial barrister baritone and with more and longer words than would be easily digestible for most English-as-a-second-language speakers. The underling paused at this verbal torrent, smiled uncomfortably, and said nothing more as he led us through another series of locked doors to an interior stairway.

The Consul General's office on the top floor was huge and imposing but understated, as befit the new Germany: thick beige carpet and drapes muted the effect of stunning floor-to-ceiling windows high over San Francisco Bay. Waiting there was Wolfgang Kepler, German federal prosecutor. He unfolded his gangly, slightly rumpled figure from a chair and greeted me in the relaxed manner and quiet voice that I recalled from our one telephone conversation, and that failed to comport with my image of a representative of the notoriously persistent and unyielding German antidrug brigades. Augie had dealt with Kepler in Germany and had told me that this was always his demeanor. The reason Kepler was able to stay in such low gear, Augie had explained, was that in the German criminal law system the prosecutor was really just a middleman, an organizer of evidence gathered by the police. The more aggressive prosecutorial tasks—arguing evidence into a portrait of criminal conduct and determining the degree of culpability to be charged—were handled by the magistrate, for which a parallel figure does not exist in U.S. judicial proceedings. The German magistrate takes statements from defendants, conducts primary examination of witnesses, and presides over all preliminary hearings, which includes ruling on the propriety of defense lawyers' questions and the sufficiency of their arguments. Finally, it is the magistrate's detailed statement of allegations against which the accused must defend himself at trial. The prosecutor merely stokes the accusatory engine; it is the magistrate who drives the train.

Lawyerly instinct is to do all the talking, in part because lawyers love to hear their own voices, but more important, to act as buffer for the client. Particularly in criminal cases, it is crucial that the lawyer, whose words cannot be used against his client, speak in place of the client, whose words can and will. Before all criminal law appearances I always gave my clients a prep-and-pep talk, the gist of which was that once we were in court they were to keep their mouths shut unless I told them to open, and that once opened, they should be ready to slam shut again if I so much as looked at them funny. But on this morning it was Augie who would be asked to do the talking. In German. And I would just have to take a backseat. Yet when Kepler greeted Augie, and Augie with obvious nerves only nodded in return, there I was leaping mouth-first into the fray. Conscious of Kepler's second language limits, I began a stream of slangy small talk about his journey over and his stay. Being addressed in English, he answered in kind, with slight falterings at which I was able to interject a word or two of the most friendly assistance.

Watching all this was not one magistrate but two. In a large, soft easy chair—beige, like everything else—was Herr Klompertz, a heavily jowled man in his fifties, pale behind the kind of tinted glasses that protect sensitive eyes, a face more wearily serious than severe. Severe was sitting next to him: Frau Lichter looked as if she hadn't unwrinkled her brow since the day she'd become a magistrate—maybe a lot longer. Her forty-or-so years were dressed in what at first seemed Lutheran black and white; when she stood up, though, I saw that the black skirt was short, tight, and leather, the black stockings sheer and seamed. The two magistrates had not stirred when we first came in; they got up only when Kepler introduced us. I immediately began a rapid nattering English but they showed no expression and offered no replies. Over their shoulders the huge glass wall framed the Bay and the Golden Gate. "Beautiful city, don't you think?" I gestured proprietarily. There was nothing for them but to agree, however tersely, in English. I exhaled deeply and continued to stare out the window, trying to make the message clear: their consulate, yes; but *my* city.

Through a different door came an elderly man whose uncertain gait and rough-edged exterior spoke not so much of his many years in the foreign service as of the subordinate ranks in which he had spent all of them. Like something out of *Grimm's Fairy Tales*, the Assistant Consul for Administrative Affairs had a shock of white hair and thick glasses that wildly magnified his yellowed blue eyes. He wore a shiny green suit two sizes too large, a wide floral tie from somewhere around 1950 and, most incongruous to both outfit and occasion but somehow seeming appropriate to the man, a hand-knit leather-buttoned Tyrolean vest with five or six pastel flowers not woven into the wool but added on, as if at one point over the vest's fifty-odd years someone had decided that fashion required a somewhat bolder statement. Herr Doktor Flink moved over on spongy shoes, leaned close, and offered a hand. As I grasped it, I did my best not to stare at the profusion of crooked, tobacco-stained teeth uncovered by his squinting effort to see me clearly.

Neither magistrates nor prosecutor paid heed to the old man's entrance. They had certainly met earlier, but there was more to their neglect than mere familiarity. Clearly, for them Herr Flink just didn't count for much: to hold such a tertiary post at his age could mean only that instead of making normal progress up the foreign service hierarchy, he had been repeatedly passed over. The old gentleman seemed not only pleased but surprised, then, when I made a point of repeating distinctly the "Doktor" of "Herr Doktor Flink" as I said I was honored to meet him. Augie, too, showed attentive respect, and with utmost old world courtesy Herr Doktor Flink thanked him so much for coming, as if Augie had been invited to tea.

Doktor Flink now apologized to Augie and me that the Consul General himself was out of town and therefore not here to greet us. He further apologized, with a touch of irritation, that the German defense attorneys had not yet appeared, so we would be a little late in starting; he gestured us toward the massive pillowy sofa facing in from the bay window. As Augie and I waited, we were watched intently from across the room by a large portrait of Goethe hanging behind the Consul General's desk. Bookshelves completely covered the side walls, arranged with commemorative plates, knickknacks, and an assortment of traditional beer steins. On only one eye-level shelf were there any books: a long row of stolid volumes with *Deutsche Politik* printed boldly on the spines, supported at the end by a glossy oversize picture book entitled *Israel*, its front cover displayed to the room.

After a few uncomfortable minutes on the couch during which Doktor Flink was out of the room and no one spoke, the underling ushered in the two lawyers for the suspect in Germany whose trial was upcoming and about whom the German authorities wanted Augie's testimony. Herr and Frau Linsmann, husband and wife team, seemed unhurried and unruffled by their tardiness. It was apparent they already knew Kepler and the magistrates. When Doktor Flink returned, they sensed right away that he wasn't necessary to know, and spoke to him accordingly. They seemed most interested in sizing up Augie and coldly said hello to him. Me they greeted with professional courtesy but not much concern—they knew their tussle would be with Augie and the magistrates, in German, and not with an English-speaking lawyer.

The Linsmanns took seats against the wall opposite the magistrates; Augie and I were on the sofa between, Kepler to the side.

Without giving the Linsmanns an opportunity to get settled, Doktor Flink called in a young woman to sit at a stenographic machine next to the Consul's desk. Flink positioned himself behind the desk, took a peek at the Goethe portrait as if to make sure the great man was with him, checked that the stenographer was ready to catch every word, then cleared his throat and began to read in a liturgical drone from a large leather-bound volume. The magistrates and Kepler sat impassively, but the Linsmanns squirmed in their chairs, unable or unwilling to conceal their impatience with the old man and his consular babble.

Augie had heard tales from Germany of the Linsmanns, this legal Juan and Evita, and had described to me their jet-setting ways, but they were even more to a type than I had imagined. Frau Linsmann was the essence of tailored understatement, letting the textures of her creamy silk blouse and pale linen suit speak in place of color or accessory. Her long blond hair was much more than a lesser professional would want to lug around, but the perfectly pinned swirls made it clear she was up to the task. It was hubby Linsmann, though, who made the real fashion statement: black hair jelled back in rows as straight and firm as the autobahn; a double-breasted blue suit, either Paris or Milan, that had instantly made me lose faith in my own; and glove-leather loafers, which I guessed as Florence or Rome. And though personally I judged pretty tacky the pale blue socks with alligators on the ankle, I was certain the current issues of Europe's finest fashion magazines would prove me grossly uninformed. As Assistant Consul Flink burbled on, Herr Linsmann opened a chrome attaché case that should have held something radioactive, took out an enormous tortoiseshell fountain pen and a stack of stationery, and began to make notes. I craned my neck to read the letterhead: "The Racquet Club, Palm Springs, California." The Linsmanns were wondrously tanned.

Doktor Flink's peroration finally came to an end and he looked to the magistrates to take the helm. Magistrate Klompertz patiently reminded the good Assistant Consul that the proceedings had been arranged not for this office but for the adjoining conference room. Flink was momentarily flustered but managed to direct everyone through connecting doors to an even larger room with the same expansive view of the Bay. We arrayed ourselves around a table the size of a local airport: the magistrates and prosecutor along one side, the Linsmanns opposite, Augie and I at one end, Flink and the stenographer at the other. As we settled in, Magistrate Klompertz spoke to the old man, and when a somewhat bewildered Flink nodded his assent, Klompertz got up and closed the drapes over the Bay.

I had told Augie to use my presence as a way of snatching a few moments before having to answer troublesome questions; whispering back and forth might buy him time to collect *his* thoughts, if not mine. And these sporadic pantomimes, plus an occasional reassuring pat on Augie's nervously bouncing leg, was the sum total of my participation. As the morning wore on, I felt myself recede further and further into the background until it seemed that despite our show of portentous whispers, everyone in the room sensed that I had no real part to play.

Not just the language but the entire proceedings were foreign to me. One of the magistrates would make a long introductory statement, referring to notes, then Augie would respond at length, after which the defense attorneys and the magistrates would argue for awhile, the magistrates sometimes asking Augie for a second response, followed by more argument and then a final, carefully enunciated statement by whichever magistrate had fired the opening salvo. Prosecutor Kepler sat a bit back from the table and entered the fray only to supply what seemed brief points of information before giving way again to the magistrates. Strange, too, was that recording the proceedings was left to a tiny dictation-type cassette machine on the table in front of Magistrate Lichter. The stenographer took down neither the magistrate's initial statements, nor the lawyers' arguments, nor, most curiously, Augie's responses; the only thing she recorded was the summary statement made by a magistrate at the end of each go-round.

At eleven o'clock, a phone buzzed on a side table, startling a somnolent Doktor Flink. He answered, then halted the proceedings: an urgent call from my office.

"Yes? . . . Uh-huh . . . . Which judge? . . . All right, tell them I'll handle it as soon as I'm finished here . . . . The judge? No, I don't want to be interrupted here. Have Collins or Bardelli call him; they have instructions. And book me a flight . . . . Right. I'll call when I'm finished. Stay by the phone."

I returned to my seat without looking at anyone, made some notes, put them in my briefcase, and only then raised my head.

"Oh, excuse me. My thanks, Herr Doktor, for permitting this intrusion. And my apologies."

The old man nodded, his gravity counterpoint to my deference.

The whole thing had been arranged, of course. A friend called the consulate and said he was from my office, requesting to speak with me immediately. And on the phone we played out an entire fake scenario, on the chance that the consulate liked to listen in.

The odds of making an impression with these shenanigans? Not great. Out of the corner of my eye I noticed Doktor Flink watching me with interest, but if the call had improved my standing with the others, they didn't show it. And as if to emphasize the interruption's insignificance, Magistrate Klompertz said that it was time for a break.

Augie and I moved into a hallway but there was nothing much to say. I hadn't understood what they'd been talking and arguing about for the past hour and a half, and even if I had, there didn't seem to be anything I could do to help him. For appearance's sake, though, with a somber expression I asked Augie to review the notes I'd been taking all morning—things like "I think Flink fell asleep" and "Linsmann's tie is ugly."

Back in the conference room, Augie went to sit down and I wound up standing next to Kepler. Although technically the prosecutor, he was the least adversarial of the bunch and we found ourselves with an odd sort of spectators' bond. We exchanged small talk, and out of curiosity I asked why they bothered to have both a tape recorder and the stenographer. Kepler seemed puzzled by the question: Well, he said, the stenographer makes an official record of the proceedings. Now I was puzzled: But she only takes down the magistrate's final statement and doesn't record my client's testimony at all. Ah, Kepler said, now understanding my confusion and being somewhat amused by it; that *was* your client's testimony she recorded. In the German system, he explained, a witness's testimony at such a hearing is no more or less than what the magistrate says the testimony is. The tape recorder, as far as Kepler knew, was merely for Frau Lichter's personal files. I was incredulous: You mean, it's the summaries, and not Augie's actual answers, that will later be considered in court? Oh, at trial a witness would be heard in person, Kepler said. But for pretrial proceedings the magistrate's summary is, well, more concise. Using the actual witness responses would give the lawyers too great an opportunity to discredit the "truth" merely by arguing later on in court about specific words a witness may have used thoughtlessly or imprecisely. A magistrate's conclusion reached after listening to both the witness and the lawyers, on the other hand, could not later be impeached. I would have to admit, he said with measured irony, that what their method lacks in subtlety it makes up for in efficiency.

I was still marveling at this phenomenon of synthesized testimony when the process itself got under way again. My bemusement quickly ended as the Linsmanns were given their first opportunity to ask Augie direct questions. Frau Linsmann had barely begun her first swings when I heard her mention the name Bert Blauser. Although Augie and I had discussed the possibility that the German authorities might try to connect Augie's old friend Bert to this smuggling scheme, we didn't expect to hear his name raised by the defense lawyers. Their client, too, was Bert's longtime friend, and Augie had never imagined him trying to slip out of the noose by hanging it on Bert instead. Apparently Augie had misjudged him. Or maybe the client didn't know what his lawyers were up to. Whichever, Augie was suddenly confronted with an unexpected and dangerous situation. He whispered a translation of the question to me, an innocuous inquiry about Augie and Bert having gone to school together. But I knew well that it was merely a warm-up question about Bert and that if Augie answered, the floodgates might quickly become impossible to close.

"*Damen und Herren*," I began slowly, "as you may be aware, this person Blauser to whom Frau Linsmann refers has been convicted of an offense in *this* country." I paused to emphasize the distinction. "I am obliged, therefore, respectfully to object to any questions of my client regarding Herr Blauser."

I had made my remarks toward all in the room and with an assuredness to suggest there was nothing more to be said on the subject, even though I had no idea if I had any legal grounds on which to base my objection. Apparently the others had no idea either, though, because the magistrates, the Linsmanns, and particularly Doktor Flink, suddenly seemed to regard me through a different lens, wondering now whether my morning silence had been no more than a tactical choice, one that just as easily could have been its obstreperous opposite. My reserve, which until this point they had considered a mark of inconsequence, now appeared to have been a carefully coiled position from which I could spring preemptive strikes. At least, I hoped that was how it appeared.

The Linsmanns were more wary now, but they were not about to back off. Herr Linsmann watched me closely while his partner-wife directed some brief remarks in German to the magistrates. The magistrates conferred for a moment and then Herr Klompertz said to me politely, almost apologetically, that while my objection might be proper in an American legal setting, we were in a German proceeding of which I was not officially a participant. Therefore, the Linsmanns had a right to ask the question.

Despite the negative content of this response, I realized that it marked the first time that morning an official exchange had taken place entirely in English. The game had changed.

"Of course they have a right to ask," I said, gazing with forced aplomb at the Linsmanns. Then I turned to Augie and said openly, to emphasize the absurdity of this mouth-to-mouth transfer, "Your reply is: 'I have been instructed by my attorney not to answer the question, and on that basis I respectfully decline to do so.'" Remaining admirably calm, at least on the outside, Augie dutifully repeated it to the magistrates in German.

This was not the response the Linsmanns had expected. Herr Linsmann glared: "We do not wish to hear from your client regarding Mr. Blauser's matters in this country," Linsmann said, barely controlling his temper. "So there is no reason, no *legal* reason," his voice rose and wobbled, "why he cannot answer us about Herr Blauser's activities in Germany, which is something we *do* wish to hear." By the time Linsmann finished, he was almost snarling. I noticed Doktor Flink looking disconcerted, his sense of consular propriety ruffled by Linsmann's tone and volume. Flink didn't know quite what to do about it, though, and managed only a mild but obvious clearing of the throat. Neither the Linsmanns nor the magistrates took any notice of the old man. But sitting directly across from him, I caught his eye and nodded in respectful agreement with his not-quite-spoken sentiments.

The substantive legal question remained unresolved. I noted with discomfort that Kepler, the prosecutor, was leaning closer to the table. Despite his lack of affection for the Linsmanns, at the mention of Bert Blauser he had suddenly become alert. I looked to the magistrates to recognize my legal point, but either because they were tilting toward German hegemony on the issue or because they, too, now wanted to hear about this character Blauser, they remained silent to let the Linsmanns duke it out with me a bit longer.

First giving Augie an avuncular gaze, I turned back to the table: "Despite any misconceptions you might harbor to the contrary, Herr Linsmann, my client is not here at your pleasure. So what *you* wish to hear is of no consequence to him . . . or to me. And I can assure you," I let my voice take on a preternatural calm, "that what you do and do not wish is, in *this* country, of no legal significance . . . whatsoever."

I peeked at the magistrates—complete equanimity. If they knew how they intended to settle this imbroglio, they weren't yet tipping their hand.

Herr Linsmann now growled something in German to the magistrates. When Frau Lichter's brief reply did not satisfy him, Linsmann again became vociferous, emphasizing his points with an insistent tapping on the table with his mammoth fountain pen and ending with a broad dismissive gesture in my direction. Since it was all too fast for Augie to translate on the fly, I just sat impassively and watched the faces. Once again Doktor Flink was frowning at Linsmann's tone and looked particularly offended by the tapping pen.

Magistrate Lichter finally replied to Herr Linsmann with a grudging agreement: "*Ja, ja das ist, aber . . .*" whereupon Frau Linsmann snatched the mantle from her husband and started in on me: "If your client refuses to answer when he has been ordered to be at this questioning, the magistrate has powers to ask from the American Federal Attorney to convene an American court hearing. And there your client *must* answer the questions."

Treacherous waters, now. I knew that the magistrates could indeed request that the local United States Attorney issue a subpoena requiring Augie to appear in U.S. federal court and testify there, which was one of the reasons he hadn't skipped this whole show altogether. To ward that off, I wanted at least to convince the magistrates that my instruction to Augie not to answer was made in good faith and that arguably we had a legitimate legal leg to stand on. If the magistrates thought I was just stonewalling, they were more likely to go to the U.S. Attorney, which would mean extra time and work for them and another long trip just to hear from this one witness, all adding up to unhappy magistrates and a far more formal and hopeless proceeding. Nor did I want to stir up the laconic prosecutor Kepler, since he could easily have the German police authorities cause Augie untold grief whenever he visited his family there. So, although I didn't know what I was going to say, I knew I had to start talking.

"Of course there is no question you have the authority to request a subpoena from the United States Attorney," I addressed my remarks collegially to the magistrates, ignoring the Linsmanns. "But then this would become a United States proceeding under the jurisdiction of American law,"—I was making it up as I went along—"which would afford my client the full protection of the United States Constitution, including the right not to answer questions that might tend to incriminate him." I glanced at the Linsmanns, who were madly making notes. "That's the Fifth Amendment to the U.S. Constitution," I said in a pedagogic aside to the husband and wife. "The *Fifth* . . . . So," I readopted a conciliatory tone for the magistrates, "I don't believe such a turn of events would get us any further than we are today. And it would have the complicating consequence of involving not only a United States Attorney but also a federal judge who, of course, would have authority over the proceedings . . . which could take crucial decisions out of German hands . . . where those decisions properly belong. After all, this affair does not really concern the United States, and I'm sure you would agree it should not be taken over by American judges . . . or lawyers."

I was rolling now, but still didn't know where I was headed.

"On the other hand, my client has appeared here to answer questions in good conscience and in good faith. And not, I might add, because of any legal subpoena forcing him to do so. Not because he is under any *legal* obligation to appear. But because, as a good German citizen, my client has honored the request of his consulate."

Doktor Flink's face animated, but still no response from the magistrates.

"We have appeared here at the *personal* invitation of the consular representative of the German nation . . . ." I bowed toward old Flink in what I imagined was an approximation of nineteenth-century manners. The Herr Doktor's eyes widened and he nodded back; through the open doorway to the Consul General's office, the portrait of Goethe appeared just above the old man's head. "And so, in the end, we shall pay due respect to consular wishes in this matter."

Flink opened his mouth but nothing came out.

"As I have stated," I went on quickly, trying to hold the floor, "we are fully aware of our legal rights . . . and we shall, if necessary, see that they are honored in a court of law . . . even should that impose considerable burden on myself and my client." Still no response; my mouth was getting dry. "Of our resolve in that regard you may be certain. For as the great Goethe himself was the first to say—before the notion became . . . abused," I flicked my eyes for an instant toward the Linsmanns, "'*Was mich nicht umbringt, macht mich starker.*'"

The old man almost lifted off his chair to hear me quote his beloved Goethe ["That which does not kill me, makes me stronger"], and in German, no less.

"But the decision, of course, is yours," I returned to the magistrates, "as to which path we will have to follow."

When I stopped, the room was momentarily silent, all of them looking at me uncertainly, wondering perhaps if they might have been suckered, if I'd understood the morning's German all along. The Linsmanns didn't tarry, though, and both began to argue vehemently, simultaneously, with the two magistrates. The magistrates were being quickly swayed toward the Linsmanns' position—"*Ja, stimmt, jawohl, stimmt.*" ["Yes, that's true, that's right."]—when from the corner of the room came a smoky, senatorial voice we had not heard before, and which Herr Doktor Flink probably had found but rare opportunity to summon in his long and anonymous career.

"These gentlemen are here at the Consul's invitation," Doktor Flink announced, rising slowly from his chair. "And decisions about how they are to be treated while on *this* German soil shall be made by the consular representative of the German state. The consulate's invitation, offered personally by me, mentioned nothing whatsoever about this Herr Blauser person and his . . . troubles. *Und so*, such a subject is a matter which these gentlemen, while here voluntarily at the consulate's request, shall *not* be required to discuss . . . . You may proceed." And he sat down.

I'm not sure who in the room was the most surprised. The Linsmanns were certainly the most shocked; they could not directly challenge the old man's authority and did not know on what grounds to appeal to the magistrates. The prosecutor Kepler would be no help to them; he had pushed away from the table again as if to say "Don't anyone look at me." Magistrate Lichter appeared to dislike Flink's incursion into her prerogative over legal decisions, but she was either not certain enough about her charter or not interested enough in the Linsmanns' sideshow to take a definitive stand. And while Magistrate Klompertz's face gave away nothing, by his silence he seemed content that the matter had been resolved one way or the other, so that finally they could get on with the hearing.

The Linsmanns tried one last gasp with the magistrates, but by now it was plaintive and halfhearted. With a brief negative reply, Klompertz nodded toward Doktor Flink and shrugged. I didn't want to let the Linsmanns keep trying, though, lest they somehow reinvigorate the magistrates, so after a moment I broke in: "While I appreciate that there may be more legal arguments to be put on the record, I assume the proper time and place will be in a German courtroom. For now, my client has been invited here to answer questions, which he can only do if a question is put to him. So may we please proceed, or should we presume that our presence here no longer serves a purpose?"

Herr Klompertz looked to his fellow magistrate and she agreed that it was time to get on with it. She said something to the Linsmanns who, with the surly air of children unfairly punished, conferred for a moment and then acceded to a new line of questioning. The session lasted all day and most of the next, but we did not again hear the name Bert Blauser.

As we left the consulate on the second, final afternoon, I spoke privately to the prosecutor. He said he really did not know whether the magistrates would bother to obtain a U.S. court order and return to the States to question Augie further about Herr Blauser. But Kepler made it clear that at least *he* had no interest in pursuing the matter. I bade a formal good-bye to the magistrates, which they returned politely and, to my relief, without any indication that we would be seeing each other again. The Linsmanns hurried out without so much as a nod.

Doktor Flink now came up to me so close that the watery blue eyes behind his glasses were like twin swimming pools seen through sliding glass doors. He thanked Augie and me for our cooperation in this "difficult business." Then he asked for my card, a version of which with home address and phone I had ready for emergencies. The old man held the card at arm's length and stared at it attentively, then tucked it away carefully in the pocket of his hand-knit Tyrolean vest.

Months went by with no word about whether Augie would be interrogated further. I had managed to put it all out of my mind, though I'm sure many a late night it visited Augie. Finally, after almost a year, Augie heard from friends in Germany that the Linsmanns had worked out a plea for their client and that the case was over. No one else had been implicated and the German government had moved on to bigger things. Augie could once again feel relatively comfortable making a visit to Germany, which he did a couple of months later. While he was away, I received an envelope from Germany addressed in his handwriting. Inside was a sealed plastic bag marked with the insignia of the German customs police. In the bag was one of the old fountain pens I had used to smuggle sauces to Augie in the Seventh Floor jail, and which after his release I had given him for good luck. The pen was in sections, just as the customs police had returned it to Augie after having taken it and everything else in his luggage apart on his arrival. They had found his name on a special list in their computer, but fortunately there hadn't been anything else to find.

Some months later Augie had to call the German consulate on other business and out of curiosity asked for Assistant Consul Flink. But the old man was no longer there. And despite his taking my card and saying that we must have lunch together, I had never heard from him again. Which is just as well. Because he might have asked me why it was he had never been able to find anywhere in his beloved Goethe the expression—*"Was mich nicht umbringt, macht mich starker"*—through which he had come to appreciate my difficult position that morning at the consulate. And I would have had to lie to him, to tell him the phrase appeared in some obscure letter or essay the location or title of which I could not remember. Or perhaps with a different lie I would have tried to save him further searching, saying that although I thought the phrase had first come from Goethe, I wasn't really certain. The truth—that it was not Goethe at all but originally, exclusively Nietzsche, and the only German lines I knew—I probably would not have had the heart to tell him.

Some Nice Young Lawyer

"Hullo?"

"Is this . . . Joseph?"

"Ah-huh. Who's this?"

"Joanne. Walters."

"Um, it doesn't . . . ."

"Your mother said I should call."

"My mother?"

"And my mother. They're friends. Sort of."

"Sorry, but it still doesn't . . . You sure my mother . . . ?"

"Mine, actually. They were talking, and it seemed a natural."

"It did? . . . You know, this sounds like a long way. Where are you calling from?"

"Yes, Chicago. But, where there's a will . . . ."

"Ah-huh. Well, listen, I think there was probably some kind of misunderstanding. I'm not really interested . . . ."

"Come on, now. Don't be so defensive. A new person, new possibilities. You've got to be willing to risk once in awhile."

"Yeah, once in awhile. But I don't think this . . . . "

"You know, you and I, there's real propinquity here."

"Propinquity? We don't even live in the same state."

"Yes, but . . . well, we're the same kind of people."

"I beg your pardon? We've never even met."

"I know enough to know. I mean, very verbal, both verbal, that's important. And professionals. I mean, you're . . . well, you're an attorney."

"Ah, listen. I'm afraid this isn't for me. Sorry you've gone to the trouble."

"But you're not . . . ."

"No, sorry, but I'm just not interested. I've got to go now. So long."

"Hello?"

"Lawyers are like that."

"Excuse me?"

"Closed down. A protective mechanism. I know lawyers. You've got to open up. Something you've got to learn."

"Wait a minute. Have I missed something here? You don't know anything about me."

"Well, I know it's difficult. But if you'd let yourself open up a little, we'd both know more about you."

"Listen, I told you I'm not interested. All right? Clear enough?"

"It's nothing to be ashamed of. A lot of lawyers have this problem."

"Look. Forget it, will you? And no, I don't want to discuss it. I'm sorry, but goodbye."

"Yes, hello?"

"You should try listening sometime, you know. Instead of always arguing, trying to be right all the time."

"No, *you* listen. The word is 'No.' Which means . . . 'No!' Which means 'I do not . . . want . . . to discuss it.'"

"You're really hostile, you realize that? Maybe you should take a look at all that hostility."

"I told you . . . ."

"Lawyers don't want to take responsibility, I know that. But you can't hide your whole life."

"Hey, I don't need this. I don't want to know you. So *DON'T CALL ME AGAIN!*"

"Hello, you've reached 919-4279. Please leave a message after the tone."

"I know you won't admit this, but you need help. You need to see someone. Because you have . . . a lot of issues. I'm a therapist . . . . Believe me. I know."

Class Mates

[Attorney Roy] Black acknowledged that Smith had the best defense money could buy.

"I flew all over the country for this case," he said. "William Smith was fortunate. He had a family that could provide the money to do these kinds of things [hire experts on meteorology, soils, acoustics and forensic fabric analysis], or he would be in prison."

Unequal justice? No, Black said. "It just reflects our society. We are a capitalist society."

—Associated Press report of his lawyer's remarks
regarding the acquittal on rape charges of
William Kennedy Smith

Monday, April 10, 8:30 A.M.:

Groggy from now chronic lack of sleep. And in jail.

It's six months into my tenure at the Public Defender's office, and jail is a regular assignment: brief interviews with people arrested the day or night before who have not yet been released on bail or O.R. ("Own Recognizance," a no-bail-required promise to appear in court). In addition to defendants held with high bail for serious crimes, public defender jail interviews also include people accused of minor offenses who have neither ready cash nor efficacious family or friends to put up immediate bail, and who thus remain in jail at least until they are brought to court and a judge considers their O.R. release. Among these minor offenders are many people who have seen the iron bars close them in for the first time. Who have awakened to find that it was not all a mistake. Who have had no sign that the door will open anytime soon. Who have no idea what awaits them. Who are sick with fear.

Mornings, the jail at its most chaotic. By 8:30 the first head-count is over and trustees are busy collecting potential-weapon breakfast utensils. Arresting cops, jailers, probation officers, and lawyers all crowd the booking room. The medic rolls in his cart to check on how the ill, the injured, the drugged, and the crazed have fared the night; shouts of "Medic!" and "Doc!" echo in and out of the cell blocks. Prisoners who are due in court are hauled out of cells, pushed through doors and chambers, shackled, stowed. Those who think they, too, should be going to court clamor for attention, shout for a deputy, their lawyer, anyone. For first-timers terrorized by arrest and a night when no one came to let them out, anxiety reaches new peaks in this morning cacophony of clanging, slamming, and shouting, in this start of every day in the local jail.

Like many other criminal lawyers, I got much of my early training as a public defender. Before becoming a P.D., I spent two years working on big cases with several extraordinary private criminal lawyers. But my inexperience kept me in the background—writing briefs, interviewing witnesses—and prevented me from developing skills in open court. So, I faced a choice. I could remain seated at the counsel table watching and listening to seasoned lawyers rise and speak, picking up the craft in small bits and pieces until eventually, but slowly, I'd be able to stand on my own. Or I could plunge into the cauldron of public defending—an overflowing swill of minor cases as well as the most virulent of major ones—and, with the meager resources provided, rapidly learn to design and float for all sorts of accused the most jerry-built, thin-hulled, and sometimes leakiest of defenses.

In the Public Defender's office of a San Francisco Bay county with a combination of crumbling urban centers, suburban sprawl, and fringes of rural poverty, I took the plunge.

"Hey, P.D. Hey! This is one of yours."

Standing next to the shouting jailer is a short, stocky, silver-haired man, motionless except for blinking eyes in the painful neon light. The jailer looks at a paper, says the name "Ledesma," and sits the man in a small open cubicle. I walk over, take a chair, and wait for the jailer to move off.

It is not merely *what* you first say, but *how.* What tone? What modulation? Facial expression? Posture? Amidst the shouting and banging and cruel laughter. Given what you know about how things go. Given how little you know about the person sitting across from you. Across from you in the jail.

"You're . . ."—I shift through my papers for the one that matches the name—". . . Anthony Ledesma."

"I know," the silver-haired man says quietly.

"Ah, yes, you do. Right. Well, my name's Matthews. I'm a public defender. And if you can't afford a lawyer, our office provides you with one free of charge. So . . . tell me, when were you picked up?"

Drifting back through the delirium of his arrest, Mr. Ledesma finally says, as if not quite believing it, "Last night."

"Okay. You might be in court this afternoon. For sure by tomorrow morning. Now, let me get some information, so when you go to court, maybe we can get you O.R.'d."

"You mean, maybe I stay 'til tomorrow? In *here?*"

"It's possible, yeah. Unless you make bail." I check my papers. "You've got a petty theft and misdemeanor assault: statutory bail's a thousand. Got anybody to put up the money?"

Mr. Ledesma shakes his head.

"Well, you could spend a hundred on a bondsman and put up a car or some other collateral for the rest. You own any . . . ?"

He shakes his head.

"Then, we'll try to get you O.R.'d. Shouldn't be any longer than tomorrow. And anyway, by then you'll have sentence credit for three days time served, even though you'll only be in here about thirty-six hours. Now, let's get some O.R. info . . . ."

"Sentence? But you don't ask me . . . . Mister, I done nothing wrong."

Antonio (Tony) Ledesma is seventy-two years old but looks considerably less: clear-eyed, still muscular, a full head of hair. His exceptionally strong hands reflect a life as farmhand, carpenter, laborer. He grew up in Texas and speaks with a slight cross-border inflection. He is a quiet, serious man with a sense of dignity seemingly untainted by false pride. There is about him, however, a subtle sadness: despite his strength, he is getting old; and he is alone.

Ten years ago Tony's wife died, and he moved to California to be near his brother. But two years ago the brother died. And his brother's kids soon left, followed by his sister-in-law. So, Tony moved into a room in the Railroad Hotel ("Single/Double Occupancy, Day/Week/Month"), a worn but reasonably clean old six-story brick building only a few blocks from the jail in which he now sits. Tony lives on a small Social Security check, on little neighborhood fix-it jobs, and on handyman work for the hotel.

It was a job for the hotel that got Tony into trouble. He had gone to the local chain variety store to get some things to repair a hotel room door. Having already begun the job, he was wearing his old work apron when he chose a lock and some screws. Then, to free one hand in order to examine some hinges, he unthinkingly dropped the packet of screws into his apron, just as he would when working. He selected the hinges, picked up some more screws, and at the counter paid for the lock, hinges, and a pack of screws. But not for the screws he'd forgotten in his apron.

The store's security guard was sitting above, behind an expensive, newly installed two-way mirror. He scurried to the front counter and without any prelude reached into Tony's apron pocket. Instinctively, Tony grabbed the guard's wrist and pushed him away.

As the security man howled to a store clerk, "Call the police!" Tony reached into his apron and discovered the screws. He tried to explain that he wouldn't steal a second packet of screws since he only needed a few for the hotel door. But the security man said only that he was tired of "all you people" coming into the store and "stealing more than you buy." Tony didn't know whether "all you people" meant the low-income hotel residents, older people, or brown people, but whichever, the remark ended Tony's willingness to explain. The cops soon arrived and started to write Tony some kind of ticket, but the security guard complained loudly about Tony's "violence" and so the cops agreed to take Tony in and book him.

Tuesday, April 11, 9:00 A.M., Department Two, Municipal Court:
Behind the railing it's packed to overflowing. Confused and worried defendants. Distressed families. Crying babies. In front, clerks, bailiffs, and yawning lawyers shuffle through papers and talk across the rail with the accused.

Each morning starts with a mash of routine judicial business: entering pleas, setting bail, scheduling hearings. And Monday and Tuesday mornings a little worse—when the weekend's madness first hits court. The pressure is always on to move quickly, to give each case the absolute minimum necessary consideration, because only by pushing hard can the court hope to get through the day's vast "calendar" of cases. As a result, the morning is a maelstrom of whirling paper and grunted code among judge, lawyers, and clerks, the mystified defendants being pulled inside the rail and then quickly turned out again as if low-grade livestock up for auction.

A public defender may have thirty or forty cases in this first round of business: drunk driving, drugs, burglaries, fights—all the assorted daily delinquencies of modern American life. And of those defendants, he or she will know only a handful by sight. For the rest, the P.D. waits until a name is called, looks to see who stands up, waves the person forward with an approximation of confidence, matches the name with a file from a huge stack on the table, listens to what the judge is already saying well before the client is standing there, whispers brief words of comfort when the client reaches the counsel table, responds to the judge with opportunity neither to consult the client nor to explain anything but the most rudimentary and essential effects—"You come back in a month; we'll talk to you before then"—and shovels the client out again while listening to the next name being called.

The process begins with the "custodies"—those accused who have not made bail or been released on their own recognizance. Though I interviewed him in jail only yesterday, I am surprised to see Tony Ledesma led in a side door with a dozen other men, all at least half his age, hooked together on a long chain. I rarely have time in this job to consider anyone or anything not immediately under my nose, and since I left the jail I have not given Tony a thought. His name is called, and I move over to the jury box—where the custodies remain shackled during their brief time in court—talking to the judge as I move: "Waive formal arraignment, Your Honor. Plea is not guilty, jury requested, O.R. motion, time waived on release."

"Your name is Anthony Ledesma?" the judge says without looking. Tony nods, lips tight. Before the judge complains, I say to Tony, "You have to answer out loud." Tony likes neither the judge's indifference nor my reproach: "Yes," he says more firmly than any of us needs.

"I'm trying to get you out," I whisper, and immediately launch my rap about why Tony should be released on his own recognizance: "No priors, Judge, and the defendant's been a local resident for ten years. Um, no relations in the area. Mr., ah . . . (I blank on Tony's name and have to check my file) . . . Ledesma is not presently working, Your Honor, but . . . ."

Tony interrupts: "That's not right. I work. At the hotel. And around. Not every day, but I work. I always worked."

"What about this hotel, Counsel?"

"His current residence, Judge. The, um," a glance at my notes, ". . . Railroad Hotel."

"And how long has the defendant lived there?"

"He doesn't know," Tony puts in. "Ask me."

"It's all right," I try to soothe Tony. And make my morning go more smoothly.

"Well, let's see what we have, then," the judge says. "No family; no employer; and a transient hotel."

"I *live* there," Tony says emphatically.

"Your Honor, since Mr. Ledesma has lived there two years, it's not transient for him. He's got no priors, and there is nothing to suggest that he wouldn't make his appearances. I mean, where's he going to go?"

I realize as soon as they are out of my mouth the forlorn sound of these words, but all I can do about them now is not look at Tony.

"Well, since he didn't exactly stick up the mint . . . ."

"Isn't *accused* . . . of sticking up the mint."

"Yes, thank you, Counsel. And in view of his age . . . ."

"Why?" Tony pipes up. "How old are you, Judge?"

Fortunately, the judge smiles. ". . . I'll release him on his own recognizance. Pretrial May 14, 1:30, Department Three."

I jot the date in my file and rapidly tell Tony he'll be released later today, to be back in court May 14, and to come to the public defenders' office before then. Tony seems bewildered at what's gone on, and at the peremptoriness with which it has ended, but I have no time to explain because the judge is already calling another name. Tony probably spends the rest of the morning in the holding cell next to the courtroom, where I could see him and explain, but I am dealing with twenty other first appearances, then with sentencings and a probation violation hearing, and by the time the morning is over, Tony has been released and, truth be told, I haven't given him another thought.

Wednesday, April 26, 4:15 P.M., Department Two,
Municipal Court:

Afternoon pretrials. The plea bargain room. Only halfway through eighty files—looks like we'll be here until six or seven. I know not to show up until three, when the D.A.s get here, but defendants have been ordered to be here at one, and some will wait out in that courtroom for five or six hours.

In many criminal cases there is overwhelming evidence that the accused has engaged in behavior that has at least some degree of illegality, but it is usually far less egregious than what the prosecutor's office has charged. The defense lawyer's primary job for these clients is to negotiate a plea bargain—a settlement of the case without trial—which minimizes both culpability and punishment. The process is a poker game, the stakes other people's lives: a lawyer bluffs and postures and barters an outcome that is measured against the likelihood of a more severe result if the case goes to trial. But how does a client assess the lawyer's judgment about a plea bargain? Particularly if they've never even met until the lawyer walks from the closed-door bargaining into the courtroom and calls the name of the defendant whose "deal" the lawyer has only five minutes to explain—the typical scenario in public defender misdemeanor cases.

Misdemeanors: crimes of bad attitude, minor transgressions of public order that cause no serious injury. The overburdened legal machine treats misdemeanors less severely and thus grants them less time and regard. And the public defenders' office, a much scorned and starved institution, is forced by the limits of its overworked resources to adhere to this hierarchy of concern. A public defender simply cannot afford much time, care, or energy to any of these less serious cases, of which there are scores every day on each P.D.'s desk.

"Less serious cases." But less serious for whom? Felony charges and significant jail time may be less than serious for someone inured to the rhythms of crime and punishment. (I've had hardened clients who have actually chosen a stretch in the violent but highly codified life of state prison rather than a shorter stint in considerably less menacing but more overcrowded, uncomfortable, chaotic county jail. As one of these career cons explained it to me, "In County, I just can't get my sleep.") Conversely, for the normally law-abiding minor miscreant, even slight criminal stigma may grievously wound. And the possibility of jail time, however short, may be utterly mortifying, nudging to the very edge of collapse an apparently solid but internally fragile life.

So now I'm bargaining pieces of lives in this horrible, airless little room. Juries deliberate in here; no wonder they convict so often. Of course, the air doesn't bother these D.A.s, Weigant and Longo—you only need oxygen if you possess internal organs. No, Weigant's not that bad: straight-laced and timid from a vacant imagination but at least willing to make concessions. And without a real taste for blood. Longo, on the other hand . . . Having to argue with Ernie fucking Longo. Cajole him. Plead for deals. Over and again, to this vicious mule. Trying to explain the sad or silly or sordid instances of people who momentarily lost control over their quotidian foibles and vices. Explaining to Longo, fundamental among whose many problems is that he believes he's *never* lost control of his.

My role—forever explaining. Always a chorus in someone else's play. Someone else's life. Each soul-wearying day dominated by other people's pathologies. But also, in the end, too much of my *own* life spent in rooms like this. In the company of the likes of Deputy D.A. Ernie Longo. Oh, am I sick of his smirky face. And if I hear him say "protecting the public interest" one more time, I'm going to leap over this table and strangle the bastard. The only interests Ernie Longo truly responds to are the call of advancement up the D.A.'s ladder and the hungers of his underfed ego. How can it be that a bend in anyone's life should depend on the character and whim of an Ernest Longo?

"Yeah, Ernie, I heard you. But I don't have the file, so it must be one of Kate's."

Kate is my office partner, who is currently out in the courtroom giving the good or bad and in any event confusing news to the

client who corresponds to the file about which she has just negotiated a deal with Deputy D.A. Stan Weigant.

"How about Anderson?" Weigant asks me.

Well, a break for Mr. Anderson—it's Weigant who has his file,
not Longo. Whoever Mr. Anderson is.

Yeah, here it is, Anderson's file, in my stack. Oh, it's *Ms.* Anderson.
Sharon. Battery on a cop, in a civil rights demonstration at a
mostly black local high school. I remember: messy scene—all white
cops, whupping school kids. Looked bad. In all the papers, TV
news. Police report makes it sound like ol' Sharon hit the cop a
pretty good lick. Looks like our office interviewed her right in
court, during her first appearance—saved an office visit. But what
am I supposed to glean from an information sheet that says, under
Describe Facts of Incident: "D [Defendant] denies"?

"Struck an officer. Can't help you much on this one," Weigant
says.

"C'mon, Stan. Kid's only eighteen. And as I recall, the boys in
blue didn't exactly do themselves proud that day."

"This officer was just standing by when he was struck by your
client."

"Standing by? Hey, a peaceful demonstration until the cops show
up."

"Right, 'peace and love'. . . ." Longo chimes in, mocking.

"Excuse me, Longo, but you remember the First Amendment,
don't you? Heard about it, maybe in law school, have you?"

Weigant doesn't want to listen to Longo and me arguing again,
and cuts us off: "I'll drop it to a 'disturbing' [the peace]," he says—
Longo turns away; I can hear his eyeballs rolling—"but I want
some jail time. Three or four weekends, anyway."

"Be serious, Stan. Girl's never been in trouble before."

"Just getting started," Longo pipes in. "Only eighteen."

"Stay out of this, Longo . . . . I mean, maybe a 'disturbing' is
right, Stan, but no way she ought to do time."

"Well, I won't agree to no jail," Weigant says. "Best I'll do is let
her plead open. Have the Turtle decide whether she gets any time."

"The Turtle" is Judge Bradley, a calm, grandfatherly sort with a habit of sitting deep in his chair, neck drawn into his robes. He's not without compassion. Plus, he tends to go easy on youngsters. If we get another judge later, the odds are likely to be worse. Besides, if we don't settle the case now, next time Longo might have the file.

"Okay, Stan, I'll give it a try."

"Candy store," Longo sneers. "She won't get it any sweeter than that."

Out in the courtroom, a sea of anxious faces. Waiting for me. To do something. To make it all go away. "Anderson," I call out to the packed room. "Sharon Anderson."

I am startled to see coming forward a chunky, baby-faced girl whose pale pink skin is set off by a raccoon's mask of freckles. Amazed because I had missed the simple but unambiguous reference in the police report—and therefore had become attached to a different image—that the girl arrested at the inner city high school demonstration was a "WF": white female.

"Hi. I'm your lawyer, your public defender."

"You're not the one I had last time."

"No, there are quite a few of us. But I know about your case. And we've got a good offer to get it over with today."

"You're not the one I saw the first time, either. At court. That was another one."

"Yes, I understand that. But I have the information here," I pat my case file as if it contains the prophets' teachings, when in fact all it has is the police report, "and we can take care of things today . . . . If you want to."

The girl looks down at her feet and says nothing.

"Well, here's the deal . . . ." I'm jabbering as if a timer's bell will any moment end the offer, explaining that the assault will be dismissed (always give good news first) . . . and that "disturbing the peace" is a very minor charge . . . and that there is no guarantee on sentence, but that Judge Bradley . . . .

The girl is crying. Her body has been shaking but her face is turned down, and I've been talking so fast I haven't noticed her muffled sobs. I look around: people are watching, doubting.

Finally she looks up, tears streaming down her puffy face: "But I tried to tell him. I only came later. Nobody asked me . . . . Nobody ever asked me . . . ."

Tuesday, June 8, 3:30 P.M., Public Defender's office:

"What sort of work is it?"

"Carpenter; electric; plumber," Tony reports. "All those."

"You, ah, licensed? You know, state license in any?"

Tony's upper lip crowds his nose. He shakes his head.

"So, then, you're not *actually* a plumber. Or electrician, huh?"

"I'm not? Then what am I?"

"Well, I guess you're . . . a laborer."

"Sure I'm a laborer. What do you think that work is, bubble dancing?"

Tony Ledesma sits across from me, his head the same height as the row of files that covers half my gray metal desk. Tony has come in for a trial preparation interview, the first opportunity anyone in my office has had to find out what he and his defense might truly be about.

Tony is here because he rejected the plea bargain offered at his pretrial conference. I wasn't at that session, but the file indicates the proffered deal: "PG 488, dis. Ct2, TS" [plead guilty to petty theft; dismiss count two, assault on the security guard; sentence, "time served"—the two days Tony already spent in jail, which is to say, no additional punishment]. Tony tells me he rejected the offer because he did not steal. I suggest that maybe I can get the D.A. to offer a plea bargain of petty theft, with Tony to do some community service, so that when it's done, the "guilty" gets removed from his record. Tony refuses. He will not plead guilty to theft. Period.

Well, what if I can get a deal with the theft charge dropped and you plead guilty to assault on the security guard, with no further punishment? "Assault?" Tony says. "I didn't assault anybody." Now I know we are going to trial.

"So, the screws in your apron. You forgot them . . . ."

"Work belt."

". . . in your work belt. You're . . ." I check the file, "what, seventy-two now?"

"What does that mean?"

"Well, just . . . people become forgetful."

"Look. You see these hands? I work them all my life. And my work belt is a part of these hands. *That's* what this is about. I forgot, yes. But a *work* kind of forgot, not an *old* kind. You see what I say?"

I see what he says. And a jury might, too. But we'll need to buttress him as much as possible because the security guard will paint him as a surly, combative old man. And under cross-examination, Tony might well stuff himself right into that frame.

The previous week I spoke with the hotel manager, to confirm that Tony would have been reimbursed for any repair parts he bought. The hotel manager agreed Tony would have been repaid, but portended nothing but trouble when I broached the manager's testifying at trial: "How do I know if he wanted other screws?" he said on the phone. "I don't know what that old man does."

Now I'm sitting with Tony, explaining that his having regular work would help with his impression on a jury. Tony says that having regular work would help more than his case. Because the hotel was his one steady source of income—and now it's gone. Tony had told no one at the hotel about his arrest, he says, knowing that even to be suspected as a thief would make his life miserable there. But somehow, he shakes his head, somehow the hotel manager found out that Tony has been accused of stealing. And so last week he tells Tony he will be getting no more work.

Wednesday, July 6, 10:00 A.M., Department Three, Municipal Court:

Luck of the draw. *Rotten* luck of the draw. Instead of the Turtle, we get the Piranha. Of course, if the odds are slim of drawing a judge both intelligent and humane, then drawing a rotten one is not a matter of luck at all.

Instead of Judge Bradley the Turtle, it's Judge William (a.k.a. Tecumseh) Sherman, a choleric, vindictive, seamlessly unhappy man with a face like a defeated nation. A man whose only saving grace is that in his presence even Longo doesn't seem so bad. Sherman considers most anyone accused of a crime to be a subversive, an unwashed Other threatening the great Traditional Middle Nation. And since he sits in an urban California court, his Other-obsessiveness suffers no shortage of incitement.

Sherman considers defense lawyers complicitous in the threat. And public defenders doubly seditious: not only are they ideologically dangerous, but while defending the indefensible lumpen they're also sucking dry the public trough. So, trying a case in front of Sherman is a struggle with much more than the usual legal rules, slippery facts, and professional mendacity of the police. At every turn, Sherman makes a defender's life miserable, doing his utmost to convey to the jury that any defense is a sham and that the very denial of guilt is an act of enormous hubris.

It's already been a fractious morning in Sherman's court, and we haven't even gotten near Tony's trial yet. I agreed to stand in for an office cohort at the first court appearance of a murder suspect. "Suspect" is even more than normally euphemistic here, since the police found the guy, gun in hand, sitting on top of the dead body of a pizza delivery man, in the middle of the street, in the middle of the day. Totally nude, our man was, head and body hair shaved in bloody swaths, covered tip to toe in a combination of motor oil and petroleum jelly, and calmly singing, "Our lo-ove . . . is he-ere . . . to staaay!" In a rare show of common sense, the District Attorney had immediately agreed that the man should be certified directly from municipal court up to superior court and from there to a psychiatric hospital for examination. Since this was all agreed upon ahead of time, the lawyer handling the case asked me to stand in for him, as he had to be in another court but wanted no delay in getting the guy to the hospital.

Tony Ledesma was nervous but grimly determined when I saw him outside Tecumseh's courtroom earlier this morning. He's wearing a black suit, though he stopped short of donning a tie. And as I requested, he brought his work belt. I explained that there would be other court hearings before we got to his trial; Tony said he's waited this long, he can wait awhile longer.

I left Tony and went through the courtroom to the holding cell where the bailiff let me in to see Ronald Taggart, the Vaseline-and-motor-oil man. I figured things might go easier if he knew in advance that I'd be the one standing with him in court this morning. Handcuffed and leg-ironed, Taggart was alone in the cell, sitting still and quiet in the corner. I introduced myself, and he said softly the one word "Hello." The bailiff stood at the door, and when Taggart remained docile, he moved off, locking me in. Docile isn't quite the right word, though; inert is closer. I explained to Taggart who I was, why the other lawyer wasn't here, and that nothing was going to happen in court except that he would be sent to another court where his other lawyer would see him. Taggart said nothing, did not move. When I finished, I asked, "Okay? Understand?" Taggart looked right through me, so I asked again, "Do you understand, Mr. Taggart?" and he said softly, "Yes." Since more discussion seemed unlikely to change the dynamic in there, "Yes" was plenty for me, and I knocked for the bailiff to let me out.

A few minutes later Tecumseh took the bench and two bailiffs brought Taggart in. As he neared me I could tell something had changed. His all-pupil eyes stared at me as if it were *me* who was from Mars, not him. Just as I began to speak, Taggart yelled, "You're not my lawyer! You're not my lawyer!" and lunged at me. The bailiffs grabbed him, and as he continued ranting, "You're not my lawyer!" Judge Sherman looked nearly as crazy as Taggart. Sherman hated our clients, hated anyone he couldn't intimidate, and hated disruption. Taggart qualified on all three.

"What is this?" Sherman bellowed at me, as if I had put Taggart up to it. "What is your office doing now?"

"My office . . . ?"

"You're not my lawyer! You're not my lawyer!"

I leaned over to speak to Taggart, to try to calm him, but he just lunged at me again.

"Judge, it's been stipulated with the D.A. that this case is to be certified to Superior Court for a psychiatric evaluation."

"Superior! Superior! . . . You're not my lawyer!"

"Are you his lawyer, Counsel?"

"Well, our office is, yes, Judge. And it's been stipulated with the district attorney . . . ."

"I have no stipulation in front of me, Counsel."

I turned to Deputy D.A. Weigant, who was cowering at the other counsel table: "Stan!"

Weigant rose and timorously said, "Ah, yes, Your Honor, that's true. That's our agreement, yes." Thank God it wasn't Longo. Who knows what crap he would have handed me?

"All right, Counsel; you've certainly made a mess of this. But all right, the matter is referred to Superior Court . . . ."

And before finishing his brief pronouncement, the judge waved the bailiffs to remove Taggart, still screaming, to the holding cell.

With the Taggart fiasco and several other, minor matters over, we moved on to the sentencing docket, which with this judge was a pitiless affair referred to by courthouse wags as Sherman's March: Tecumseh considered "the quality of mercy" nothing more than a perilous Papist construct and "mitigating circumstances" merely a page to turn in his judge's sentencing manual. This morning I was facing Sherman with William Tarua, a Pacific Island kid of twenty-one whose drug problem had left him an empty-eyed ghost of his formerly robust South Seas self. Weeks earlier, William had agreed to plead guilty to a reduced charge of misdemeanor drug possession—in his case, a kaleidoscope of pills—in exchange for the D.A.'s acquiescence to a sentence in a residential drug treatment program. It was the kind of no-jail deal that Sherman hated and often refused to accept. So, the D.A. Weigant had agreed to postpone the actual plea and sentencing until I already had the kid accepted to a program and we could present Sherman with a virtual *fait accompli*. Now William stood slack-shouldered and silent next to me as I outlined the deal to Sherman.

I had to argue with Sherman about the *bona fides* of the residence program and even about William's need for treatment—as opposed to a "good stiff drink of deterrent," as Sherman so quaintly put it—though only a petrified sea slug or a presidential candidate could fail to notice William's sorry drug-debilitated state. Finally, Sherman grumblingly agreed to the deal and was in the middle of stating its terms for the record when suddenly he leaned over the bench, pointed at William, and barked, "*Where* did you get *that?*"

Even the somnolent William blinked.

"Get what, Judge?" I wondered.

"That jacket!"

William started to speak but I stopped him with a hand.

"Judge, what does this have to do with anything?"

"*That* happens to be a regulation Marine Corps flight jacket, issued only to the few fine men who have earned it. And I want to know where someone like *him* got one."

I asked in William's ear about the jacket and he whispered that he'd bought it in a flea market.

"It is my information," I said to Sherman, "that he came by it secondhand, Your Honor, from a flea market."

"Not on your life!" Sherman thundered. "No Marine aviator would *ever* sell his flight jacket."

"What about a broke ex-aviator, Judge? Maybe one of the county's two or three people without a job?"

"Don't hand me any of that," snarled Tecumseh. "And I want an answer: Where did you get it?"

Again I stopped William from speaking and said, "Excuse me, Judge, but how is this relevant to his sentencing?"

Sherman drew himself up and spoke with his best imitation of judicial dignity: "All matters pertaining to a defendant's character may be considered in determining whether a probationary disposition is appropriate. Now, where did you get the jacket?"

I whispered to William, then turned back to Sherman: "Your Honor, given the court's suggestion that there is no lawful means by which my client could have obtained the jacket, the court's question necessarily raises the specter of self-incrimination and on that basis I am obliged to instruct my client not to answer."

I thought Sherman was going to have a coronary.

"Fine, Counsel. Fine. We'll just see about this. Let the record reflect that the defendant has failed to cooperate regarding presentence information, and on that basis the court refuses to accept the terms . . . ."

"Judge, wait a minute. *I'm* the one giving you the grief here, right? Not him. I mean, you and I don't always get along too well. But you wouldn't hold that against my client?"

"Are you suggesting that this court would allow personal feelings to enter into a sentencing decision?" he croaked. "Because if so, that is contemptuous of this court's . . . ."

"No, no, Judge. I know you wouldn't. Just the opposite. But that's what the record is going to look like if you suddenly reject a negotiated plea right in the middle of this, well, difference of opinion you and I have had . . . . Won't it?"

Sherman was absolutely livid but smart enough to see the point. He looked down at his file and, when he again had his composure, readopted that drippingly officious voice, as if the written court record would somehow register his change in tone.

"Let the record reflect that I have *not* rejected probation for this defendant. But I have not finished setting its terms and conditions. I see that the defendant is scheduled to enter the drug program on August 1. Is that correct?"

"That's right, Your Honor."

"Well, that's a good three weeks or so from now. So—as one of the conditions of probation—I will order that the defendant spend twenty-five days in the county jail. If he goes into custody immediately, he will be out the night of the 31st. Just in time to start being 'rehabilitated.' Rehabilitation—that is what your client wants, isn't it, Counsel?"

The son of a bitch. I was granted a few moments to speak to William and explained the bind to him. Sherman had covered his judicial ass by keeping the drug program in place; and the jail time was not technically improper because it was made part of the same probation package. If William didn't take the whole deal, he would get no probation at all and no court referral to the drug program.

And if he didn't enter the program on the scheduled date, there was no guarantee of an available place for him there when his case came back to court. Besides, all deals would be off then. And he could count on Sherman to make sure I didn't slip the case over to another judge in the meantime. In other words, William was skunked: he had no defense to his case; he badly needed this drug program; and after the jacket episode, he couldn't risk facing the amount of jail time Sherman might lay on him next time around. William understood the situation pretty quickly and, though stunned at getting three-plus weeks—starting immediately—in jail, agreed to the deal.

"Damn, I feel bad about this, William," I said as we returned to face Tecumseh.

"Why?" William slurred. "It ain't *you* going to jail."

Another paper cut to the heart. How much more all these little wounds hurt than the few and meager victories can heal.

But, that was a whole ten minutes ago. During which I did two more sentencings and now I'm out in the hall to tell Tony Ledesma to get ready for the start of his trial. But first I have to tell Bobby Alonzo that although I'll probably be going to trial with Tony, if for some reason Tony's case doesn't begin today and my partner Kate's trial also folds, Bobby's drunk driving case would be next in line to begin.

Oh, and there's Sharon Anderson over in the corner—the high school demonstration girl. She's way down the list, after Tony, Bobby, and two of Kate's cases. I explain to her again, as I had on the phone, that although she is scheduled for trial today, it won't actually happen. But until another trial starts and the judge formally lets her go, she's got to stick around. Sharon responds with monosyllabic grunts that manage to convey that she doesn't distinguish me from any of the other characters in this nightmare that refuses to end. Well, I'll deal with that another day.

Tony is ready. And, I guess, so am I. Our defense will consist first of challenging the security guard: getting him to admit that installing the new two-way mirror meant he had to come up with enough "thieves" to justify the expense; that taking a seat behind the mirror makes him suspect everyone of stealing; that he had automatically categorized Tony as one of "those people"; that he never gave Tony a chance to explain; and that he, not Tony, had initiated the physical contact.

Then I'll put the hotel manager on the stand, to confirm that Tony was doing repairs and was to be reimbursed, and so didn't need to steal. And more, that Tony wouldn't be reimbursed without a receipt, so stealing extra screws wouldn't have meant extra cash—emphasizing the mere eighty-nine cents worth. But the hotel manager has been so generally hostile that I'll have to get him on and off the witness stand quickly, leaving Tony still an unknown quantity to the jury, which will bring it down to Tony himself to make a good impression. And if he falters on the stand or loses that temper . . . .

When we'd met to prepare, Tony had given me the names of a number of character witnesses. Unfortunately, none of them is here to testify. There were plenty of folks back in Texas, but neither they nor Tony had money for them to come to California. There were people for whom Tony did odd jobs here, but most had only one or two minor contacts with him and were unwilling to come to court. As for the two or three who gave him regular work, Tony was afraid to have me contact them: they might react as did the hotel manager—and several local shop owners to whom the manager had passed the bad word—by giving him no more work. And that was something Tony just couldn't afford.

There *was* the city councilman, though. After the first time Tony's trial had been postponed—at the D.A.'s request, but virtually automatic in the overcrowded courts—Tony reluctantly told me that for seven or eight years he had worked as a handyman for Robert Trujillo, newly elected to the city council. Reluctantly, because Tony was embarrassed to have Trujillo know of his arrest. I convinced Tony to let me contact him; an elected official can make an impression on a jury.

It took me two weeks of phone calls to get through to Trujillo's first-in-command, who agreed to pass on my request. After two more weeks the councilman finally called me back. Trujillo said that indeed Tony had been a great worker and honest as the day. But when I brought up the possibility of him testifying, he rapidly changed his tune: "After all," he didn't know Tony "terribly well"; he was reluctant to appear "in these circumstances"; and he had a busy schedule that might just otherwise "commit" him during the week for which the trial had been rescheduled.

However, it turned out that the D.A.'s office had again requested a trial postponement—an unavailable witness, Longo said. And when Tony turned down Longo's sweetened offer—drop the assault, plead guilty to petty theft, no jail or fine or community service, and clear Tony's record after a year's probation—I convinced Tony that the delay was not a bad thing. Although it would leave Tony in limbo, it would allow me to give Trujillo lots of advance notice. And after I went over with Trujillo on the phone the simple testimony I wanted (and mentioned that the press didn't bother covering misdemeanor trials), he had grudgingly agreed to appear on the new trial date. Which was today. But now it's 10:00 A.M., and where the hell is the guy?

The courtroom door opens and Longo sticks his head into the hall. Says he wants to talk, so I join him inside.

"Say, some powerful folks your people know."

"What folks? What do you mean, 'my people'?"

"Well, your old guy out there. Seems a councilman called our office last night to see if there wasn't some way we'd be willing to dispose of this thing."

"Called *your* office? . . . Well, okay, so?"

"So, seeing as how it's just been Fourth of July, I thought I'd show your Mr. Ledesma what this country has to offer him. So, I'll drop the petty theft to a disturbing the peace. Three months probation, then we dismiss, and he can tell all his grandchildren his record's clean."

I'm furious at Trujillo for not showing up, but the truth is his call's gotten something good for Tony. Disturbing the peace is a rarity from Longo, and only three months probation with no terms, then clearing Tony's record: in all, as low as the D.A. can go without dropping the case altogether. Longo is never going to drop it, not with the security guard actually seeing Tony put the screws in his pocket. And without any character witness now to back up Tony, going to trial would be a major gamble. So, I go out to give Tony the face-saving news.

Nope. Not pleading guilty to something I did not do, Tony says. I tell him he'll never get a better deal. And explain how risky trial is with no witness to support him. Then remind him that it's Sherman he's going to face. If Tony gets convicted, Sherman is almost certain to send him to jail again. Jail, Tony. Remember jail?

Longo sticks his head into the hall: "Five minutes, judge says. What about it, is he gonna plead?" I wave Longo away.

I want to go to trial with Tony, let him tell his story, then shape it in closing argument and offer it to a jury. But my experience of the courts, and particularly of Sherman, smothers the rush toward righteous resistance. I can't just go down swinging, because it's not *me* who'll go down. No, my job is to be a buffer for Tony, and in this case I'm convinced I know best. So, I try again. Remember, I tell Tony, if you're convicted of theft, the word will go out through that hotel manager, and you won't get any work at all. You can't afford that. And if you go down on assault, too, Sherman will give you more jail time, for sure. Tony, be sensible—take the deal.

But Tony is adamant. Stubborn, frozen with fear, I don't know, but he will not budge. I can't hide my frustration, and without speaking we march into court. I shake my head "No deal" to Longo as Sherman takes the bench and calls the case.

"Defendant's personally present in court, Your Honor. We are ready for trial."

"Well, I understand there's a disposition offer in this matter. Have you transmitted it to your client?"

"I have, Judge, but we're going to trial."

"Approach the bench, Counsel . . . . Listen, Matthews," Sherman hisses, off the record, "D.A. is giving away the store, so you start explaining to your man how, ah, things work around here."

"Judge, he won't plead. That's just the way it is."

"Well, then, you have to change his mind, don't you? I've got other trials and I don't want to waste my court on this."

Feeling thoroughly soiled and disdained from all sides, I sit Tony down at the counsel table and listlessly start to dun him again. After a moment he sets his work belt on the table, puts a strong, calloused hand on my arm, and squeezes. Not hard enough to hurt, but enough to stop me in midsentence.

"Your Honor," I stand up, "We're ready for trial."

The judge glares, then looks at Longo, who slowly gets to his feet. "Your Honor, the People have a motion. Due to an unavailable witness, we request that this matter be continued."

I look over at Longo: What the hell is going on here?

"Your Honor," I say, "we're prepared to go to trial. This is now the third time the D.A. wants a continuance. Since they obviously cannot put together a case against my client, I'd ask that the matter be dismissed for want of prosecution."

One thing is in our favor: Sherman hates delay almost as much as he hates defendants and P.D.s.

"For the record, Mr. Longo, what witness is it?"

"The complaining witness, Judge, a Mr. Stephen Baldwell."

The security guard. I start to argue again for dismissal but Sherman looks disgusted with everyone and puts up his hand.

"Have you subpoenaed him, Mr. Longo?"

"Ah, no, Your Honor. He now resides . . . out of state."

"Out of state!" I blurt. "Longo, you . . . . How long have you known . . . ?"

"Save it, Counsel," Sherman says. "Well, well, Mr. . . . Ledesma. Seems you played the right card; your lucky day. But let me strongly suggest that I not see you here on any other day. The charges are dismissed. You are free to go."

Tony does not look at me, starts to walk out.

"Tony, if I'd known . . . I'd never have told you to plead." I start to follow him out. "Tony, I didn't know . . . ."

"Counsel," Sherman calls to me, "we have other matters."

I stop. "Tony, I'll be out in a couple of minutes. I need to talk to you. Wait for me, will you?"

Tony looks at me with a rigid mask I cannot see behind. He nods slightly and goes out the door.

Longo is heading for the judge's chambers. I chase after him, to confront him about the game he ran on me—pretending the councilman was forcing him into a soft plea bargain when he knew all the time that he didn't have the key witness to go to trial. But Longo makes it into chambers, where Sherman is moving on to the rest of the trial calendar, and for the moment all I can do is glare. My office partner Kate is there, along with Deputy D.A. Weigant. Kate is next in line for trial—a "joy riding" case—but the client picked up a new beef over the weekend and she and Weigant have just agreed to package the two cases and take this trial off calendar. So, I'm up again, this time with Bobby Alonzo's drunk driving case. But the court clerk has a message that the arresting cop was involved in some shoot-out this morning and is not available for court today. So, Bobby Alonzo is postponed, and Kate and Longo are up next with another case. They quickly complete a plea bargain, however, and so that trial, too, has now folded.

All right, Sherman says, what's next? Nothing, Judge, I say; I'm not ready on anything else. What do you mean? he scoffs. Your office has another case set for today; let's see: Anderson. If the D.A.'s ready, it's going to trial.

Weigant tells Sherman that his two police witnesses are not here, but can be within an hour. Well, then, Sherman says, we're going out on Anderson.

"No way, Judge," I shake my head. "Can't do it."

"What do you mean, 'can't'?"

"Judge, I prepared two other trials. There's no way I'm ready to try this one, too."

"Listen, mister, your office has an obligation to be ready. And besides," he suddenly lards his voice, "it's a simple assault. You can do that on one leg."

Echoes of a career public defender to whom I had once bemoaned the chronic lack of time and resources to properly prepare for trials: "Well, just fly by the seat of your pants," he'd said, beaming. "Hell, that's the fun of it."

"Can't do it, Judge. I've barely looked at the file."

"Well, I'll give you a half-hour, so go talk to the girl. She's here, isn't she? Or maybe she wants to plead. Either way, I've got an empty courtroom, and we're going to use it."

Kate says she'll stick around to help, and I drag myself out to see Sharon Anderson. I take a moment to look at the file, but see again that there's virtually nothing in it. I've briefly spoken to Sharon on the phone, but all she said was that she had nothing to do with the demonstration—which seemed to be stretching things a bit, since she'd been arrested smack in the middle of it. Because these other trials were ahead of her, though, I hadn't bothered to press for details or speak to witnesses. Nor had I sent out one of our office investigators: with staggering overwork on felony cases, they almost never get to bother with misdemeanors, and then only to track down evidence the lawyers can't. So, the file is bare. And we're going to trial in half an hour. I need to get a story from her right away, then work with her on it at lunch while we're still picking a jury, and again this evening, before I head home to whip up a closing argument: ". . . the rising wave of people in this country, young and old, just like you and me, ladies and gentlemen, who are standing up not only for racial justice but for the fundamental and sacred American right to be heard . . . ."

Such suspicion in Sharon's eyes: "I told you, I wasn't at no demonstration." Anger brings out her Dust Bowl accent.

"Well, Sharon, how did you get caught there, then?"

"I wasn't demonstrating. I was . . . pregnant."

So much for my closing argument.

Turns out Sharon had gone to school that day just to find her boyfriend. She had learned for certain that morning that she was pregnant. She needed to talk to her boyfriend but didn't like going to his house—he's black, she's Okie cracker—and she thought the demonstration was where she could find him. And there he was, in a crowd of kids under arrest next to the gymnasium. She had to see him, couldn't wait—what if he went to jail for awhile? So, when the cops wouldn't let her get by, she sort of pushed her way through. Of course, she hadn't told all this to anyone before—not the cops, not our office—because she didn't want her family to know. And, she now said emphatically, wouldn't tell it in court, either . . . .

Well, a few minutes ago I had some notion of slogging through a trial. But I sure as hell don't anymore. And Sherman will just have to deal with it. I march back into chambers and announce that there is no way I am going to trial.

"No way?" Sherman says fiercely. "Did I hear 'No way'?"

"Afraid so, Judge. Couldn't give her a fair trial today."

"Not a fair trial? In *my* court?"

"Not any court. At least not until I can . . . develop some things."

"And just what, exactly, do you have to 'develop'?"

"That . . . I can't say, Judge. Attorney-client privilege."

"You want a continuance so you can so-call develop something, but you won't say what it is. And you have no other excuse for not going to trial? Well, I have a word for that—it's called Contempt. Contempt of this court and its processes. Just so we're clear before we go out on the record and you refuse this court's direct order to proceed."

Contempt. So, what the hell's he going to do? Ban me from his courtroom? Hallelujah. Let's go put it on the record.

We go out into the courtroom and I bring in sullen Sharon Anderson. Sherman calls the case and asks if the D.A. is ready to proceed; Weigant says he is. Then Sherman glowers at me, and I say that the defense is not prepared. Sherman says to state my reasons, and I say, "In order to protect my client's right to a fair trial and to adequate representation by counsel, our office needs more time to prepare." Sherman asks if the defendant is the cause of the delay. I quickly say, No, it's our office. And that, Sherman counters, means me. As a final formality, he directly orders me to begin trial. And I refuse.

Sherman draws himself up in his chair: "This court hereby finds attorney Joseph Matthews to be in direct contempt. And forthwith orders him into custody for a period of forty-eight hours, or until he purges his contempt by agreeing to proceed with trial in this matter."

"Judge, I . . ."

"Miss Anderson, you are ordered to remain in this courthouse and available to this department until further order. Bailiff, remand Mr. Matthews into custody."

What a joke. Old Collins the bailiff doesn't know what to do, and neither do I exactly, so I pick up my files and start to go with him back to see Sherman again in chambers. My partner Kate comes back too, but Sherman is waiting in his doorway.

"I don't want him, Collins. Put him in the holding cell."

Now this is really ridiculous. Kate says not to worry, she'll call our boss to straighten it all out. Actually, I don't even mind. I'll sit in the stupid holding cell and work on my files. An embarrassed Collins unlocks the cell door and I pause to see Kate scoot off to the phone. "No hurry, Kate," I say, and Collins closes the door. Only then do I turn and see that I am not alone. Crouching in the corner of the cell, quiet and peering like a nocturnal animal, is Taggart—the motor-oil man. Who, three days before, blew away a pizza delivery guy. And who, when last seen, had been trying to get a grip on my esophagus.

Have I soiled my pants? I don't think so. But these are some of the longest seconds of my life. Before I can call out to Collins, Taggart starts yelling, "You're not my lawyer! You're not my lawyer!" The bailiff doesn't bother to check with Sherman before opening the door. Fortunately, Taggart never lays a paw on me; in fact, he never leaves his corner.

Even Sherman now realizes the folly of putting me in the holding cell with Taggart, and so he has Collins put me instead in the empty jury room. It's a short stay in any event. My boss calls Sherman, and after some harsh words between them I am brought back into court where Sherman belittles me and my office but withdraws the contempt and sets a new date for Sharon Anderson's trial. As the proceedings end, Sharon says just one thing: "Judge, next time . . . can I have a real lawyer?"

Friday, July 29, 6:00 P.M.:

I stroll again by the Railroad Hotel, hoping to bump into Tony Ledesma. On my fourth or fifth pass—like a schoolboy by the house of his first crush—I spot Tony in the lobby and wave through the scratched and yellowed glass. I can't tell whether he takes awhile to notice me, or sees me and doesn't particularly care. Finally, he comes outside.

"Hey yah, Tony . . . . So, ah, how you doing?"

"Getting along."

"Well, you always do that, huh?"

The muscles in Tony's face relax a bit. I'm not sure what I'm going to say, but now is the time to say it.

"Tony, listen . . . . I gotta tell you, I'm really sorry."

"For what?"

"For, well, I don't know. You know—everything. The work you lost. The long hassle. You know, the way it all came down."

"Sorry?" he says. "Sorry's if you could do something different." He looks back at the hotel, down the street toward the jail. "So, tell me. Is there? Something different? Tell me."

A Permanent Dye

We had been walking for nearly an hour, wending up deep ravines canopied by stands of massive primordial redwoods. The air was cool and damp, our steps muffled by the soft red ground cover shed by the lordly trees, the strain on our legs helping to keep us from profaning with chatter the forest hush and beauty. Above the redwoods, we moved along a sun-mottled trail through scrub oak and Monterey pine, passing finally through a last gorse thicket and emerging into shimmering autumn light. High on a bluff the four of us stood, the late morning sun massaging our shoulders and bringing up to us in sharp relief the curling Big Sur River, the rocks and surging surf, and the endless Pacific beyond.

We sat without speaking on a rough granite outcrop, the hike and the view each breathtaking in its own way. There was Anna—whom for the past three months I had been seeing almost as often as I could rally myself, which in truth is to say only once in awhile—her sister Connie, and her brother-in-law Jeff. It was the end of my first year as a public defender, and over that time these two days in Big Sur were the first weekend I had not spent at least some part of writing a brief, working on files, or preparing for a hearing or trial.

It was Anna who finally broke the silence, saying simply and softly how glad she was we had come. Jeff passed around some bread and cheese and the three of them began quietly to converse, but I found I wasn't yet able to join them. It was a rare thing for me to be without glibness, my sword-and-shield of words. But I was overcome by the enormous distance between the feral beauty of this spot and the sordid, sorry world in which I had been immersed every waking moment the past year: a world of jails and courts; of endless broken lives laid bare; and of my triage ministrations with the crude and blunted tools of public defense.

For reasons beyond reason, I suddenly saw the face of my father, the face from the photo I had always known. The face of the man whose death in my early childhood had left me without a certain ballast by which to take the measure of myself. The man I'd never known but whom nonetheless I had always believed I could keenly feel—through the kindness of that face in the photo and the unfailing tearful adoration with which my mother would speak his name. The face of a man who had never managed to escape the gnawing of his inner demons; who had known love but never peace. What would you make of me, Father? What I care about? What I do? What would you tell me about this tight and aching knot inside my chest?

Somewhere sounds were faintly forming. I couldn't tell what they were except that they seemed unconnected to the distant conversation around me. After a few moments—minutes, perhaps—the amorphous sounds coalesced in my mouth and without a thought came bumping out, round and whole:

> Some Days retired from the rest
> In soft distinction lie
> The Day that a Companion came
> Or was obliged to die

An Emily Dickinson, recited for school and secretly, confusedly cherished. And which, despite the relentless American maleness of my youth, had survived in some hidden cave of memory. Venturing out, unbidden, for the first time, here and now.

So sweetly startled by its reanimation, I was unable to explain to the others my sudden murmur but could only turn and smile.

"Just like a lawyer," Connie said, "always spouting something."

O, Margaret

"Tell me something, will you? What's a punk?"

Since I was certain that Willis, of all people, had had the common epithet hurled at him often enough throughout his youth, I assumed that for some curious reason he must be after its more particular prison meaning. Without looking up—I tried to look at Willis as little as possible—I said, "It's the guy who catches . . . instead of pitches. You know, the one who . . . takes it . . . ."

"No, no, not that," he said with puckered lips. "England. . . . Some new thing."

I was the youngest in the office, still in my twenties, and therefore considered the one to ask about Some New Thing. It was 1974, maybe early 1975, and the English Punk scene was known in the States only to a few devout followers of anything from London involving haircuts or amplifiers. It didn't mean anything to me. And as always by mid-afternoon of a day spent lawyering, I was grouchy. Besides, Willis was a weasel.

"Don't bother, Willis. Just give it up. I mean, there's no fucking point . . . ."

"Right, right. That's the kind of thing. I knew you'd know."
Weasels have a notoriously poor ear for intonation.

The lawyers for whom I worked rented Willis an office—one of
the former bedrooms—in our converted three-story Victorian. I
had nothing to do with him, didn't know much about what he did,
didn't want to know. Willis's law practice seemed to consist not so
much of cases as of deals, his only lawyerly service being to
"review" documents generated to close these deals. As far as I could
tell, he never did a lick of work he could pawn off on someone
else—all too often I overheard his blustery phone litany, "All right,
then, have your people draw up the papers; I'll review them." And
his only actual legal expertise was in evictions and foreclosures.
Mind you, he claimed not to hire himself out indiscriminately to
handle such sordid proceedings. But for deals he had a piece of
himself, well, it came in handy once in awhile . . . .

This time the deal was called "O, Margaret." And although the
details I got from Willis were a bit muddled, essentially this is what
happened. Willis's connection had begun two years earlier at a tax
shelter seminar in the Cayman Islands, which was itself, of course,
tax deductible. There Willis had met and found instant mercantile
affinity with one Stanley Bob (*né* Bobovich), a Jersey City native
who had sufficiently tamped down his accent and hipped up his
wardrobe to insinuate a small entrepreneurial toe into the lower
Manhattan music scene. One night not long after the Caymans,
Stanley was in the Bowery sniffing at commercial possibilities when
a girl dressed entirely in torn and artless black slammed her shaved
head against a wall and threw up on Stanley's shoes outside a club
so trendy that even Stanley, whose job it was to know, had heard
rumor of it only hours before. As a direct result of her two-pronged
paroxysm, the girl had immediately gained admittance to the club
while others who fit perfectly what Stanley thought were that
week's fashions had been summarily turned away.

Stanley was impressed. Quickly he made some calls, heard his
first murmurs about something called Punk, collected a couple of
names, bought a plane ticket (standby), and within a few days
landed in London.

It's a marvel how people who deserve each other, find each other. Willis had found Stanley. And now Stanley found O, Margaret.

Reading through Willis's extensive clippings file on O, Margaret— or "the Maggies," as they were called by the underground press—I came across several different but equally impious versions of how they got their name. One related to that most nondescript and hence abusable member of the royal family; another to the Tory Party leader soon to begin her pillage of the realm; and a third to the horrified shriek of an unsuspecting shopper to her sister Margaret as they stumbled upon the Maggies' lead vocalist and a young woman of dubious majority *in flagrante delicto* near the back door of a Holloway Road fish and chips shop: "O, Margaret!"

I am unable to describe in great detail what the Maggies looked like, because the only photos Willis had were taken mid-perfor- mance—for lack of a better word—in some of East London's more subterranean venues. And the lads were not exactly enamored of the camera: one rare close-up of lead singer Furious Chaz swinging a microphone stand had cost the photographer twenty-seven stitches in the head. Actually, it wasn't that easy to distinguish between Chaz and the microphone stand, though from other pho- tos one could make out short stiff black hair, thin lips with a seem- ingly permanent ring of spittle, and a remarkable facility for doing away with his shirt, which revealed three battered crosses pinned through the flesh of his sunken, hairless, twenty-year-old chest. Thank you, Chaz.

Then there was Rat H. Difficult to say what Rat H looked like because in every photo I saw he was lost in the recesses of stage rear, head down, playing one sort or another of electronic noise- box, seemingly with his nose. Music director.

And finally, there was Boo Gluteus, bass guitar. Shaved skull like a spotty white bowling ball, and body to match, across what would have been Boo's hairline was tattooed a brief exhortation that finally I managed to put together from a composite of several photos: "Fuck" . . . "Off."

Stanley returned from England to find the hippest clubs in New York, San Francisco, and Los Angeles desperately wanting a "real"

English Punk band. Stanley immediately booked his new clients into half a dozen places even though none of the club managers had ever seen or heard O, Margaret. Stanley's approach was to play the club a brief snip from a Maggie performance, then quickly cut off the tape—claiming poor recording quality—and in its stead spread out the lads' pictures and a fistful of write-ups from the London alternative press, carefully culled encomiums ranging from the ecstatic "Maggies'll bleedin' rip your face off!" to the more ambiguous "O, Margaret, new truth of Britain's lie."

For the artier clubs, Stanley also winnowed some quotes from a self-described "sensor of modern music's mobile gestalt." Formerly a doctoral student of modern European politics, this seer had dropped his scholarly pursuits to write for the emerging music press when he realized that slinging postmodern cant about rock and roll would be more fun and considerably less work than studying politics. It seemed, though, that he had never ceased being somewhat embarrassed by his choice, and so relentlessly endeavored to demonstrate that in fact rock music *was* politics—not so much to convince people to take rock and rollers seriously as to have them take *him* seriously. From this character's slavering piece on O, Margaret, Stanley was able to mine such nuggets as "An irremediable breach in the historical fabric of representational art"; "Self-expressionist refutations of mass culture codes"; and "Dada thug rage poems." The Europhile clubs ate it up.

It was after the bookings were signed, however, that Stanley really went to work. From the clubs he managed to extract advance money, something normally unheard of: trans-Atlantic expenses, Stanley explained. He also convinced a record label that puffed itself on having "performance artists" in its fold to advance money for the Maggies to do a demo tape in New York. Stanley even got Willis involved. It happened that Willis had recently foreclosed on an old building in San Francisco that happened to house a hot underground club; Willis had just begun eviction proceedings. Stanley quickly turned Willis's leverage to good purpose, getting the Maggies booked into the club in exchange for Willis agreeing (temporarily) to let the club stay.

Once all the advance monies had been paid, Stanley moved to phase two. He flooded the clubs, record company, recording studio, and the music and underground press with a new set of clippings and photos, this time featuring the Maggies' penchant for inciting club-destroying mayhem among their adoring and despising fans. These reports added tremendous fuel to local proto-Punk anticipation of the tour, but also seeded considerable trepidation among club management and recording people. A record company executive, the recording studio manager, and several club owners called Stanley for reassurance. All Stanley would give them, however, were genial remarks like "Boys will be boys" and vague references to the saving graces of insurance, limited liability, and local law enforcement.

As time drew nigh for the sure-to-be-legendary American tour, Stanley upped the ante. O, Margaret unwittingly helped out by kindling a near riot in an East London club—not, in fact, a terribly difficult thing to do at the time—which the London tabloid press eagerly trumpeted as further proof of the imminent downfall of civilized life in Britain. Stanley not only had the newspaper articles rushed to his office but also numerous lurid original photos of the chaos-in-progress. It seems that Stanley had commissioned a photographer to attend this very engagement and to focus not so much on the Maggies as on their frothing, rampaging public. (In recounting all this, it should be noted, Willis vehemently denied any knowledge of Stanley having invested directly in crowd provocation.)

Stanley thoughtfully distributed photos and newspaper coverage of the devastation. His phone immediately started ringing: club owners clamored to cancel the engagements; the recording studio feared for its equipment; and the record company foresaw having to pay not only for the studio's losses but also for the injuries surely to ensue when these East London Punks got stroppy with the studio's New York security lugs.

Suddenly, though, Stanley wasn't taking calls. And after a calculated anxiety-producing delay, it wasn't Stanley's voice that the troubled businessmen heard but that of Ormond "Mincey"

Whipple. Stanley understood that the right trial lawyer can alter the balance of nature, and Mincey was known in New York legal circles as a man who would happily sue his own mother (a reputation somewhat slanderous since he had only sued his mother once and had not, in fact, been all that happy about it since she had proved to be a ruthlessly formidable opponent).

Mincey began negotiating with the club owners and the recording people from a position of strength encapsulated in the two phrases he alternately intoned for their edification: "*Caveat emptor*" and "Well, the lads will be here soon." Within ten days, Stanley and Mincey had settled with all the clubs, the record company, and the recording studio, on terms decidedly favorable to the O, Margaret entertainment consortium: each club coughed up an amount equal to what sold-out performances would have grossed; the record company paid twice the amount of expenses advanced; and the studio paid the estimated (by Stanley) cost of recording at an equivalent London venue. All in exchange for the promise that the Maggies would *not* make their scheduled appearances. The total was something over forty thousand dollars. 1975 dollars.

It's often said that information is the key to a lawsuit. And Stanley had once again proved the axiom. Because by the time Stanley unleashed Mincey Whipple, they but not their adversaries knew that all that remained of O, Margaret was its infamous name. Furious Chaz had by then become Chazzam!, a black-leather human installation artist, and had left for Berlin. Rat H was in the hospital after scorching off his body hair and doing considerable damage to his eardrums when he connected a synthesizer to a London Underground track-switching box. And Boo Gluteus? Boo was beginning three years behind bars for torching his mother's apartment while, due to his drug-stupored miscalculation and much to his chagrin, she was out at the shops—*caveat emptor.*

Call Me Willie

I wasn't really surprised when Willie's desk blew up. Stunned, certainly—of all the crises that might beset a desperately sinking lawyer, explosion and fire is not one you are prepared for. And once the shock wore off, depressed—how bad could things get for the poor guy? But surprised, no. Because by that time Willie's capacity for disaster seemed as great and out of control as was his swollen, overloaded heart.

I hadn't known Willie for very long, at least not well. Still, within a short time of working for him two days a week as I gradually withdrew from practice, I felt an uncommon warmth and loyalty toward Willie, which translated into Sisyphean efforts at keeping him and his practice on their increasingly wobbly legs. And that was the thing for Willie, both his unrelenting need and his particular genius—getting people to like him. Even when he disappointed them, did them wrong, over and again. And not simply to like him, but to care about him. A remarkable talent. And gangway to his ruin.

I'd met Willie through his law partner, Eric, my former colleague in the Public Defender's office. Willie and Eric had met in

Mississippi during a "Freedom Summer" voter registration drive, their friendship forged in that special, superheated air breathed by people who not only find themselves *in extremis* but who derive satisfaction from picturing themselves so. After they finished law school, Eric coaxed Willie west to join him in a Legal Aid office. A year later Eric shifted to a public defender job while Willie hung out a solo shingle doing bits and pieces of small-time legal work: petty crime; landlord-tenant; divorce; personal injury. When after two years Eric had cut his trial teeth as a public defender, he left the P.D.'s office and joined Willie to form their own two-man private practice.

Willie got the clients. Eric did the work. It was an arrangement that suited them both. Not that Eric didn't bring in some cases nor Willie ever write a brief or go to court. But from the beginning their roles were heavily weighted by their personalities, and as their partnership lengthened the imbalance became more pronounced. Eric was organized, diligent, and jurisprudentially articulate but otherwise dull. Whereas Willie was, well, charming.

Irish charming, some people said. But that was only partly right. He was half-Irish, true enough, his father over on the boat. Ulster Protestant, Willie's father had been, but of that a shifting shade. During his youth in the North, Thomas MacElveen had worn Orange bright and wide, yet later in Dublin he'd been Green as any Padraig or Sian. That Tom MacElveen recoated himself with a republican brush in the South was due in part to an obvious taint: MacElveen is a Scots name and so, despite the elocution and airs he acquired at ruinous cost to his tradesmen parents at a Trinity College preparatory school, forever disqualified him—certain markers were clear and ineradicable in Ireland—from full membership in Anglo-Irish Protestant society and its Dublin power grid.

But the mouthing of republican sacraments worked no Green miracle in Dublin: whatever else he had become, in the South Counties he was still a Northerner. So, Tom MacElveen decided to get off the emerald rock altogether. And as he disembarked at Boston harbor, he brought to a new life his old chameleon ways: when asked his name, he pronounced it Thomas M. Kelveen, and

the pachydermatous immigration officer duly followed Tom's pho-
netic lead. From that day on the "Mac" was gone, and Tom
Kelveen was able to step onto New World streets with one less peb-
ble in his shoe.

He was, of course, still recognizably Irish in heavily Irish Boston,
but the exact wheres and whats of his history were now more easily
maneuvered. So, Tom Kelveen was Tommy-as-could-be in the
working class streets of his Dorchester home, but slipped smoothly
into Tom and Thomas as he made his way deeper downtown. By
the time he married Willie's mother—a first generation Polish-
American Catholic whose South Boston family of eleven was far
more concerned about whether he would take over the care and
feeding of this pregnant fourth daughter than which church he'd
marry her in—Tom's pronunciation of Kelveen had evolved into
something remarkably close to "Calvin." And when he signed the
papers to move his wife and new son Wil into a flat in the less
Irish-identified Brighton area of central Boston, the second "e" had
mysteriously gone missing from Kelve(e)n.

Willie was delighted to find that he and I had Boston, even
Brighton, in common. Or, sort of in common. I had left the East
Coast while still an adolescent, and teen years in California had
obliterated most lingering Boston aftertastes. By age ten Willie,
too, had moved from Brighton, though not nearly so far. His father
had managed to shift the family a couple of miles upscale to
Brookline. But because Willie was initially uncomfortable in these
posher confines—parts of which were home to the Cabots and
Lodges and to Irish like the Kennedys—he continued until high
school to hang around the haunts of nearby Brighton. So, for
Willie, Brighton was his youth, memories of it primal and hallowed. Evocations of this Brighton, however, had found no echo in
Willie's Northern California life and so had languished unspoken
and sorely missed. Until he met me.

Willie would take me to lunch at Bip's—the nearby formica and
Naugahyde diner where he felt most at home—and something

about the waitress, the food, or the homely clientele would spark for him a flash of Brighton, and he'd be off on a reminiscence. It usually involved some ramble around back-street Boston with his peripatetic father, the telling of which would begin in hilarity but eventually and invariably would leave Willie sobered and somber, and for virtually the only time I ever spent with him, silent.

It was from these tales told over extended lunches—digesting Bip's food made it difficult to get up quickly, a process that Willie would in any event prolong, my rejection never withstanding, with two orders of ersatz Boston cream pie—and during Willie's coffee breaks, snack breaks, shopping breaks, and breaks to handicap horses, in all of which I served as the company he craved, that I stitched together the family saga of Willie Kelven.

No longer obviously either a Mac or a Mick, Willie's father Tom worked both sides of the street in several parts of town—not easily accomplished when the town was 1930s Boston where by name, speech, and somatic tics everyone knew immediately where you were from and made sure to keep you there. But Tom had experience of Belfast and Dublin, and soon understood that while Boston's class compartmentalization might not allow you to be someone other than you'd always been, its immigrant porosity permitted a clever enough fellow to be several of who he'd sometimes been. So, Willie's father undertook the careful cultivation of separate, parallel lives. In the warehouses and docks of Boston's North End, he was a broad and lilting Tommy Kelveen (". . . as in 'Green'"). In the garages and storage yards of Mattapan, he was Ulster Tom ("That's *Kel*ven, if you please"). And in later years, as a guest in oak-paneled office suites on Beacon Street, the Brahmins certainly knew he wasn't one of them, but—by his embossed card with a decent enough name (Thomas Mansfield Kelven) and business address (though not if they'd known he lived there, too), and an accent that passed in New World ears for something near enough to "class"—he was just acceptable enough for an occasional lunch if not dinner invitation, which is to say, for them to drop him business crumbs without worrying that he'd use the wrong fork.

It was metalware of another sort that had gotten Tom to their table. He'd heard tell of the Laughlin family's Irish-American fortune in steel, and figured that might be his ticket, too. And so it became—though from the opposite end of the line. Dublin Tommy/Ulster Tom made his living by scouring docks and warehouses for scrap iron and damaged machine parts, setting up salvage and repair operations in the off-hours of garages and workshops. And when the Second World War brought shortages of both raw metals and finished machinery, Tom Kelven's back-street network was able to nudge itself into the bigger business world downtown.

It was Willie's mother who held this ship of progress on course. From their Brighton kitchen and then Brookline dining room, Magdalene Kelven (maiden name Palawski) handled the books and billing and, perhaps most crucially, worked the "office" phone with a subtle, shifting set of phrases to match with each contact and customer the particular demographic connection her husband had carefully forged in person.

Magda also steered through other shoals: she chose to bear but one more child after Willie, and only ten years after, when the family fortunes had significantly improved. In the heavily Catholic Boston of the 1940s and '50s there was an extreme dearth of birth control assistance, and whether Magda's success in limiting the number of mouths to feed was managed with or without the blessings of the Church—or of her husband, for that matter—Willie never inquired. But in great part because of such restraint, and despite the demands of business, Willie and his little sister Beth received from Magda all the care and attention that this fourth of nine children had missed from her own numbingly poor and overextended immigrant parents.

After the first few rough years in Brighton, life for Willie—and for his sister born in Brookline—was comfortable and relatively carefree. Their father provided them increasing material support and security, though work kept him away for long hours most every day and many nights. And while Magda may have wished for more of Tom at home (or perhaps not), she knew that he made his interminable rounds entirely for the family's sake. Knew that, despite the considerable opportunities presented by his far-ranging encounters and protean charm, Tom Kelven resisted—except for an occasional card table stint and a passing amount of whiskey in the cause of Irish-American commerce—both gewgaws and vice.

During his primary school years, Willie often made weekend rounds with Tom of his Irish network of sheds and workshops, docks and yards. Tom Kelven knew the Hibernian solidarity value of a bright and impish flame-haired son, but he also just enjoyed showing young Wil how cheerily his father was received all over town. And Wil saw very well: the boy quickly picked up his father's knack for evoking an easy chumminess among varied sorts. Wil had a child's innocent pride in so easily pleasing all these adults. But more, since he could not fathom the depths of his father's manipulations nor details of the transactions, what he read in the grown-ups' relations was both simple and deeply impressing: that his father Tom's mood rose and fell in direct proportion to how well Tom was able to instill in each cohort a feeling that whatever life brought the man's way, Tom and he were in it together.

By high school, Willie's forays with his father were less frequent, in part simply because Tom Kelven's networks were by then so well established that he made fewer personal rounds. Nonetheless, Tom would have liked to keep bringing his son along, to continue Wil's real-world education and to groom him—this Willie assumed, his father never actually saying so—to take over the business Tom had so painstakingly built from scratch.

No, the slowing and eventual end during high school of Willie's trips around town with his father was not of Tom's choosing. Rather, it was part of a larger separation between father and son, a natural and common progression of teenagehood: breaking away from parents, their authority, their old-fashioned ways. For Willie, this need for distance arose in a particularly painful form. In the boisterous but nuanced world of teenage social relations, Willie's parents proved to be a distinct if mostly unspoken liability. Willie's father had by now made enough money to provide Willie with many of the obvious trappings—nice clothes, a car—that most children of Brookline's well-to-do families had. But by high school these scions of the Boston oligarchy already knew the distinction—long established in this oldest of New World cities—between the families that own and those that merely buy and sell. So, despite a big house and Mr. Kelven's ability to turn on a cultured Anglo-Irish voice and manners, Willie's tony schoolmates understood in the same way as did their parents that Tom Kelven had to work for his money. It was an understanding that peeled away the senior Kelven's present from his past, the Anglo from his Irish, and rendered unwinnable Willie's struggle for full acceptance by the kids who "mattered" at Brookline High.

But if in high school Willie resented from on high his parents' immigrant roots and petit-bourgeois success, in college this perspective turned on its head. It was now the Sixties, and by the end of his fevered years at university Willie had only contempt for the old high school elite and its judgments. But while Willie's view of his parents now came from an antipodal position, his verdict was not much improved. Tom Kelven's single-minded life of accumulation was antithetical both to Willie's new politics and to the spirit of the age. And more, Willie's high school experience had led him to a conclusion his father had never reached: that earnings alone were never quite enough to gain the kind of security Tom strove for, a security that only a change in where your money comes from—a move up in class—could guarantee.

That is, Willie *believed* that his father never reached such a conclusion. For it was with much left unsaid between father and son that Tom MacElveen—a.k.a. Tommy Kelveen, Ulster Tom Kelven and Thomas Mansfield Kelven—died.

Immediately after college graduation, Willie had left for the Freedom Summer in Mississippi with his father ailing and a huge gap of silence between the two men. And though surely Willie's mother had known how perilous was her husband's condition, she did not stop Willie from going south. Despite what seemed its rather reckless direction, Magda saw Willie's first step out of

Boston as an opportunity for him, and she wanted nothing to stand in the way of his moving still further from where she and Tom had begun.

During that summer, Willie was so mesmerized by the civil rights hothouse of Mississippi that he gave barely a thought to his family. Following him to Mississippi, though, were lessons he'd learned back home. For example, he'd always been William in school and Wil to family and friends. But much like his father at immigration four decades earlier, when first meeting Freedom Summer comrades he had found himself blurting, "Hi, call me Willie," with a slight, unobtrusive drawl.

This new moniker notwithstanding, Willie was acutely aware during that summer of the degree to which he didn't belong. Not that he wasn't appreciated by local civil rights veterans for his street smarts and verve. Nor that he wasn't popular with the other young volunteers who admired the ease with which Willie mimicked and melded with their hosts. But shaped by exposure to his father's commercial performances and by his difficult high school days, Willie suffered from an inability to view himself except as he believed others saw him. And despite relative success among his Freedom Summer peers, his being a callow white Northerner in Mississippi meant that any picture of himself that he might truly relish inevitably remained out of reach. So, by summer's end he was doubly pained: by what he'd seen of the nation's racial morass, and by uncertainty over which of his already several identities truly belonged to him. Before he could get home to sort things out, his father died.

What happened after Tom Kelven's death both heightened Willie's insecurity about how others saw him and deepened his conviction that lucre was not so much filthy as ephemeral. For awhile, his mother was able to keep the family business going. But whatever Irish romanticism Willie harbored from the success of his father's emerald network was now spectacularly disappointed: neither shared Celtic spirit nor long-years' relations with his father generated much in the way of economic empathy among Tom's former cronies. By the time Willie took his law degree, his mother had been forced to sell for a song what was left of the Kelven business.

Willie now had a difficult decision to make. He was being coaxed to California by his Freedom Summer buddy Eric, and the chance to leave Boston was immensely attractive. It was 1968, and San Francisco—with its beatnik, hippie, and political tribes—looked mighty good to a young man from a city whose dominant cultural progenitors were the Puritans and the Catholic Church. But Willie was uneasy. He'd left Boston once before, and his father had died with much unresolved between them. Willie didn't know exactly what he needed to resolve with his mother or wanted to impart to his sister, but he felt that leaving might keep him from finding out.

Magda urged him to go, to start a new life. And while Beth was excited by the imagined picture of her big brother in California, she could not hide her sense of impending loss. Finally, Willie decided to leave. But to assuage his guilt, he promised Beth that when settled he would bring her out for a long visit and together they would explore the wild West. When Willie saw Beth's thrill at the idea, he embroidered for her elaborate descriptions of the things they'd do together in California. Lavished her with itineraries right up to the moment he climbed into his car for the long drive west. And who knows, he said to Beth from behind the wheel, when you get out there you might just have to stay. When this elicited an excited if embarrassed laugh from Beth, he blew a kiss to her and his mother and drove off quickly, Beth's grinning face his last image of leaving them behind.

"Damn it, Willie, you're driving me crazy!"

"Sorry . . . sorry . . . right . . . right . . . sorry."

It was about six months after I had begun part-time work for Willie. We were in a break from a hearing in a serious criminal case, and for the past hour as I cross-examined a witness, Willie's ceaseless manic scribbling on a notepad—copper health bracelet clacking away—had maddeningly rocked the counsel table where we sat. I was ready to throttle him. Particularly because his note-taking was pointless: I was the one examining the witnesses and preparing the briefs, not him. Perhaps the furious writing was intended to give client, prosecutor, and judge the appearance that Willie was in charge. All I knew was it was making me nuts.

As best I recall, this was the first time I sensed there was something seriously wrong with Willie. More seriously, that is, than with his usual chaotic, procrastinating self. Maybe I should have noticed it earlier, in the map that unfurled on his body. Willie was small-boned and had always been thin, an underwhelming physical presence about which he'd been mildly embarrassed as a youth. But in college he had heard himself described as "lean" and "slim"— adjectives newly flattering to males in the anti-matter Sixties—and from then on had taken pride in his lightly carried frame. Over the few months I'd worked for him, though, he'd refused to recognize a sorry new bloatedness, and his stubbornly held self-image had begun literally to cause him pain. Instead of changing either habits or trouser size, Willie cinched his belt tighter and tighter to hold in his increasing girth, which resulted in a misconceived trek through shelves of antacids and in a decidedly pained expression following his favorite lunches at Bip's.

Willie's entire appearance was becoming slovenly and lax. While limited income and a political antipathy for conspicuous consumption had kept Willie from being a serious clotheshorse, he'd always liked stylish, well-made threads. Now, however, Willie was likely to come to work in polyester shirt and slacks bought on the run at the local Save-Mart store. And often the same stained clothes several days running, because even though he'd buy three shirts at a time, in the mess of his house and his car he wouldn't be able to find the other two. Eyeglasses were the same: always lost, bent, or so scratched that they only contributed to Willie's now frequent, mysterious nausea. In fact, if it hadn't been for Jenny's vigilance at keeping an extra pair at hand—as well as spare sets of his keys—it's doubtful Willie would have ever made it home at night. As it was, on increasingly frequent occasions he didn't make it home anyway.

Although he was married when I'd first met him years before, by now his longtime secretary Jenny was the woman of Willie's life. I say "of" rather than "in" his life because they had never become lovers. Not physically. There was an intimacy and mutual dependence, though, a deep familial caring that I have no hesitation calling love. Jenny was immensely good at what she did, which had progressed—or deteriorated—from being Willie's legal secretary to serving as his personal amanuensis, apologist, and steward. And Willie was in considerable need of all three. Because by the time I arrived to help with what Willie described as his "overflow" legal work, he was nearly incapable of doing anything for himself.

It hadn't always been that way. The original Willie had been the engine of his and Eric's practice. A marvel with people of all sorts, he'd been able to quickly find common ground with them, and more, to convince that he'd do right by them. Willie loved his role in the law—people came to him because they *needed* him. And for at least their first few meetings, he and a client could both believe that he'd be able to help.

Willie not only brought in the clients but also was the one who blathered up the insurance adjusters and opposing lawyers, the D.A.s, probation officers, and judges. In any one of these legal opponents Willie first and foremost searched for something the other could recognize they had in common, some way to the soft human center of the hardened legal heart. It was Willie's special talent, this chatting up the bad guys: if he could get them to talk, he could get them to like him; and if they could like him, they could like his client. Or at least do Willie a favor despite what they thought of his client. So, Willie would do lunch, do coffee, discuss baseball, gardening, God. He'd laugh at bad jokes and tell them, smile at lies and lie back, smiling. It could be a tremendous strain, this being likable to all the sundry cold-eyed legal bastards, but it was the way Willie knew to make things work. And while most lawyers feel somehow unfulfilled by compromise, bargain, negotiated plea, Willie actually took extra pleasure in it: not only did he achieve something for his client, but he could also believe that on the other side he might have made a friend.

Of course, Willie's efforts didn't always pan out. And then Eric would step in for the battle. Not that Willie couldn't engage, if necessary, in the aggression and heated disputes of litigation. It's just that he so much disliked to, was never comfortable letting that part of himself take over. Besides, that's what Eric was for, what Eric did well.

After awhile, Eric began to suffer from Willie's capacity to like— and therefore to sign up—every potential client he met. As their reputations grew and Willie hustled up more business, Eric faced grinding trial after trial and was wearing out from the struggles— especially the more serious criminal cases that, win or lose, took such a chunk of his flesh. He was starting to make noises about slowing down.

At about the same time, after several years in practice, Willie suffered a blow the effect of which it is difficult to gauge. His first year in California Willie had spent adjusting to his new life and to his demanding Legal Aid job, and so had put off his sister Beth's trip west. The next year, plans for the visit were beginning to take shape when Willie met his wife-to-be, and once again Beth's trip was put on hold. In the third year he and Eric opened their own practice, an all-consuming task, and so he postponed the visit once again. A year later was Willie's divorce and another delay. Finally, Beth was set to come out. But she fell ill just before her departure. The doctors didn't know what it was and began a series of tests. Willie wanted to fly back to Boston to be with Beth and his mother, but a case was coming to trial and for the first time in a long while Willie had agreed to handle it. He could have asked Eric to take over the case, but Eric was already overwhelmed, so Willie postponed his trip east and instead went to trial. On the third day a call came: Beth had a brain tumor, inoperable. Willie flew immediately to Boston, but Beth had lapsed into a coma and never woke up.

Willie stayed off work for a month. And soon after he returned, money became a problem. Not that the practice wasn't making enough. But Willie seemed incapable of hanging onto it. He had never believed that income bought security, and now more money seemed to mean just more to spread around. Among other things,

Willie was constantly buying the latest gadgets (a sunglasses/radio; a TV/watch), both as toys to distract himself and as presents (my first was a calculator/pen, useless as either) to stroke his often-exasperated friends and associates. Gambling, too, served a dual purpose: an adrenaline rush, plus the fawning attention paid a (losing) gambler by both bookies and touts. And then there was always another business lunch or dinner, with adversaries as well as clients; Willie always picked up the tab.

The result of all this spending was that Willie needed to generate more business. But while Willie was now procuring more than ever, he was litigating not at all, leaving the increasing number of courtroom battles exclusively to Eric. Willie had reached a point where he no longer merely preferred negotiation to litigation but avoided legal conflict completely. Eric was already burning out in the crucible of trial work, and he was seriously chafed by Willie's total avoidance of the fires. Whether Willie taking back some of the trial load at this point would have staved off Eric's decision I don't know. But Willie wouldn't or couldn't get back in the courtroom, and after six years together Eric left both Willie and private practice, going to work in a legal department of the Catholic Church.

With Eric gone, it was just Jenny and the kindness of strangers. Willie's practice slid slowly, then precipitously, downhill. His now total reliance on chatty personal relations with his adversaries and their hoped-for willingness to compromise—which is to say, his unwillingness to engage in formal legal battle—left him with a growing backlog of unfinished cases and unhappy clients.

"Oh, he's in deposition," Jenny would deflect phoning clients and lawyers time and again. "Don't know when he'll be back." With remarkable dexterity she would cover for him while the phone-message slips piled up on his desk. Until finally she'd reach a point when she could take the angry voices and her own lies no longer. Then she'd step into Willie's office, close the door, and demand that he either immediately make some calls or look for another secretary.

Having Jenny threaten to quit didn't worry Willie much; they'd been through so much that it was now just another part of their bond. And besides, it gave him a chance to make it up to her. But worried, restive, or furious clients were a different matter, painful for a man who needed to be liked. So, every couple of weeks he'd sit down to make desperately conciliatory phone calls—"Hi-hello-good morning," he'd begin rapidly, "I've been trying to get you . . . ."—craving from the clients even the most reluctant kind word, latching onto the thinnest straws of forgiveness. Inevitably, he'd end the call with a promise to wrap up the case "in the next week or so" and to see the client for lunch "as soon as I've got a free minute." He'd often follow up with flowers to the client and some costly new gadget—an electric cat-food dispenser stands out—for Jenny. And the rest of the day off for himself.

His criminal cases, however, could not be so easily finessed. Willie used standard excuses to request one and then another delay, and the overburdened courts would regularly oblige. Willie hoped that in the interim his blarney and blandishments, plus diminished interest in the now-stale cases, would lead prosecutors to offer reduced pleas that Willie's clients could live with. And often it worked. But in serious cases, getting repeated delays was problematic. And a decent plea bargain was usually beyond reach unless and until one prepared for and verged on trial. Major trials were well beyond what Willie could handle, but heavy criminal cases were now his only source of substantial income and so he continued to take on new ones. As a result, he had a festering backlog of these cases—referred through his gambling circles or by former clients from Eric's days—with some unpredictable, menacing defendants.

Menacing to Willie because, like other criminal lawyers, he demanded his fees up front. In other words, Willie had long since taken and spent large sums of money from these clients but had done little or nothing to earn it. And by now most of the clients *knew* he'd done nothing: no witnesses contacted; no defenses mapped; no legal maneuvers filed in court.

It was at this point that Willie got in touch with me to help him out. But since part-time backup work was by then as much law as I could stomach, I could only be so much help. I would prepare drafts of legal motions, but they would sit on his desk untouched; and if, between Jenny's hectoring and mine, Willie somehow eventually managed to file a motion, he would wind up indefinitely postponing its hearing. Or I would plan out trial preparations for him and he would listen and discuss them with passionate attention; then two or three weeks later I'd find that he hadn't done a thing. After awhile I wasn't doing any new work for Willie, just repeating old conversations, and those more cautionary tales and pep talks than discussions of law.

Often I would come to work only to find Willie gone, Jenny not knowing where—"He's in court," she'd report to callers—and so I would spend hours doing little more than organizing the incredible mess of his desk and files. When Willie did come in, he'd be nervous, scattered, and disheveled. The ringing phone was a terror to him: in constant money trouble, he now dodged bill collectors as well as clients. Willie's only contact was with a few drug clients and a selection of bookies and gamblers, but most of the time he avoided even their calls and hid, ashen-faced, from their occasional drop-in visits.

Increasingly, when Willie would step out of the office for a few minutes, he wouldn't come back. He could never be reached at home, though sometimes he'd call in to Jenny. Evasive about his movements, he'd want to know only whether a particular person— one of the bookies or drug clients—had called. Occasionally he would leave a number for one of the select to call him; most often it would be a room at a local Holiday Inn.

In the nine months I worked for him, Willie went through three car accidents, a stolen briefcase, a lost wallet, chest pains, a broken finger (on his writing hand), and a purported case of gastroenteritis, each buying a grace period during which he was excused from work by both clients and courts. Eventually, however, Willie's ability to stall the major criminal cases ran out: three were coming to trial within the next two months. Willie was sweating heavily but making no progress. Finally I urged him to face the music: tell the clients to get other lawyers and file court motions to withdraw himself from the cases based on medical reasons I was sure his doctor could truthfully ascribe. But to withdraw from the cases would mean having to return large sums of money, money Willie no longer had. And perhaps more painful still, it would mean publicly admitting that Willie Kelven could no longer be of any help.

It happened on a Thursday, but since I only came to the office a couple of days a week, I didn't see the devastation until Monday. Even then, Willie's inner office was still a remarkable mess: scorched shards of files and charred bits of paper all over the floor; walls and ceiling smirched with soot; a yard-wide, caramelized circle seared into the top of his desk. Jenny was there, tight-lipped and grim, a new layer of anger piled onto years of frustration and creasing her face. Willie was there, too, dazed and somber, yet also somehow elated. His eyebrows were singed, one hand bandaged, but otherwise he seemed physically unscathed. I stood by Jenny's desk, not understanding what the hell had happened, not knowing what to do. As Willie darted past, he gave me an oblique staccato of the event—"Working late. Fell asleep. Could have been killed."—but did not look at me or stop to explain. He spent the morning on the phone telling clients, courts, and prosecutors about the fire, then ran out, bought a Polaroid camera (deluxe model), and took pictures of the destruction for Jenny to send along with his requests to postpone all his cases.

I was sitting in the little library I used as a work space, wondering what to do with myself, when I heard Willie and Jenny arguing. He had on his jacket and was heading for the door.

Jenny was near tears: "If you can't stick around, I'll be damned if I will."

"Fine," Willie growled. "That's fine. Real loyalty. After all I've just gone through."

"Gone through? Whose fire was it, Willie? Whose?"

"Well, but I have to see some people. Fine. Wait . . . ."

Jenny was out the door, Willie trailing her. I didn't see either of them again that day, which I spent sorting through burned papers and files. The next day I called in but got only the answering service. I tried Willie at home; no answer. The same at Jenny's house.

On Wednesday I went into the office and found Willie on the phone with one leg propped on his desk and resting on a pillow. At Jenny's desk sat Gloria, who used to do extra secretarial work back in the office's busier days. From Gloria I learned that when the cleaning man had come in early that morning, he had heard groaning and banging in Willie's office. There he'd found Willie on the floor with his leg "stuck" under a tipped-over file cabinet. Willie, claimed to have come in during the evening to get his office back together when somehow the cabinet toppled and trapped him there, out of reach of the phone, all night. Strange, the maintenance man had mentioned to Gloria, but when he'd found Willie, there had been an open can of cola and a stack of magazines on the floor right next to him.

Willie had called Gloria to come in for the day and asked her to try to reach Jenny, giving close instructions to tell Jenny that he had been injured while cleaning up his office. Willie spent the morning on the phone, and when Jenny didn't show up by lunch, he limped out and didn't return.

I came in again the next day to continue sifting through the wreckage; Jenny still wasn't there. Willie came in late, carrying a large box the contents of which he proudly displayed for me: a wide-brimmed gardening hat inside the high crown of which was set a tiny electric fan. "Solar-powered," Willie grinned and held it under a desk lamp. In a few moments, the blades began feebly to turn. "Jenny's probably been out in her garden," he added in apparent reference to why she hadn't answered her phone. Then he swept out the door. Phone messages piled up all day, and when I left, there had been no more word from him. Or from Jenny.

I called in each of the next few workdays to see how things were going; Gloria was answering the phone. There were signs that

Willie had been in at night, she said, and occasionally he called in for messages, but Gloria hadn't actually seen him. When I showed up the next week, Jenny was back and Willie was in his office on the phone. I didn't ask about the garden hat, but Jenny seemed ready to bolt again any minute. She and I went out to lunch, and she confirmed what I had suspected: Willie's drug clients were now his suppliers as well. I knew Willie had for some time been "chipping" small amounts of cocaine, both to escape his unrelenting stress and to establish good graces with the dealers from whom he had taken large fees but to whom he had yet delivered nothing on his legal promises. Now, though, Jenny reported having several times found Willie slumped in his chair, a pipe, burned screens, and cocaine residue on his desk. She was sure the office explosion had been caused by chemicals used to "freebase" cocaine. When I asked whether it might have been intentional—to buy him time and sympathy—she shrugged and said that at this point, she really didn't care.

For more than a year I had been planning and saving for some extended travels, and the time had finally arrived. I spent extra days before my departure trying to piece Willie's files and practice together. Jenny resumed her stalwart defense against the attacks of clients, courts, and bill collectors, but it was clear that Willie was losing the war. On some days he would come into the office with apparent good intentions, make some calls, shuffle some papers, and raise some hopes. On most days, though, he would arrive late, nervously check messages, spar with Jenny, and leave soon after. Many days he didn't come in at all.

The delays he had obtained via the office fire were now running out and the pressure was back on, full force. His big cases were once again coming up for trial, but he was incapable of preparing for them yet unwilling to have someone else take them over. He was rarely in the office for more than a few minutes at a time and, when there, was barely communicative.

One morning Jenny found on her desk an envelope with her name written on it. Inside was an unmarked key and a note in Willie's handwriting. The note said that Willie—described in the third person—had been "held" overnight at the 10th Street Motel, that his hands were bound with wire and tied to the bathroom sink, and that Jenny was "requested" to come and get him. The office receptionist could tell Jenny only that the note had been delivered by a somewhat bedraggled woman who didn't leave her name. Jenny took it all for another of Willie's delirious productions and did nothing.

An hour later the phone rang. It was Willie, and he was furious at Jenny. "Where are you?" he demanded.

"Well, where are you?"

"I've just been released. If the cleaning lady hadn't showed up, I'd still be in there! Where were you? In ten years I've never asked you to do anything for me . . . ."

Jenny hung up on him. A few minutes later Willie staggered into the office and tried to show us how red his wrists were from having been bound all night. Jenny wanted no part of the story, but Willie followed her around like a dog that won't go home, alternately trying to tell her "the whole story" and berating her for "deserting" him. When he sputtered about how much "integrity" he'd shown at the motel by refusing to take part in some sort of drug deal, Jenny howled with grief and derision, snatched her things, and stormed out. As the door slammed behind her, "loyalty" was the last word she heard.

I was out of the country for two months (accompanied by the self-everything camera Willie had bought for me on my departure, even though he couldn't pay the rent). When I returned, I wasn't greatly surprised to find Willie's office closed, his apartment empty, no forwarding phone or address. I got in touch with Jenny, and a few days later, we met for a drink. She told me that after I'd left she had come back to the office and tried but failed to get Willie into a drug rehabilitation program. She had left the office soon thereafter, and though Willie continued to call and stop by her house, she had refused to have anything more to do with him until he sought help. The State Bar had moved against him on behalf of long-languishing clients, and the courts had removed him from his criminal cases. She wasn't sure, but Jenny thought some bookies and drug dealers were looking for him, too.

The last Jenny had seen of Willie was a month before, on his way out of the state with a few belongings packed into his now-battered car. He had told her that he was cleaning himself up, but she'd heard it before and he'd driven off mumbling something about "integrity."

Jenny told me what a good thing it was for her to have gotten away from the whole mess. Then she cried and said she missed him.

One day about six months later my phone rang and there he was. It was almost the voice of the lively, ingratiating Willie I had once known, but given all that had happened, a voice in the wrong key. With forced cheerfulness he told me he was living with friends "way out in the country" and doing well. I asked no details, he offered none, and we said without conviction that we'd get together the next time he was in the area.

An hour later the doorbell rang. Willie. And a huge box. Speedy and a bit rough around the edges, this was not the easy charmer I used to know but neither was it the near-derelict I had last seen. He set the crate down on the living room floor—jabbering away about how he knew I didn't have pets and probably didn't want these but if I gave them a chance they were really amazing—and removed a three-foot-wide aquarium. Not just any aquarium, he told me, but a self-cleaning, self-oxygenating, and self-something-else one. Still chattering about the wonders of the equipment and the beauties of the tropical fish he had brought in a small plastic bag, he cleared off my old wicker table, and with slightly trembling hands, set up the aquarium, plugged in its various attachments, filled it with water, and put in the fish. Then, unable to speak about what had happened but too embarrassed to remain and do otherwise, he beat a retreat, struggling to hold onto a Willie-like smile until he'd made it safely out the door.

A little while later I looked in at the aquarium. It had leaked all over the table and the floor.

Professional
Courtesy

That riveting national farce came to be known as the Anita Hill hearings. To differentiate it from the earlier Clarence Thomas beatification process, a pathetically pale charade successfully choreographed to fade quickly from public memory. "Could someone please tell us," the Senators asked at the earlier hearing, "just what it is that demonstrates this person's place among the very best legal minds in the nation, and therefore qualifies him to join the highest court in the land?" (Come to think of it, maybe they didn't ask that.)

What enthralled and enraged about the Anita Hill hearings differed, of course, with different people. For multitudes of women to whom the phenomenon is distressingly familiar, it was the ignorance, hostility, and consequent belittlement with which the all-male committee greeted Hill's accusations concerning a dirty secret of patriarchal public life. For millions of African Americans, particularly embattled males, it was the sight of all those white faces airing for ridicule on national television yet another cartoon version of black sexuality. And for most everyone, I suspect, it was the sorry satisfaction of watching these otherwise sanctimonious clerics

of power having to chew publicly on mouthfuls of the grossly salacious, permanently staining their pinstripe bibs.

One of the little-noted sideshows in this circus was a clown act
of hyperbolic self-regard. Although most had either never actually
practiced law or had long since given it up for more aggrandizing
roles in "public life," many on the Senate committee and most of
the witnesses identified themselves as lawyers. And more,
demanded that the viewing nation be moved by the fact.

Consider Orrin Hatch, for example, the Senator from Utah and
one of feudalism's foremost representatives on Capitol Hill. When
not, at crucial moments during the setting of the hearing's ground
rules, conveniently in the men's room, Hatch took upon himself
the position of committee social psychologist. The charges of sexual effrontery could not possibly be true, Hatch gestured grandly
toward Thomas, because they were plainly inconsistent with the
man's character.

And how were we to know this?

Well, after all, Hatch sniffed, *the man's a lawyer. And,* he added to
clinch the matter, *attended one of the four or five best law schools in
the nation.*

Then there was one of Thomas's old friends, nearly apoplectic in
attack on the proceeding itself. *The whole thing's an outrage!* he
railed. Not because of inherent weakness in Ms. Hill's evidence,
mind you, but because Clarence Thomas—the committee seemed
to have forgotten—was A Man of Standing.

Why, Clarence Thomas is not just some foreman of a machine shop,
the old friend excoriated the senators. *He's a lawyer. And what's
more, a sitting federal judge!*

(The implication being, I suppose, that the higher one goes in
the legal profession, the more latitude one is to be allowed for sexual
improprieties. Although this no doubt accurately describes the way
in which such crimes and peccadilloes truly are measured in the cor-
ridors of power, it seemed extraordinary to hear it openly proposed
as the formal basis for public accountability. Indeed, I found the
notion so novel that I lost the rest of this witness's testimony to a
reverie about just how such seniority standards for Bar and Bench

might be transformed into a code of conduct: "Section (3)(b)(ii): State judges, superior court level (min. 5 years experience)—two hands, above the waist; or, one hand above, one below . . . .")

For my money, though, the most entertaining of the clowns was the one who crawled out to claim that ten years before, when they had both worked for a management consulting firm, Anita Hill had told him that she had "fantasized" about him being "interested in her romantically." No doubt to place this episode in proper context for the committee, this character found himself obliged to describe similar treatment he had suffered at the hands of numerous other women. And to vouch for his impartiality in the matter, the witness assured the committee that although he was now a Republican, he had until recently been a Democrat. (He did not explain, however, whether this conversion related to any anticipated flow of business toward the management consulting firm he now owned, the name and address of which he carefully enunciated for the national television audience. Nor was he asked the questions that most intrigued me: Did his change in party affiliation alter the frequency or intensity of attention paid him by awestruck females? And if so, in what direction?)

Reporters later caught up with this beleaguered soul and asked who it was that had recruited him to testify about Ms. Hill.

No one, the witness claimed; he had simply volunteered.

The intrepid reporters pressed on, asking what had moved him to volunteer.

The witness looked incredulous: *Why, I'm an attorney*, he replied.

There was a momentary silence. Apparently none of the reporters had been admitted to the legal sanctum. And therefore none quite understood how being a lawyer—or more precisely, being a management consultant who had gone to law school—had compelled this person to take the witness chair in order to occlude Anita Hill's credibility . . . and, only incidentally I'm sure, to lay before the American public his swain's song of swooning females and the lustrous details of his climb to success. Noting with some pique the reporters' lack of comprehension, the consultant-*cum*-law-degree deigned to explain: *Attorneys take oaths, and this is one attorney who remembers his.*

Well, this put the reporters in their place, and they asked nothing more. But it puzzled the hell out of me. What oaths, exactly, was this guy talking about? I couldn't recall any oaths upon becoming an attorney that had anything to do with volunteering as a Congressional witness, or any other kind of witness for that matter. Trying to sort the thing out, I went over in my mind his testimony to the committee, or as much of it as I had been able to stomach. And it occurred to me that amidst all this guy's tales of advances, come-ons, and fantasies among lawyers, of prurient innuendo and lurid commentary, none of them seemed actually to have engaged in any. Sex, that is. And then it struck me—this must be what he was referring to. The oath. That lawyers are sworn to *talk* endlessly about sex . . . but never to *have* any.

Personally, I was stunned. To think of how many years I had violated this sacred trust. But where was I when this oath had been administered? Like Hatch, was I in the men's room? In any case, I reminded myself, my sins had been unknowing, so my moral qualms were eased. And legally I was consoled by the success I'd seen of the Hatch toilet defense—you can't violate an oath you'd skipped out on. Besides, when I looked at the matter in practical terms, I felt safe in the knowledge that I no longer practiced. Law, I mean. Of course, in the committee's eyes I am still and forever a lawyer. Which brought me back to the hearings' final sordid twist on the politics of professional identity.

It was Arlen Specter, Senator from Pennsylvania, who was designated to examine Anita Hill closely on the details of her accusations against Thomas and on the extraordinarily difficult situation in which she alleged she had found herself. Was he so designated because he was familiar with the dynamics of sexual harassment? Because he was experienced in the rocky terrain of workplace discrimination and employee rights? Oh, no. Despite his immense difficulty in forming even minimally coherent sentences, he was chosen for the subtle and complex task of elucidating the relationship between Hill and her former boss Thomas because . . . the Senator had once been a lawyer, a criminal prosecutor, in fact.

And so, what were the depths of understanding this lawyer/ solon managed to illuminate for the public during his hours of cross-examination? What was he able to elicit, through his lawyerly skills, about the largely hidden relation between workplace sexuality and the imbalance of economic power between women and men?

Well, Specter sputtered his dramatic rhetorical conclusion, *why didn't she press charges against Thomas at the time?* And lest this polemic prove less than sufficiently devastating, he followed it immediately with his *coup de mort,* the ineluctably damning confutation intended to bring down with a single blow the edifice of Hill's hysterical heresy: *After all,* the old Constitution State prosecutor swelled and trumped for the national cameras, *she's a lawyer, isn't she?*

A Technicality

The Seneca River runs hard and clear through the Cascade Range of the northern Sierra Nevada. In February, the river fights a merciless battle against the encrusting ice. It numbs, so cold is the mountain water. To touch it is to feel nothing.

Annie Kinsella was born near the hamlet of Dunfirm on a bleak stretch of north Scotland coast. Annie's mother died when the girl was only six. Her father knew far more about draughts than daughters, so there were nods of understanding in the village when two years later the girl was packed off to live with relatives in the U.S.A. The sea had brought little enough joy to Dunfirm Bay, and someplace in the mountains of America must surely be a change for the best.

Annie was strictly raised by a God-fearing American aunt and uncle. There were few distractions in the grimy Colorado mining town where the only visible deviations were among shades of gray. Annie grew straight, knew what was right, rarely did wrong. Conscientious, polite, exceedingly pious—people referred to her in ambivalent tones as a perfectionist. But Annie's moral vigilance and religious devotion were balanced by ingenuousness and a sweet disposition. She never set herself apart in her piety and she remained popular with her peers. Especially the boys. By fifteen, Annie had emerged from adolescence with fine pale skin, Celtic curves, and a secret pleasure in the attention she attracted; at sixteen, she was chosen princess of the church's spring bazaar.

In her senior year of high school, Annie's uncle died—the second father to quit her. The blow hit Annie hard, but she steadied herself by redoubling her efforts at righteousness; she made a special point to stifle her interest in boys, which, though never acted upon, she sensed must still, somehow, be sinful. When, after graduation and with much trepidation, Annie went off to college several hundred miles from home, she immediately sought out the ministries there for support and guidance. The rigor of one particular evangelical group gave her a feeling of relative security, and so over the next two years she became deeply involved with this new church.

She also became involved with Boz Davis. Ten years her senior, Boz worked for the management company that sold church real estate holdings: remote mountain land to hunters and survivalists; more accessible lots to the well-to-do for holiday or retirement homes; shares in the Mexican desert to the fuzzier of the church's flock. With a boxer's bravado and an affecting drawl curiously broader than any Southern limb of his family tree, Boz was the church's—or, technically, the company's—best salesman.

It was during a promotional swing through a church retreat that Boz first spotted Annie. Impressed by her bearing, Boz thought she would make him a winning domestic complement. And told her so. Annie was dazzled by Boz's sophisticated attentions and mesmerized by his unabashed approach, at the same time she was alarmed by both. On the other hand, he was a substantial member, even a sort of official representative, of the church.

Not long after Annie and Boz met, Annie's aunt died, her only relative in America. Soon thereafter, Annie accepted Boz's marriage proposal and was carried off to the Cascades, where they moved onto a remote five-acre parcel, near the Seneca River, that Boz's company sold them at a reduced price and entirely on credit. They lived in an old shack on the property while saving to build a real house of their own.

The saving went poorly. Boz was doing well, traveling throughout the Western states and receiving heaps of praise from the church and company. But there never seemed to be much left over from his monthly commissions: the church took a large tithe; the land payments were stiff; and Boz always managed to run up more than his allotted travel and entertainment expenses—a price they had to pay, he explained a bit testily to Annie, if he was to make his mark in the ecclesiastic business world. And then the twins were born. Colin and Katie meant still more expenses and pushed further into the distance the day Boz and Annie could escape the shack.

Despite the strain of being so often left alone with the twins in the cramped and isolated little shack, Annie remained an unfailingly devoted and doting mother. And when Boz made it home—churlish, distracted, soon gone again—Annie was an attentive and, at times painfully, compliant wife. Whether Boz was home or away, the long days and nights were increasingly a trial. More and more, Annie looked to her religion for comfort. She kept in touch with local church women—her only adult contact—and clutched a silent faith that, Lord willing, things would get better.

Boz was clutching something else. It was on the twins' second birthday that Annie learned he was unfaithful. Relentlessly unfaithful. Now she saw with sudden and brutal clarity what all those expenses had been, then discovered that even the meager house money they had saved was gone. And soon after, so was Boz.

Annie and the twins faced a bleak winter: two payments on the land were overdue; other debts Annie had never even known about had piled up; and Annie was named in a lawsuit that claimed Boz had sold the same twenty shares in church desert land to sixty-seven different people. Annie began to wait tables at a local diner, leaving the twins with church women; she also took in sewing. Then the pipes froze, water heater cracked, no money to fix them. And the holidays coming. One night, the cook at the diner saw Annie collecting discarded pine boughs and wiring them together—a Christmas tree for the twins.

As a bitter new year iced the shack, Annie's emotional walls began to crumble. Huddled inside with the twins, trying to sort through the web of her life with Boz, Annie began to obsess about the evils with which he had soiled her. His lying to people and taking their money—money that Annie and the twins had lived on. And the things he had made her do with her body. Searching further, deeper, she reached back to her original sin, the vanity and lust, yes, even lust, that had kept her from seeing Boz for what he'd always been—unclean. Boz, and now all of them, unclean. The misery she and the twins now suffered was surely God's wrath at their abominations.

From time to time Annie would find a moment's solace in one of the television ministries that had become her only company. But late one night, the solace turned to ashes. Annie knew the preacher was looking right at her when he raged from the television screen:

> *The Infernal One's evil He only will sow*
> *In souls where He knows that such evil will grow.*

It was the very word Annie Kinsella Davis had most dreaded—that she was, and must always have been, a daughter of Perdition, lost to the church and to Christ for eternity.

Annie no longer feared for her own soul; she now knew damnation to be certain, inescapable. But a still greater terror remained for the fate of her children. There was no hope if they remained with her—they'd continue to be stained by her evil, stained forevermore. Round the clock, Annie kept a pan of water heating on the woodstove, washed the twins five, ten, twenty times a day.

In late January one of the church's "home advisers" visited the shack and found Annie at the very edge of madness. No hope, Annie kept mumbling, No hope in the world. The adviser bundled up Annie and the twins, took them to his home, and called church authorities. The next day, a pastor from the church's "emergency ministry" arrived. He prayed with Annie and she was relieved—the church understood and would surely save her children by taking them into its bosom. But when evening came, the pastor told Annie to take her children home. In moments of doubt, he said, prayer would help her through. The pastor also advised her of the time and channel on which their very own church's TV ministry would soon be appearing, told her to watch without fail, and said to get in touch if her set had trouble with reception.

Annie barricaded herself and the children in the shack, afraid now that the least contact with the outside world would push the twins into the waiting arms of Perfidy. She tried desperately to believe that faith could protect the children, but she was constantly assailed by the fear that her vigilance might weaken, as it had when she'd met Boz. And if ever it did, she knew she'd be condemning Colin and Katie to lives in sin and afterlives in the Inferno. Day after day she spent searching stacks of the ministry's pamphlets for some path to the little ones' salvation. And finally, tragically, she found one. Church dogma declared that small children bear no responsibility for their own evil, and thus shall suffer not damnation when they die. No matter the sins with which they are marked, children of God are taken without judgment into the Celestial Kingdom—if they die before the age of six.

The official weather report recorded well below freezing that February afternoon when Annie bundled the twins into the old pickup truck. Later it would be colder still. For hours Annie drove around aimlessly, stopping to change the twins, to feed them. Stopping for long periods. Moving again to keep the truck heated, the children warm. About two in the morning, Annie drove past the diner and across an old loggers' bridge. She turned the truck around and drove slowly back across the bridge. Turned and crossed again. Then again. There was another car; Annie pulled to the side and waited. By 3:00 A.M., she was sure no one else was around, and with headlights dark she rolled the truck onto the bridge.

Katie Davis was asleep on the front seat when her twin brother Colin was dropped from the bridge into the Seneca River. Katie followed moments later.

"They just went kerplunk. I didn't hear a cry out of either one of them . . . . At least, I don't think I did." It was the quickest way, Annie thought, the water so cold they'd feel nothing. When you love someone, you don't want to hurt them. And Annie Kinsella Davis loved her children to death.

She drove around the rest of the night, then slowly began to consider what might happen. The Lord would understand. And her church. But what about the others? For the first time Annie thought of the police, imagined that when they found her they would shoot her down. Immediately she drove to the police station, buoyed by the notion that they would quickly end her torment.

In his report, the officer who took Annie's terrible confession described her as disheveled, gnawing her nails until they were raw, nearly incoherent except when she called out to the Kingdom of Heaven. "Subject Davis," he wrote, "appears to be in a state of mental breakdown." Momentarily stepping out of his role in the face of this incomprehensible tragedy, the policeman tried to reassure Annie: "Somehow things will work out. They always do." For the only time that long morning she looked up at him: "No they won't."

As murder cases go, the Annie Kinsella Davis trial would be fairly simple: the facts were virtually uncontested; the only real question was what, legally, those facts meant. Under the state's newly streamlined rules regarding criminal liability—designed to ensure that the judicial system is not bothered by the social sources of individual pathology—one is either legally insane or fully responsible. Middle ground is messy. So, the new law says, no middle ground. The effect in Annie's case was a rare occurrence in a criminal trial—both sides saw the crucial issue in similar light: Assume a young mother loves her small children more than anything else on earth, yet one winter night takes them to a bridge over an icy river and drops them in. Does that mean she'd lost her mind?

The prosecution opened with the testimony of the officer who had found Annie standing outside the police station waiting for them to gun her down. The officer recounted Annie's confession, readily admitting that Annie's account of it had been rambling, disjointed, almost unintelligible. The officer described her demeanor as dazed and ghostlike, but the D.A. objected when the officer used the word deranged, and the judge instructed the jury to disregard it. Nor would the judge permit the officer to repeat for the jury what had seemed so obvious that he had put it in his report: that on that morning Annie Kinsella Davis clearly had suffered some kind of mental breakdown.

The next witness was the county medical examiner, who described in detail the children's cause of death. This gruesome testimony could almost certainly have been kept from the jury by Annie's attorney: if he had offered to stipulate—to agree in a legally binding way—that the children had died by drowning abetted by impact with the water, the judge almost surely would have blocked the detailed medical testimony as superfluous and thus unduly inflammatory. But its very gruesomeness was what the defense attorney wanted. With a totally vacant Annie sitting in front of them, the coroner's testimony could only underline for the jury the utter insanity of what she had done.

The defense began its own case by presenting the church home adviser and a series of local church women who described Annie's precipitous decline after she'd learned of Boz's invidiousness. The jury also heard about Annie's overwhelming love for and devotion to the twins, about how even in the worst of times she'd never raised a hand to them. Next, Annie's lawyer called the church's emergency pastor, in part to have him corroborate Annie's mental state and concern for her children, but also to establish how this church sought to dominate totally each member's individual will, to take from the believer her capacity to make decisions about what is right and wrong. The prosecutor objected to this line of questions on the grounds that there was no evidence the church explicitly instructed its adherents to violate secular law. The judge sustained the D.A.'s objection, ruling gruffly that "the church is not on trial here"; the grateful preacher rushed out of the courtroom without the D.A. bothering him with a single question.

The defense next offered the expert testimony of three psychiatrists, each of whom had spent hours observing and examining Annie. Though none had spoken to the others about the case, each psychiatrist testified in strikingly similar language that Annie had suffered from the delusion that she was under the Devil's sway and that, as a result of her evil, Colin and Katie would quite literally burn in Hell. In this condition, prompted by her church's teachings, she had acted purely in the belief that she was saving the children. Medically, the psychiatrists agreed, her pathology was an "acute psychotic depression with paranoid tendencies"—without doubt at least a temporary form of, in common parlance, insanity.

The prosecutor asked few questions of these psychiatrists and challenged their conclusions not at all. The D.A. seemed content when he had elicited from each doctor a statement that what each had done was to render an expert opinion regarding Annie's medical condition.

The prosecution's rebuttal to these doctors consisted of one witness only. Dr. Wesley Tynan was a forensic psychiatrist who testified that Annie had indeed been "mentally ill, mentally disturbed, and mentally affected." But, he continued, she had premeditated the acts, had sought to avoid detection while committing them, had known that the law would condemn her. In other words, Annie had known that society's right and wrong were different from her own. And therefore she was technically, *legally*, sane.

Under cross-examination by Annie's attorney, Dr. Tynan admitted that he had based his opinion solely on the police reports, the confession, and the reports of the defense psychiatrists. He had never once spoken to Annie, had never even seen her before this day in court. When the defense attorney asked incredulously how it was possible to make a medical diagnosis without even so much as a single examination, Dr. Tynan replied, without affect: "I was not asked to make a medical diagnosis." The simplicity of the law's definition of insanity, he explained, meant that written materials alone were sufficient to arrive at an expert opinion of a defendant's *legal* state of mind.

And Dr. Tynan was indeed an expert. Exclusively an expert—not in the diagnosis and treatment of mental illness but in *testifying about* mental capacity. For many years he had maintained no clinical practice, had seen no patients. Yet he had worked on more than a hundred criminal cases involving the question of a defendant's mental state. And in ninety-eight percent of those cases, Dr. Tynan's opinion had been that the defendant was legally, though not necessarily medically, sane.

In his final argument to the jury, Annie's attorney focused first on the unequivocal and unchallenged opinions of the three practicing psychiatrists that Annie had been severely mentally disturbed. Then he spoke passionately of Annie's love for the twins and thus of how incomprehensible—that is, how insane—were her actions. The jurors, and everyone else in the courtroom, were visibly moved.

In a criminal case, however, the prosecutor has the final word. And this D.A.'s closing argument to the jury was a somber reiteration that the case was *not* about whether Annie was mentally disturbed, nor indeed whether she was medically insane. Rather, the prosecutor reminded the jury over and again, the *only* issue was whether under the technical rules on which the judge would precisely instruct them, Annie Kinsella Davis had been *legally* sane or insane.

The judge immediately followed with the very instructions to the jury that the prosecutor had promised. In deciding Annie's guilt or not-guilt—as in all criminal trials, "innocence" was not the question—the jury was to follow a legal standard of insanity based on a concept known as the M'Naghten Rule. Though universally discredited by the medical community as hopelessly simplistic, some form of the antediluvian M'Naghten Rule is used in most states—in fact, reinstated by several during the 1980s wave of lock-'em-up hysteria—precisely because of its simplicity. In Annie's case, the judge's M'Naghten Rule instructions were virtually word for word the same terms used carefully by Dr. Tynan and the prosecutor: Had the defendant been able to distinguish societal right from wrong?

Despite the narrow technical bounds of the M'Naghten Rule, veteran trial observers predicted a verdict of not guilty by reason of insanity, which would result not in Annie's freedom but in her commitment to a state psychiatric facility. "Bonkers is bonkers," one spectator said, "and everyone knows that if a mother like that throws her kids off a bridge, she's bonkers."

But there was no quick decision. Four and a half days the jury deliberated. And when finally they returned, their ashen faces and downcast eyes betrayed the verdict: Annie Kinsella Davis, two counts of murder, guilty as to both counts. The courtroom's stunned silence was broken by the jury foreman. In a quavering voice, he read a prepared statement: "We, the members of this jury, hereby denounce the instructions we were bound to follow as morally repugnant." So saying, the jurors rose from their chairs. The flustered judge quickly dismissed them without the usual treacly speech about them having done their civic duty.

Outside, several shaken jurors spoke of their burden. "We had to do it," one man said with tears in his eyes. "We didn't want to, but we had to." In the courtroom, Annie's lawyer spoke to her quietly but, as throughout the trial, she seemed to register nothing. At the other counsel table the prosecutor gathered his papers, careful not to look in Annie's direction.

Instead of treatment at a psychiatric hospital, Annie Kinsella Davis was sentenced to state prison where, at best, she might receive sporadic counseling in what can safely be described as a less-than-therapeutic environment. Annie was twenty-nine years old when the verdict was read. If given a normal parole date, she will be well over forty by the time she is released. Her likely mental condition after a decade or two in prison was not, by law, a part of the trial proceedings.

During the years I practiced criminal law, I was frequently met by remarks, and by that sidelong glance that so often accompanies received wisdom, about getting criminals "off on a technicality." There were plenty of stories like Annie Kinsella's. But usually I was just too tired to tell them.

What Are Friends For?

The call from my office answering service came at ten o'clock on a Friday night, as such calls so often did. (The police know that if they arrest you on a Friday, you won't come to court until Monday or Tuesday. And if you are unable before then to post the grossly inflated bail the cops themselves have set for you, they will have summarily imposed on you a three- or four-day jail sentence regardless of whether you are later found guilty of any crime.)

The woman I reached on my return call was hyperventilating: "My husband Peter . . . been arrested . . . in jail . . . it's crazy . . . he's a professor, college professor . . . they must have the wrong man . . . it's a nightmare, a nightmare . . . ."

I was able to calm the woman, Allison, enough to find out that her husband had been arrested at his ex-wife's house, charged with some sort of drug offense. I took brief background information on Peter—assistant history professor, late father a prominent local doctor—then hustled over to the jail. There I found Peter distraught: he had never been near a jail before and had no idea what was going on, except that the cops had said something about cocaine. Worse, he was frantic about his eight-year-old daughter, Hilary, who had been with him at his ex-wife's when he was arrested and who had been taken into protective police custody. I told him the first thing I would do would be to make sure his daughter was all right. With that assurance, however thinly supported, Peter was able to tell me a little about his arrest, and that of his ex-wife and her boyfriend, when Peter had gone to the ex's house to drop off his daughter as part of an alternate-week child custody arrangement. More than that he just didn't know, and I left him with a promise to get him out of there as soon as possible.

From the jail I called the night-duty judge and made a strong enough pitch about Peter's background—references to the markers of social status can be extremely effective, although you mustn't actually use the words—plus a plausible enough argument that he had simply been in the wrong place at the wrong time, that the judge lowered bail from $50,000 to $5,000. Then I went to a bail bondsman to whom I sometimes sent business and prodded him into the favor of putting up a bond without any immediate collateral. While the bondsman went to the jail to take care of the paperwork, I took information over the phone from Peter's mother, hoping to get Hilary released to the grandmother's custody. Then I went back over to the jail, waited for Peter to be released on bond, and drove him home. It was now 5:00 A.M.

I sat with Peter and Allison at their kitchen table, trying to allay their fears about his daughter and his arrest while at the same time trying to sort out what had gone on. We talked until shortly after eight, when I was able to get in touch with a juvenile court referee who agreed to review Hilary's situation at ten o'clock. I left Peter and Allison huddled together on their sofa, drove over and picked up Peter's mother, went down to juvenile court, got Hilary released to the grandmother, then drove them back to Peter and Allison's. I disappeared into the background for a few minutes while they reunited, then had to remind them of the juvenile court's order that, at least temporarily, Hilary was to stay at the grandmother's. I told Peter I would meet him first thing Monday morning in my office, then drove Hilary and her grandmother back to the grandmother's house. I got home at three o'clock Saturday afternoon.

It took awhile to sort things out. Once the law enforcement machinery has you in its clutches, it is loathe to let go. It became readily apparent that Peter's only connection to the house, and therefore to the boyfriend's drug business, was the regular picking up and dropping off of his eight-year-old daughter. The police report, however, had characterized this as highly indicative of criminal behavior:

> *Late model blue Camry 2-dr., observed arriving and leaving surveilled premises on four occasions. Suspect, WM, remains inside premises for short period, long enough to complete transaction. Each occasion, suspect delivers or picks up small suitcase and is accompanied either into or out of premises by WF, possible juvenile.*

The district attorney seemed unable to distinguish this "eyewitness" myopia from evidence of crime, and so would not immediately dismiss the case. So ingrained is it in prosecutors that anyone arrested must be guilty of something, so conditioned are they never to "give" a defendant anything—in this case, to drop an absolutely unfounded charge—without in return exacting some retribution, or at least contrition, that it took three months and four court appearances finally to get the charges dismissed. Freeing Hilary from the tether of juvenile court and its social services network similarly took ten weeks of interviews and three more court appearances.

During those months, however, Peter, Allison, and I got to know each other. We spent long hours jointly preparing our presentations to the juvenile court, and we went as a unit to all the interviews and court appearances. We also got in the habit of decompressing together afterward, sharing a bottle of red wine at their house and on one occasion at mine. Toward the end of the case we extended our debriefings into dinner, allowing the food and drink to humanize us again after our strained and artificial performances in courtrooms and bureaucrats' offices. And it turned out we had much in common besides their case. Peter, about my age, taught history at a local university and had done his graduate work with some of the same faculty I had known as an undergraduate. Allison taught poetics at a small alternative college and was active in the local poetry scene, through another denizen of which she had been initially referred to me. So, our conversations moved easily from the absurdities of the legal system into the absurdities of the academic and poetry worlds, and then on to whatever subjects, both topical and personal, the wine and conviviality led us.

As it became clearer that Peter's case would ultimately be dismissed and that Hilary would soon be out from the net of juvenile court none too worse for wear, we began to manage a few laughs together. And on the night after the final dismissal of Peter's case, we wound up getting happily soused on two celebratory bottles of champagne that accompanied the expensive dinner Peter and Allison treated me to. Outside the restaurant, they slurred their gratitude once more and said that now, at last, the three of us would be able to spend time together without the judicial bogeyman lurking over our shoulders. We hugged warmly, then sank into separate taxis.

I was busy with and exhausted by a trial over the next several weeks, but when I again got a breather I called Peter and Allison to see about getting together for dinner. They weren't in, so I left a message on their answering machine, making the point, so they would not worry, that it was purely a social call. I didn't hear back from them for a few days, and the following Sunday morning I thought I'd give them a call to see what they were up to that evening. Peter answered the phone. He seemed surprised that it was me and asked if everything was all right. I laughed and assured him the case was really over, that this was not a business call. He was relieved, but there remained a tinny distance in his voice. I asked if they were interested in a movie or some dinner that night, and Peter hesitated.

"Um . . . just a minute," he said with a clumsy pause. "I'll, ah, speak to Allison."

He called to his wife in the other room, but his hand didn't quite cover the mouthpiece all the way.

"Allison! Allison! It's the lawyer . . . ."

"God, I Wish . . ."

In one way, my friend Gabriel was not unlike most other lawyers, which is to say he'd much rather have been doing something else. But how much rather? Recent American Bar Association surveys found that seventy percent of the lawyers responding would rather do something, anything, other than practice law, and that only one out of four would advise their children to join the Bar. And since most of the disaffected lawyers I've known—that is, most of the lawyers I've known—don't bother to belong to the American Bar Association, let alone participate in its surveys, the percentage of lawyers-in-misery may well be much higher. Mind you, what we are talking about here are lawyers who *would like* to do something else; the conditional is key—though they all thoroughly dislike what they do, they still do it.

Which brings me back to Gabriel. Although he found himself worn, disillusioned, and at times nearly unhinged by the pressured combativeness of his litigation-strewn law practice, Gabriel's remarkable character refused to permit work, or anything else, to make him unhappy. Gabe was, if not always cheerful, at least unfailingly capable of cheer. Whereas most trial lawyers are ferociously involved in their cases, nerves tightly compressed, every minute closely organized, Gabe just bumped along in a creaky barouche of good will and good humor, mustering sufficient focus to overcome his chronic disorderliness and habits of digression only when imminent legal disaster absolutely forced him to. And whereas most trial lawyers found solace in temporary escapes but could imagine no life beyond law, Gabe ignored trivial distractions and opted for the big dream instead.

Swami G (as I called Gabe because of his unfashionable full beard and the unconventional and mischievous wisdom that roamed behind his eyes) was never without some scheme or other for complete manumission—not just from his law practice, but from the wider dehumanizing world. "Well, it's only for a little longer," he would say when one of life's monsters raised an ugly head. I'd look at him doubtfully. "You see," he'd continue, "I have a plan . . . ."

Once, the plan had been to run an import-export business from a seaside hacienda in his wife's native Costa Rica; six months later it had been a yacht-for-charter plying the waters between California and Hawaii; and a year after that, a construction business building *gringo* retirement houses on the west coast of Mexico. Of course, he never made it beyond the "By this time next year . . . ." and "I'm getting in touch with some people" stages. But during the time each scheme remained afloat, it permitted him to feel that his sentence in the over-modern world was only purgatorial, and left his sunny disposition free from the clouds of long-term doubt. Whenever I'd hear the latest plan, I'd say, straight-faced, "But Swami, what happened to the yacht?" And with serious mien he'd give a sensible reason why the previous scheme hadn't material-ized—usually perfectly obvious from the beginning, if he'd chosen to look—and I'd just say "Mm" and "Uh-huh" until he'd break into a grin that spread his beard wider and wider until finally it encompassed not just his own folly but the entire human comedy of false promises and empty dreams.

I first met Gabriel through a mutual friend when I was in law school and Gabe was enjoying the manifold pleasures of residence in the Haight-Ashbury. In my obdurate radical eyes of those times,

Gabe was a hippie. And contrary to the mass media's muddled melding of the love child and the militant, for the most part the former was disdained by the latter. But despite my aversion to his milieu, there was something about Gabe I could not help liking: a deliberate, thoughtful manner behind which twinkled a quick and lively mind; an utter lack of self-importance; and an ability to see the absurd lurking beneath any purportedly serious moment, plus an anytime, anywhere willingness to bring that absurd to the surface. His physical presence, too, was a combination of the distracting and the disarming: a perpetual squint that made him appear to be in a constant state of slight confusion; a prematurely bald pate that topped an Ichabod Crane figure so long and floppy that I sometimes peeked to see if there might be an extra set of joints somewhere along the line; and the grin that would unexpectedly part his beard, liven his crinkly blue eyes, and deflate whatever dirigible of self-aggrandizement anyone happened to be riding nearby.

Not long after I met the Swami, our mutual friend, Andy, reported that Gabe was applying to law school. I later heard that this seemingly anomalous decision had materialized while he'd been under the influence of psychedelics, which proved doubly curious: one doesn't normally associate "mind-expanding" drugs with mind-limiting life choices; and more, once straight again, Gabe actually went through with it. I was skeptical that this overgrown elf would stick with his choice when exposed to the rigidity and humorlessness of law school. And if he managed to get through school, I certainly couldn't imagine him coping with the daily practice of law.

I saw little of Gabe over the next few years: I was a criminal lawyer who had little time or energy for anyone, and our one mutual friend, Andy, had moved out of the area. It was only after he'd been in practice a few years—Gabe served a brief apprenticeship in a firm, then hung out his own shingle—that Gabe began to get in touch. He would call from time to time for advice on the odd criminal case he took on, and I would occasionally refer him a client: a divorce; a will; a simple contract. Not long after, I left full-time practice and put on my law hat only to do itinerant research and writing for lawyers too busy, too lazy, or too confounded to handle all their own work. This was a perfect arrangement for Gabe, who was often too lazy or too confounded, and we began having fairly frequent visits as he fed me his backlog of work.

Although it was always an exchange of work that brought us together, Swami G operated under the principle that there had to be social gab before, and usually for twice as long as, any business talk. And since his commentaries were wide-ranging, unpredictable, and punctuated with that spirit-lifting grin, I was always happy to oblige. Given most lawyers' difficulties with the world of litigation, Gabe's side of our palavers was surprisingly free of complaint about his practice. There was the occasional tale of woe about this or that rebarbative lawyer or obstreperous client, but it never spiraled into the all-out "I've got to get out of this fucking business" rant one heard regularly from so many others. Despite a distaste for the battleground of trial work and a mind that constantly wandered from the tasks at hand, Gabe seemed to have made passable the potholed road his professional life had taken. Of course, there was always the latest far-flung escape plan. But after awhile I sensed that these fantasies were more about holding onto the Swami he had always been than about throwing off the lawyer he had become.

Our discussions ranged over a broad array of topics. But "belief" was not among them. Neither Gabe nor I nor the people we knew well were much interested in such matters, and if one discussed them at all, it was usually in short shrift disgust over crimes committed in the names of organized religion or the passivity engendered by various brands of faith. About the time Gabe reached age forty, however, for the first time I began to hear him talk about Judaism. He had grown up in the suburbs of Los Angeles an unarticulated Jew like so many others of the second or third generation in America: vaguely aware of and alternately pleased and embarrassed by his cultural heritage but without much sense of Judaism's religious or historical foundations. Of a spiritual—as opposed to a mere formally religious—component to Judaism, Gabe had never had more than a glimpse, and without ever having it named, on the faces of a few elders during his once-yearly High Holidays foray into the synagogue. And Judaism's global history had been reflected for him in nothing more extensive than an occasional somber reference to someone having survived the camps, and in the slavish attentions paid by most older Jews to anything having to do with Israel. Not that Gabriel wasn't aware of the separate cultural current along which Diaspora Jews moved—regular reference by his parents' generation to the antics of the *goyim,* plus the inevitable if infrequent slaps of suburban anti-Semitism, kept Gabe vaguely conscious that he was different, though leaving him in considerable doubt as to which side was the Chosen one.

And that is where his awareness had lain, both unchallenged and undeveloped, until somewhere near his fortieth birthday. In the meantime he had married Yola, a Costa Rican–American ensnared by an odd pairing of passions for salsa music and mock Colonial furniture, and completely devoted to Gabe. I don't know that there was a causal connection, and if so in which direction, but at the same time Gabe began showing an active interest in Judaism, he and Yola began showing an active interest in having a child. This manifested itself in all the usual technical twitches for a couple each of whom was passing forty: compulsive calendar-watching and temperature-taking; expensive pokings, proddings, and microscopic examinations of their most intimate fixtures and effluents. Gabe's growing interest in Judaism, meanwhile, was manifested in readings of cultural history and religious canon, plus tentative attempts to engage those whose thinking he appreciated, both Jews and not, in discourse about being religious in general and Jewish in particular in the modern Western world.

Gabe's early conversations with me on the subject centered on the equilibrium a "traditional" culture might provide someone otherwise adrift in the waters of anomie (this was the mid-1980s, the reign of glut and greed and devil-take-the-hindmost, for many people the depth of backsliding from former commitments to the common good). I was deeply antagonistic to religious structures, but separate if sometimes related questions of "identity" did seem of particular moment, and so Gabe and I began lively debate. Gabe was willing to open up to me on the stirrings of his Jewishness because he knew that I would provide him with the same sorts of counterarguments he would have provided himself. And I was willing to wrangle at length with him because I believed he would chew hard on my rebuttals before he'd swallow the tenets of faith.

One day as we sat down for a prework confab, Gabe mentioned that he had recently attended a synagogue High Holidays service, his first in more than twenty years. He had been exhilarated by the sense of community there and had been surprised to find nothing about which he felt hugely uncomfortable: yes, the references to God doing this and God saying that were a bit hard to take, but after all, the language of religion had always been metaphor; and yes, mention of the Chosen People had made him wince, but he was willing to think of it merely as an enduring myth that helped hold together collective pride through ages of persecution. Despite Gabe's deep-seated resistance to institutional verities of any kind, he seemed willing to take on these rationalizations in exchange for the obvious pleasure he had received.

Soon Gabe reported that he had been attending Saturday Sabbath services and that he was relishing the regularity of participation, the growing sense that he was a part of something. It was a Reform synagogue, he assured me, not too heavy on direct orders from God and full of younger to middle-aged people of liberal views, many of whom, like Gabe, had found themselves returning to the fold after a long hiatus. We discussed what such congregations were about, and whether one couldn't just as well share cultural values and a sense of community without performing these modernist pantomimes of devotional rituals. And while Gabe admitted that the whole notion of Reform religiosity seemed not merely a half measure but somehow a hollow one, he would not repudiate the experience he'd found there.

The way Gabe resolved this discomfort with the mixed metaphors of Reformism was not what I expected. The next time I saw him, he told of leaving the Reform *shul* (synagogue) for a more traditional Conservative one. But this only whetted his interest, and soon he had left the Conservative congregation and was attending not only an Orthodox synagogue on both Friday night and Saturday, but also its Talmud class.

At first, the Swami's delve into Orthodoxy seemed to me just the latest, albeit more extreme, eccentricity of a man who by virtue of such curlicues maintained his sanity in what had become for him an otherwise maddeningly conventional life. Soon, though, it became clear that this was no mere whimsy, that he was seriously immersing himself in the powerful mysteries of collective energy and religious faith. This meant, among other things, that Gabe now had to struggle not only with the idea of a Higher Being but with a particular Higher Being who spoke directly and only to Jews. So, regularly now, he would sit me down to worry the question of whether his "becoming" a Jew again meant having to accept the full raft of Orthodox imperatives and, more difficult still, making that mystical leap into faith that truly being Orthodox seemed to require.

What of the millions of Jews who are not particularly religious and certainly not Orthodox, Gabe would ask rhetorically during our discussions, but who share a common history and culture? People who feel themselves to be Jews, for whom being Jews is an essential and ineradicable part of their lives? People who are considered Jews not only by themselves and their secular fellow Jews but also by those non-Jews who identify, segregate from, and yes, would even expel or exterminate them as Jews? Were they not *really* Jews? Who the hell says not? Some rabbi somewhere? Which one? Who chose *him*? And why should some self-righteous sect or other get to define who you are? Tell you whether you're a *real* Jew or not? Isn't that just the flip side of Gentiles telling you whether or not you are a *real* something else? Whether you are worthy or not? Fit to live?

Gabe's responses to these and other questions raised by his embrace of Orthodoxy eventually devolved into one compellingly compact argument. For him to be a Jew, Gabe finally decided, he must accept unequivocally the full panoply of Orthodox beliefs and dictates, because without an undiluted religious core, Judaism could not survive. Diaspora assimilation, intermarriage, and the lack of a unifying language, Gabe declaimed, left religious belief as Judaism's only certain defining element. That is, not counting Israel.

Israel. Homeland. Zion.

Gabe had always been a man of Left instincts and persuasion, and his sympathies had long—albeit quietly—lain with Palestinian rights, as against the hegemony of the Israeli state. Now, however, he was faced in the Orthodox community with constant reference to Israel as every Jew's spiritual and cultural home.

Except for specific tactical questions—greater or lesser negotiations, more or less repression—Gabe was unable to discuss with others in the Orthodox community his doubts and discomfits about Israel. The large questions had been settled among the Orthodox faithful so thoroughly that even to raise them again was to tar oneself as pariah. Moreover, Gabe was still a neophyte in this community; he had yet to achieve full standing, and perhaps just as important, did not own the moral authority of having been to Israel. Nevertheless, basic questions about Israel's place in both the Jewish and the larger world remained for Gabe a source of considerable uncertainty, and for a year or more he and I frequently wrangled with them.

The opportunity to discuss and argue was afforded by the growing load of legal work Gabe was giving me. He was his small congregation's only lawyer, and his new ties had begun to provide him with clients. But while more business came in, his energies were increasingly consumed by commitments to the *shul*—Sabbath and holiday services and social gatherings; administrative meetings; helping hands to others in the community and to visiting Jews; weddings, ritual circumcisions, mourning—and by his study of religious history, Hebrew, and Talmud. With so little time left for law practice, more and more work got farmed out to me.

The trend of more work for both of us, however, soon began to reverse itself. The cases he was gaining from his new brethren were now more than offset by the cases he was losing. He had no time any longer for the socializing with lawyers and former clients required to sustain a flow of new work. Of the potential clients who did make their way to his office, many shied away from the now chest-length beard, the devotional wrappings that bulged obviously under his shirt, and the beret—Gabe's remaining external mark of individuality; the others of his community wore old-fashioned black fedoras—that his religious tenets now forbade him to remove in the office or anywhere else. And the clients he still had were becoming increasingly exasperated—such that a number of them took their business elsewhere—by the degree to which his religious tasks made him even more dilatory than normal in attending to legal chores. Gabe continued to give me research and writing for the cases he held onto, but there was less of it all the time.

Gabriel seemed only passingly disturbed by his dwindling practice: he had put away some money over the years, and his and Yola's lifestyle was modest (mock Colonial furniture notwithstanding). The only immediate impact of his drop in income seemed to be that the current get-away-from-it-all scheme—a move to Buenos Aires, to set up as a counselor in U.S. matters to the large Jewish community there—was referred to in an expanding future tense. Besides, a few clients were all he could handle: with something now of real meaning to him, the comparative barrenness of law practice made it more difficult than ever for him to get any work done.

But one kind of work did get done. "From your lips to God's ear" was an old Yiddish expression Gabe had recently become fond of invoking (in English) when someone verbalized a wish. I don't know what the anatomo-celestial equivalent might be for a wish to procreate, but after two years of trying, Gabriel and Yola were expecting a child. The impending birth also pressed them ahead on another quest: for Gabe to be a member of an Orthodox community, his wife had to be a Jew. And while being a lapsed rather than practicing Catholic may have made the transition more likely for Yola, it didn't make it any easier. Conversion required immense amounts of study in order to pass rigorous examination by the rabbis. But more, before you could be admitted to the faith, the rabbis must somehow understand by your evident righteousness that you have already achieved the faith; that is, you could be deemed a Jew only if you showed that you had already been Chosen.

It was in the midst of the pregnancy and the push toward Yola's conversion that I was finally persuaded to have Sabbath dinner with Gabe and Yola. Gabe had been dunning me for months to join them for an evening meal, and for months I had been making excuses. Since it was specifically Friday nights to which Gabe always coaxed, I assumed it was their home Sabbath celebration as much as his and Yola's company that the evening was intended to share. Which was exactly what had been holding me back: I was uncomfortable at the prospect of seeing Gabe's new Orthodox persona fully on display without the leaven our free-flowing discussions had always provided.

I arrived just as it was getting dark and was ushered into the house by a distracted Gabriel, who was trying with difficulty to maintain the bearing of dignified beneficence appropriate to a Sabbath host. Sundown was imminent; as soon as it was dark, all work had to stop; and his house was not yet ready. Gabe had still to finish cleaning up the kitchen and laying out the Friday night finery—best tablecloth, dishes, and silverware—as well as the accoutrements for the ritual *shabbes* (Sabbath) blessings. In the midst of his last-minute chaos—not unlike the way he practiced law, it occurred to me as I watched him scuttle around, pick something up, stop to think, then put it down again—Yola came into the kitchen.

Although my relationship with Gabe was long-standing, it had always been limited to our rambling discourses at his office, at my apartment, or at a neighborhood cafe, and I had never had more than a few brief encounters with Yola. What I remembered was a lithe, cheery woman with searching black eyes and a quick but soft-edged tongue. I was totally unprepared for the kerchiefed, long-sleeved, floor-skirted woman who slid quietly into the room. Even her body shape seemed to have changed, now round and low to the ground, and while her fourth-month pregnancy might have accounted for part of it, some other, longer term change had also occurred.

Yola greeted me warmly and with a wholesome hug: Orthodox
Judaism being unrepentently patriarchal, I was relieved that she had-
n't been transformed into someone with downcast eyes who did not
speak until spoken to. Benignly she began guiding Gabriel in the
tasks of arranging the Sabbath table, not because she was mistress of
the kitchen—Gabe had always prided himself on his culinary talents
and had often told me he did most of the cooking—but because she
seemed to know, when he wasn't sure, exactly how the ceremonial
items were to be arranged. Gabe accepted her correctives, although
without the good-humored self-deprecation with which he would
normally accompany an exposure of his flummoxry; I kept expecting
him to glance over and flash me that trademark beard-splitting grin,
but it never came. This was serious business.

The table was laid and the rituals began. With a beautiful white
tallis prayer shawl over the shoulders of his best blue suit, Gabriel
stood and read in halting Hebrew the blessings that opened the
Sabbath meal. My attention was drawn away from Gabriel's best
efforts, though, and toward Yola, who sat across the table silently
davening, eyes closed, head and shoulders rocking to and fro, lips
moving fluently in unuttered fervent prayer sent, I had no doubt,
on a direct path to God.

A particular ritual corresponded to each prayer: a certain way
with a certain knife to slice the first piece of bread; a certain cup
from which to sip the first wine. And while it was Gabe who conducted each small ceremony, at several points he looked to Yola for
counsel. She gave it easily and surely, and without the least hint of
chastisement at Gabriel's lack of facility. Finally it was time to eat,
and Gabe brought to the table one of two identical crock pots sitting next to the stove. He explained that the second pot would
steep—sitting on an automatically timed hot plate—through the
following no-working, no-cooking Sabbath day until it served
them upon their walk back from synagogue the next afternoon.

The lid came off the pot and a hearty aroma steamed up. As
Gabriel served, Yola proudly pronounced the word *tcholent*, a
beef, bean, and barley stew. In Lithuanian *shtetls* (rural hamlets)
like the one Gabriel's family came from, she continued, *tcholent*

was traditional on *shabbes.* They would start it the day before, then deliver it before dark on Friday to the *shtetl's* communal ovens where it would cook all night until retrieved by the family on the way home from *shul* the next afternoon.

"Family tradition"? "From the *shtetl*"? Gabe's father was born in Hoboken, his mother in Chicago. And though there may have been a Lithuania-born grandparent somewhere, until recently Gabe hadn't had two Yiddish words to rub together and had never tasted *tcholent* on Saturdays or any other days. I kept my gainsaying to myself, though, and took a peek at Gabe: he was holding the serving spoon in midair, watching Yola intently, proudly, as she continued her disquisition on *shtetl* life. A dollop of barley sauce hung suspended from the end of the spoon. I watched to see if it would drop harmlessly on Gabe's plate or fall to the just-cleaned floor, but Yola handed me something and I had to turn my head.

As we ate, I asked about the rituals, each question first answered by Gabe and then filled in or gently revised by Yola. Then all the standard questions about getting ready for the baby—not revealing that Gabe already told me Yola had ordered a luxury model Colonial crib—mixed with a few queries about the patterns of their new existence: how they managed to follow kosher cooking and eating rules; how often they went to the synagogue; how often to Hebrew class; what Gabe did in the sessions with his special Talmud tutor. Their answers were earnest and thorough. Dinner was endless.

All three of us were just about asleep, I'm sure, when Yola said that next month they were going to Israel for three weeks.

Gabriel hasn't told you? Yes, we'll be shown around by some people there who are connected to our *shul.* It will be marvelous to feel what it's like to be surrounded by so many other Jews. And to experience the Homeland . . . .

This was Yola speaking. I peeked at Gabe watching her, and if he felt any sheepishness at her effusion, or at his not telling me of their trip, it was hidden by a glow of gratification tinged with wonder. As Gabe gathered the dinner dishes, Yola continued to describe their upcoming Israel trip. When he got up, I could see that the glob of barley that had hung perilously from the serving spoon had reached neither table nor floor—it had been halted by Gabe's beautiful white *tallis*.

Back from Israel, on the subject of his Orthodoxy in general and Israel in particular Gabe was considerably more circumspect with me than before the trip. He did say that he had been struck by many things in Israel, the force of so many Jews in one place, and in power, foremost among his impressions. When I asked gently about the extraordinary conundrum of Israelis and Palestinians, Gabe said only that he remained confounded. He looked sad when he said it.

Of his life here, Gabe told me that he would continue to study with his Talmud tutor, be involved in all aspects of his *shul*, and practice law. His erstwhile volubility was gone now, and our conversation subjects were limited: people we knew in common; work we were doing; cases we had handled before. It was almost never about his daily life. It was almost always brief. And there were no more invitations to Friday night dinner.

I didn't see Gabe for awhile after their daughter was born. He was too busy with baby, household, and synagogue, plus his personal religious tutelage, to give his law practice even the minimal attention required just to pass work on to me. He went to his office only rarely, to see an occasional client or to drop off a bit of work for his secretary. He now did virtually all his work at home, which is where I saw him next.

Yola greeted me and brought me to the living room where baby Rachel was ensconced in a porta-bed that apparently she preferred to the $3,000 Colonial crib. Yola smiled at the baby, then turned the same maternal smile on me and said that the Talmud told of the angel Gabriel showing Joseph the way. Before I could mull what this was supposed to mean, Gabe called to me through an open door and I went into the room he now used as an office.

The only other room I'd ever seen that looked quite like this was one that had just been searched by a SWAT team: drawers open, contents spilling out; papers and books strewn over desk, chairs, and floor; one telephone off the hook while Gabe spoke into another. I moved some papers off a chair and sat down. On the phone, Gabe was doing far more listening than speaking, and when he did speak it was only to contradict or take exception. By the increasing color behind Gabe's beard I could tell that the tone was considerably more heated on the other end. "Well, you do whatever you think you have to," Gabe finally said and banged down the phone.

Sensing that the call had been with a lawyer, I knew enough to keep quiet. After a moment Gabe slowly unfolded from his chair and moved over to some shelves swarming with files, papers, and books. He knew exactly where in the mess he was reaching, though, and pulled out a small, well-worn volume. He flipped through it, then nodded and read silently before handing it to me and pointing to a passage. "Victory cannot tolerate truth," I read, "and if one displays a true thing before your eyes, you reject it for the sake of victory. He, then, who wants the truth in himself drives away the spirit of victory, for only then is he ready to behold the truth." Martin Buber, *Tales of Rabbi Nachman.*

I commiserated with Gabe about belligerent, deceitful lawyers like the one on the phone—I believe "slimeball" was the technical term Gabe employed—but then Yola called for help with something and when he got back the phone rang and when he got off the phone we both realized we had better skip any attempt at a social visit and get right to the work he wanted me to do. I had just gotten the gist of the project when the doorbell rang and Yola ushered in Gabe's Talmud tutor. Gabe apologized with a harried smile, and I left them to it.

A few months later Gabe told me of a new plan: he and Yola would move to Israel. At first I silently dismissed it as simply the latest in his long string of schemes. But while this plan seemed no more practical than any of the others, I soon realized that it was considerably more likely. The year before, Gabe had said that only by becoming Orthodox, by practicing Judaism to its religious fullest, could he find out what being a Jew truly meant. Then he had done it. And now he would take the next step. The daily practice of Judaism was one thing, he explained, but in Israel he would immerse himself in it, study Talmud in a *kolel*—a religious community—and get to depths he had not yet reached. I tried to tug gently at the loose threads of the idea, to touch on the impracticalities of it all, but Gabe had ready if unconvincing responses and spoke with such tenacity of purpose that I quickly let it go. To mark my surrender, I asked whether they'd make him get circumcised again. He gave a little smile, but the Swami grin was nowhere to be seen.

Gabe talked of nothing now except winding up his practice and selling their house. He managed to close out some cases, but a year went by with no obvious movement toward Israel and I came to believe that like all the other plans, this one, too, had fallen apart. I was wrong. Gabe made a final push to settle as many cases as he could, actually doing a fair amount of legal work. Then in rapid succession, they accepted a bid on their house, Gabe closed his office and turned over his remaining cases to another lawyer. When he told me that Yola had gone to Macy's, bought a Colonial dining room set, and had it shipped to Israel, I knew it was for real.

It happened that Andy, the old friend who had introduced me to the Swami many years before, was back in town at the time Gabe was packing to leave. The three of us gathered for a farewell breakfast at the local café where Gabe and I used to meet before his religious food restrictions had made it a less inviting spot. I sat quietly at the table as Gabriel explained to Andy the primary purpose of his move to Israel: it was there, he said, in a religious community, that he would immerse himself fully in the study of what it meant to be a Jew.

Andy had spent the previous six years as a reporter for a major newspaper. So, he had a tremendous unrequited need to ask the kinds of questions a modicum of thoughtfulness made obvious but his job did not allow. Where exactly was this community? Andy asked. Not one of those new settlements in the occupied territories, he hoped.

Oh, no, Gabe assured him. It was in the Old City part of Jerusalem. And a religious community, not political; they made it a point to "keep out of things."

Andy reminded Gabe that just the week before there had been a huge flap in the Old City when a band of right-wing Jews had pushed their way into the Arab quarter and, protected by the army, had physically thrown several Arab families out of their homes and moved in themselves, claiming ancient rights to the property. They were "religious," too, Andy said.

Gabe was aware of the incident and, though he had assiduously avoided discussions with me about the political situation in Israel, now confessed a growing unease over placing himself amidst these intractable problems. "Keeping out of things" doesn't seem very likely, I said, taking care to avoid reproof in my voice. No, Gabe admitted mournfully, it doesn't.

Breakfast came and our fussing with it provided momentary respite. I'm sure Andy meant no more in ordering sausage than I did in bacon, but when Gabriel looked at our plates, I thought I heard a wistful sigh.

"So," Andy began again cheerily as he and I ate and Gabe sipped his second cup of tea, "what's your apartment there like?"

Gabe blanched a bit. "Well, housing in the Old City is pretty tight. But it's been arranged. It's a, um, furnished room . . . until we can find an apartment."

"Sounds a little cramped with the baby," Andy said. "And what sort of place will you finally wind up with?"

"Oh, hard to say," Gabe mumbled into his tea. "Maybe three rooms . . . or two."

"But Yola just bought . . . ." I blurted out before biting my tongue.

Andy's curiosity was aroused and he looked back and forth between Gabe and me. I demurred.

"Yeah, well, Yola, you see, she bought this . . . furniture," Gabe admitted. "And had it shipped over."

"But you won't have anyplace to put it?"

"Well," Gabe shook his head slightly, "I guess . . . we all pay a price."

Andy and I joined Gabe in silence for a few moments before Andy asked what seemed another obvious question: Just what were they going to live on over there?

"Oh, we've got enough for a year. Or so. Thought I'd have more but, well, just didn't work out that way."

That wasn't what Gabe had told me. With their savings and the sale of the house, he'd been claiming as recently as a couple of weeks ago that they'd have enough for at least two years, plus a year's reserve in case nothing new was coming in by then.

"But I've got this client," Gabe quickly added. "Worked out a big deal for him a couple of years ago, and now he thinks I'm a genius. Anyway, he's thinking about starting a business in Europe, car diagnostic machines. I'll be his Southern Europe guy. And you don't have to sell a lot of these things."

I'm not sure whether Andy or I was more incredulous, but my shock was two-edged: for the sheer fancifulness of the idea; but also because this was the first I'd heard of it despite a year of listening to Israel plans. Andy was out quickly with a string of protestations: The client's only "thinking" of starting a business? Do you know how long it could take to get going in half a dozen different countries? And you don't know anything about machinery, Gabe. Or about cars, for that matter. Besides, what makes you think people over there will want these things? And what do you mean, Southern Europe? You think Jerusalem and Rome are twin cities, fergodsake? You just gonna hop across the Mediterranean every time you get one of those little pink message slips? Gabriel, what are you talking about!?

Gabe had sort-of responses to all this but none rose even close to the level of an answer, and as they piled up, each sounded slightly more ridiculous than the last. We all just sat there looking at one another, not knowing what to say. I gazed down at my plate, thinking to find some distraction there, but the bacon had gone cold, the fat around the edges had curled up uninvitingly, and suddenly I didn't want to eat any more.

Finally I broke the silence, trying to let Gabe recoup some of the losses Andy had inflicted. I mouthed something about how maybe it would all be worth it given how strongly Gabe felt about the learning he could absorb in Israel. Andy nodded, happy to get back in Gabriel's corner, and asked Gabe about his study: Was it an actual school he'd be attending?

"Not exactly a school," Gabe began slowly, looking only at Andy. "It's in people's homes, other members of the community."

"And they speak English, these people?"

"Oh, they all speak English. Actually, they're all Americans. It's connected to people here. They set it all up here, to take in Americans who want to go over."

Andy peeked at me, but I was intent on Gabriel's face, waiting for a sign of some telltale emotion.

"So, and what sort of teaching . . . ?"

"Well, it isn't exactly teaching. You see, you work at your own pace. It's more . . . an opportunity, to study as deeply as you can."

"Huh. So, is it a rabbi? I mean, leading the study?"

"No, not rabbis, actually. Teachers aren't necessarily rabbis, you know. Or the other way round. But anyway, it's, well, other members of the community . . . who've also been studying. You see, that's the idea. An organization there works with my *shul,* with lots of *shuls,* and they just help you get over there and get settled . . . with other people who are coming over . . . who all want to study . . . and so you study together."

"You mean, with a scholar, like your Talmud guy here."

Gabriel took a deep breath, let it out slowly.

"Well, not necessarily. I mean, maybe, sure. But actually, the teacher I have here is more of a, well, major scholar."

"Wait a minute. I thought that's why you're going? To study Talmud and Torah and whatever. Right?"

Gabriel closed his eyes briefly and nodded.

"So you're going all the way to Israel, selling your house and everything, just to go study . . . and you don't know how you're going to make a living, or where you're going to live, or how long your life's savings'll last . . . but you're telling me you could do the exact same study, in fact with some high-powered teacher, if you stayed right here?"

Gabe closed his eyes again. When he opened them, his face showed the calm of a man who had already been studying for years.

"Well, not *just* to study," Gabe said evenly. "Because over there, you see . . . I won't be practicing law anymore."

For the first time since Andy had begun to ask questions, Gabe turned and looked at me. Then slowly, and for the first time in many months, the grin, that Swami's grin, spread his beard wider and wider and wider.

Labor Pains

Around a corner named January or habit or husband,
a door has opened slightly.
The light we call life forgets to wear a tag.
Of course we have believed in miles,
in beginnings and middles and ends,
in tragedy and untimely death
as if the gift
were like an infatuation,
poignant
and out of reach.

We have been wrong.

—Flora Durham
from "For As Long As We've Worn Our Bodies"

You will have noticed, I am sure, how few women trial lawyers have appeared in these pages. Not an accident of random distribution, of course. In the 1970s and 1980s out of which many of these tales are told, few women trod the courtroom boards, and current numbers are still exceedingly small. My 1971 law school graduating class was typical: of roughly two hundred students, fewer than a dozen were women, and of those I know of only one who became a trial lawyer. (After two decades of tenacious, immensely wearing, and barely remunerative legal toil on behalf of women's rights, that one classmate litigator closed up her practice, left a tape of bird songs on her office answering machine, and enrolled in art school.)

Criminal law has been somewhat ahead of the game as far as women in the courtroom is concerned. Most criminal lawyers begin their careers as public defenders or prosecutors, and these government offices have been notably better at hiring and developing women trial lawyers than have private law firms. For example, in the early 1970s, when women comprised only five percent of the total lawyer population and a much smaller portion of trial lawyers, about a third of the public defenders in my office were women. Only in the last decade has there finally been a substantial rise in women trial lawyers, though the comparative number remains quite low: by the late 1990s, the number of women lawyers overall has grown to about 25 percent, with an analogous if not proportional increase in the number of women who actually try cases.

Sociologists of the legal profession have by now explored and exposed the factors that continue to steer women lawyers onto certain professional tracks—notably family law and government bureaucracy desk-work—and away from trial law. What seems to remain unexamined, however, are changes that may have been occasioned by the entry of women *into* the trial court world: on one hand, how "femaleness" may be affecting the nature of the practice; and on the other, the gender-specific vitals of women attorneys that may be proving more or less vulnerable to the pathologies of trial lawyer life.

Despite a number of deliberate conversations on the subject with women lawyer friends, I had no real sense from them of even tentative conclusions on these questions. So, when happenstance was about to send me through a certain Midwest city, I got in touch for the first time in a long while with Angela, an old friend who had left her public defender job and then private criminal law practice, and for several years now had been teaching in a social science department of a small university there.

"Oh, I can tell you exactly what convinced me to do it," Angela said. "I'd had the idea for quite awhile. Vaguely, anyway. But I'd never actually pictured myself. No image of myself as a lawyer, you see. So, I never did anything about it. And then by chance I watched this hearing, with Beverly Ansthallen one of the judges. Well, not exactly by chance. Typical—it was this man I was seeing. In those days, I seemed to get involved with more than my share of lawyers . . . ."

Angela and I both smiled at the recollection. We, too, had been briefly "involved" when I was just out of law school, shortly before the period she was now describing. But despite broadly shared values, mutual respect, and a shimmering physical attraction, we found ourselves arguing far more than embracing. Not the best of beginnings for the perfect relationship. And since Angela and I were of a generation that believed that the perfect relationship would be the next one to walk through the door, we soon ended ours.

"So, this man—Jeff Balkin. You remember him?"

"With the motorcycle?"

Angela laughed. "I hadn't thought of that. But yeah, that's the guy. Anyway, he asks if I want to watch him argue a case in the court of appeal. And he mentions that Beverly Ansthallen—at that point she's one of the only women anywhere on an appellate court—will be one of the judges. So, okay, I show up. And during the hearing, Judge Ansthallen asks Jeff to respond to a line of cases that ran against his client's position. Now, Jeff had already told me that he was going to hang his whole argument on a single case, a 2–1 decision from Beverly Ansthallen's first year on the court, and although she hadn't written the opinion, she'd cast the deciding vote. So, when Ansthallen asks him about these other cases, Jeff glosses over them, and with this charm-boy act of his starts gushing about the 'compelling logic' of the early Ansthallen case. But ol' Beverly keeps asking him about this other line of cases, and after the second or third time he gives her this 'compelling logic' crap about her early case, Beverly's had enough. She yanks off these giant clip-on earrings she's wearing, slams them down on the bench, and almost climbs out of her chair to glare down at Jeff: 'You know, counsel,' she growls, 'something tells me that if I had it to do over again, I'd vote the other way on that case! Now, do you have any *other* logic you think might be compelling?'"

Angela told me this story as we sat on the front porch of her three-room cottage, a modern little A-frame that squatted alone and anomalous on ten acres of scrubland almost an hour outside the city. Around the house lay miles and miles of remarkably flat fields and pasture, broken only by the occasional fence and at a great distance two dots that were an old clapboard farmhouse and barn. Far to the west, worn hillocks of mottled browns and greens were the only clues to perspective.

"Part of it was that I was sick and tired of the men I knew always driving the car while I just rode along."

"You mean motorcycle, don't you?" I teased. Shortly after splitting up with the motorcycle-riding lawyer Jeff, Angela had bought an even bigger bike of her own.

"Yes, I did love bikes. The power was, well, right there. Like climbing onto a new set of muscles. But after awhile I realized it was a bit too heavy on the, ah, metaphoric."

"And when you got to the real thing? Your time trying cases, I mean?"

"Well, but the struggle just getting the chance . . . . Did I ever tell you about my job interview with Thompson & McCreavy?"

"No. But I meant . . . after you were actually in . . . ."

"You know, that big civil litigation firm? It was amazing. This stripe-suiter sitting there—silver-haired gentleman type, you know. Doing the recruiting for this big-time firm of his. And since I was almost top of my class, I thought I'd have a good shot at a job with them. So, he's sitting there, doing the interview, and after a minute or two he says, 'Tell me, do you really think you're cut out to be a trial lawyer?'

"I ask what he means, exactly. And he says, 'Oh, I'm sure you'd be a good lawyer. But it's the life, you see.'

"So I say, 'No, actually, I don't see.' And he says, 'Well, women get married, of course. And husbands get jealous . . . of the time the wives have to spend litigating. And of the prestige.'

"And then when I don't say anything—because I can't believe what I'm hearing—he bumbles right along: 'And women have kids,' he says, 'and the kids get jealous, too. Because of the time Mommy spends on her work.'

"Well, I'm sitting there still speechless, and so this clown gives me what he must have thought was the clincher.

"'To be honest,' he says, 'there's another problem. Sometimes you have to travel. And that means men and women lawyers together . . . .'

"Now, I expect him to say something about the women getting hassled on trips, or maybe some line about women not feeling comfortable traveling with men. But oh, no, that's not it.

"'It's the wives,' he tells me. The wives of the male lawyers. They get jealous. And cause problems. Have I considered that? he wanted to know. Do I really want to be in the middle of all that . . . ?"

The sun was disappearing behind the recumbent hip-and-shoulder hills, their faded-gingham browns turning vaguely blue. I wanted to nudge Angela to talk about her years in practice, but she'd gotten so steamed by thoughts of that job interview fifteen years before that I didn't know what to say. Angela got up from her chair and collected my iced-tea glass. She came back with two gin-and-tonics.

"Well," I said after we had worked our ways down the gin, "I'm sure you brought something different to the whole thing."

"How do you mean?" She eyed me over the rim of her glass.

"I don't mean anything . . . in particular. Just . . . well, okay, for starters, all that hideous trial lawyer aggression."

"You mean, could I handle it?"

"No, I know you could . . . ."

"Well, then what *do* you mean? Could I *be* like that . . ."

"No, not . . ."

". . . if I needed to?"

"Look, I wasn't saying anything. I know you were good. Come on."

"Thin-skinned," Angela laughed.

"What?"

"Women. They say women are too thin-skinned to be trial lawyers. Too emotional, you know. And here we are, a little heat from me and *you're* the one getting all defensive." She smiled, but I wasn't sure whether her expression was comradely or sardonic. It was getting dark.

"Easily intimidated," she continued in a somewhat less bumptious tone. "Meek. But you want to do stereotypes, how about 'Women love to argue'? Of course, that leads to their favorite *bête*, the New Woman. You know: pushy, hard, and blunt? . . . Now, there's a law firm for you—'Good morning, Pushy, Hard, and Blunt.'"

"And what about 'Women are too direct'? I added. 'Too forthright, so they always get taken by crafty male lawyers.'"

"Crafty males?" Angela said with mock incredulity. "Come on. Have you forgotten Eve and the apple? I mean, Original Sin—whose work was that, for godsake?"

Angela was making us dinner. While peeling and chopping as she seared and sautéed, I urged her to talk about her life when she was practicing criminal law. She responded with stories of D.A.s and other lawyers, of judges, cops, and clients, and of gender restraints both subtle and crude. What I couldn't manage, however, was to get her to speak about what she might consider as elements of her femaleness, about how they may have affected, and were affected by, her life in court.

After supper we were back on the porch. The moonless summer sky had exploded into countless twinkling possibilities. Since I hadn't been able to get Angela to talk about what trial lawyering may have done to her sense of herself, her "identity" as a woman, I shifted to a different lens: Did she feel, I asked, that the presence of more women lawyers was humanizing criminal law?

Aware as soon as it was out of my mouth of the hopeless mush of "humanize," I immediately tried again: What I meant was, did she think any of the mutilating saws of criminal justice had been blunted a bit by the infusion of values specifically female?

This was as vague and stilted as my first attempt, but Angela understood pretty well what I meant. I knew she understood— even without the porch light, I could see her face twisting in distress.

"You know," she spoke wearily, "whenever one of my students says something about 'Americans do this' or 'Americans think that,' I say: 'There are 260 million Americans. Which one, exactly, do you have in mind?' So, let me ask you: Which women, exactly, do you have in mind? Or which values?"

"Well, all right," I backpedaled. "I'm not talking earth-mother essentialism, here. But are you saying there aren't any gender particulars that might make a difference to criminal law? Or at least to criminal lawyers?"

"Such as?"

"Such as? I don't know. You tell me . . . . Well, all right, how about . . . compassion? There's an awful lot of talk about the 'caring ethic.'"

"Excuse me? When you think of the women prosecutors you've run up against, is compassion a word that leaps to mind?"

"Well . . ."

"Or women judges in criminal cases?"

"Okay, major dragons, most of 'em, you're right. But they're playing to the role, aren't they?"

"Precisely. The position: D.A.; lawyer; judge. There are women in all of them now. But it's still the same people getting busted. The same people getting shit on the same way in court. And getting put away for even longer. I mean, it's like saying that with more women soldiers, armies will kill people 'nicer.'"

"Yeah, okay, GIs, but . . . ."

"Or, you want to move up the ladder? The decision makers? You mean women in the boardroom won't plunder for profit? Women in government not just as capable of callousness? Of monstrousness? You mean they won't serve the worst imperatives of power? Tell me, which one do you want, Maggie Thatcher or Eva Peron? Or since you mentioned 'caring,' how about the exquisitely compassionate Madeleine 'Bomb-'em-to-their-knees' Albright. Or my hero, Judge Beverly Ansthallen? Last I heard, she'd left the bench and was representing some chemical company—against women who'd been crippled by one of their toxic medications. So, go on, take your pick . . . . And take your time."

Surfacing from our distant past together was an uncomfortable memory of this same tone of voice, the same forward-tilting head and rising brow. An atavistic burning arose in my chest as I recalled how often we used to argue and how Angela would press on unwaveringly until either I gave in or we parted with sizzling skins. Then, in a day or two or three, she would make peace and pay her respects to those of my arguments she thought worthy; she was always good about that. And by then reflection had usually shown us that we agreed far more than disagreed.

But this time we didn't have another day or two or three. And for the most part, again, I agreed with her. Besides, giving in or not wasn't really a problem—skin was no longer at risk. So, I kept quiet. And when I didn't respond, Angela leaned back and slowly exhaled.

"Did you know," she said softly after a minute, "that fish that are hooked and then released develop permanent psychological problems? . . . See how great it is reading academic journals? I mean, you'd never learn that in a law book."

"And no more twenty-hour days," I chimed in. "Or midnight phone calls. You get to have a life now."

"Pardon me, but I *had* a life. That was one of the raps, too: trial lawyering follows you home, and 'women can't handle that.' You know, relationships suffer, and 'those things' are too important to a woman. So, in the end she'll give up the gig. Well, relationships have changed. And what's important has changed, too . . . . Right?"

We sat in silence, closely felt. I could almost hear Angela's jaw working. The country sky had spread a huge blanket of stars, but too distant to give comfort.

"But . . . you did give it up," I finally said.

After a moment, Angela got abruptly to her feet and went inside. Noisily she banged around in the kitchen. The sounds seemed to carry a long way over the fields, nothing around to stop them. In a few minutes she came out again and sat down but said nothing.

I looked toward an old MG parked on a dirt path at the side of the house: "You still have a motorcycle?"

"No," she tried to laugh. "I'm a professor now."

"Oh, right." I tried to laugh with her. "So, what do you do with yourself . . . out here?"

"Well . . . a lot of riding."

"You mean, horses?"

"A horse, yes. Most every week. Cross-country: six, eight hours in the saddle. Sometimes I go the whole weekend. Extra muscles are okay out here . . . as long as you get them from a horse."

Images were just beginning to form a line—Angela on a motor-bike, Angela in court, Angela on a horse—when she spoke again.

"Yeah, horses, I know," she said sternly. "That's another facile lit-tle metaphor, isn't it? But frankly, I don't care . . . . Women are like that, you know," she added in afterthought. "Not caring." And managed a smile.

Find a Need

And then there is the old story, not so much revived here as told yet again, about the only lawyer in a rural area's county seat, who simply did not have enough work to survive. Until a second lawyer came to town.

Getting It Right

When I think thus of the law, I see a princess mightier than she who once wrought at Bayeaux, eternally weaving into her web dim figures of the everlengthening past—figures too dim to be noticed by the idle, too symbolic to be interpreted except by her pupils, but to the discerning eye disclosing every painful step and every worldshaking contest by which mankind has worked and fought its way from savage isolation to organic social life.

—Oliver Wendell Holmes

Many archaeologists view written materials as secondary, suspect even, because they know that until very modern times writing was the exclusive province of elites, and therefore both an inaccurate record of the spoken language and a distorted reflection of the broader social world. Clerical elites in particular have long cloaked themselves with language both confounding and inaccessible, thereby arrogating the tasks of interpretation exclusively to the few who knew that language—that is, to themselves. And since most legal codes were initially stretched on ecclesiastic frames, lawyers were early and well instructed on the benefits of obscurantist language.

For centuries, the legal profession concentrated its efforts on convincing the propertied and merchant classes to submit their major transactions to lawyers, who would reduce the agreements to highly stylized documents. The process consisted of torturing common language into stilted, abstruse legal-speak, thereby creating a chimera of critical meanings to which only the lawyers were privy. After the fact, of course, a competing version of reality would force the lawyers to reveal that there existed not one but, arguably, several competing meanings. And that would require several competing lawyers to sort out—meters running. (My first year of law school was so consumed by a lexicon of Latin and Old French that one disgusted fellow student took to ending all his classroom utterances with a mumbled "*nun quam igas*," a revisionist phrase of his own making that a few of us were able to translate as "Not that [*nun quam*] I..give..a..shit [*i..g..a..s*].")

As nineteenth and twentieth century commerce spread money into wider segments of society, the always enterprising legal community stretched the law's tentacles after it. In recent years, lawyers have pantingly accelerated their pace, shoving legal muck and mire into the most distant and formerly unlitigated corners of human behavior. Thereby, of course, insinuating themselves as self-proclaimed indispensable corner-cleaning tools. "Call my lawyer!" has become the quintessential opening volley of modern private warfare—technographic violence unleashed by proxy. In some circles, the relative viciousness of one's personal mouthpiece is even seen as a measure of social status—a sort of vicarious machismo.

Like sidewalk dog piles, the hideous legal lingo is now everywhere you step: a neighbor's noise is no longer just an annoyance to be discussed but a "noxious interference with property utilization" to be "equitably abated"; a bad conduct mark given to a third-grader now "the intentional infliction of emotional distress." But nowhere, perhaps, has the seizure by lawyers of daily life's ground rules been so intrusive as in the realm of domestic relations. Divorce has long been a legal matter (the courts necessarily stepping in to address economic gender inequity), but now every aspect of formerly married life is dissected and examined, bartered and monitored, made a part of "the record." And prenuptial agreements, postnuptial declarations, and midnuptial tax arrangements have made marriage itself a legal affair. Affair? That, too, as "palimony" arrived on the scene.

Of the many creatures to emerge from this juridical swamp, one of the most curious is something called the "living-together contract"—a phrase the oxymoronic nature of which may be worthy of some musing. This nouveau-legal construct finds its niche among people who have refused to play by established marriage rules but who eventually feel the need for some rules of their own: accumulations of money and property, they discover, may soon outweigh their stocks of consideration and trust. Since these are often well-educated folk duly exposed to the spreading legal stain, most have been indoctrinated that in matters monetary it is always best to write things down. Of course they know that some things just can't be reduced to paper. But this contract is about cohabitation, they say. A separate issue. It's not, they insist, about love.

During my years in private practice, when a domestic dispute occasionally neared my desk I would immediately refer it to a "family law" specialist—even if I could easily get up to speed on a simple enough legal problem, the woolly battleground of contentious mates was something I wanted no part of. Nonetheless, in one extraordinary lapse of judgment I allowed a former client—a woman who had attended a year of law school before switching to public relations—to hand me a living-together agreement she had drawn up for herself and the man with whom she shared a house. As to what else they did and did not share, the document speaks for itself.

NON-NUPTIAL COHABITATION CONTRACT

CONTRACTUAL AGREEMENT is made this day by and between CONSTANCE LAGRANGE, Party of the First Part, hereinafter referred to as "Female Party," and WALTER STAGNO, Party of the Second Part, hereinafter referred to as "Male Party."

Recitals

BE IT KNOWN that the parties are an unmarried woman and man of sound mind and body who hereby choose, of their own free will, to cohabit the same residential real property in NON-NUPTIAL RELATIONSHIP, each agreeing to provide amorous, companion, property management, and standard of living maintenance and improvement services to the other.

Notwithstanding any of its specific terms, the parties declare that nothing in this CONTRACT is intended to conflict with or restrict the parties' pursuit of their respective careers. The essence of the CONTRACT is *in limine*, in no way restricting the conduct of the parties *ex contractu*.

Notwithstanding any of its specific terms, the parties further declare that COGNIZABLE AFFECTION and MUTUAL RESPECT are attendant to this document and are inherent herein.

WHEREFORE, IT IS MUTUALLY AND IN GOOD FAITH AGREED:

Abbreviations

FP: female party	BP: both parties
MP: male party	OP: other party
EP: either party	TP: third party
NLT: not less than	OPM: once per month
NMT: not more than	OPW: once per week
T&A: tidy and arrange	C&R: clean and reposition

Definitions

SOCIAL CONDUCT: Non-pecuniary personal, telephonic, electronic, written, or Platonic physical, contact between EP and any TP.

SEXUAL CONDUCT: Non-Platonic physical contact between EP and any TP, with specific intent to arouse EP, TP or both.

STANDARD OF LIVING: Possession and use of real estate, commodities and services which make life more pleasing, including such matters as may contribute style or other social grace, to EP.

I. Separate Property

Except as specifically provided herein, all assets obtained by EP through her or his individual efforts shall remain separate property outside the purview of this CONTRACT, including but not limited to personal property marked with identification numbers and listed on identical signed documents held in the separate safe deposit boxes of BP.

II. Extra-Officio Personal Relations

BP hereby reaffirm that mutual respect is at the essence of their CONTRACT and therefore EP shall make an *honest* effort to abide *in good faith* with the terms of this Section.

Social Conduct—EP may engage in any SOCIAL CONDUCT with any one or more TP. But should EP engage in frequent SOCIAL

CONDUCT with any TP, she/he shall, with due diligence, keep OP informed as to the nature and frequency of that CONDUCT.

Sexual Conduct—EP may limit OP's SEXUAL CONDUCT with any one TP to NMT OPM. EP may limit the total number of OP's TPs to NLT four PM. EP shall, within 48 hours, notify OP of any instance of more than OPM SEXUAL CONDUCT with any one TP, and more than four SEXUAL CONDUCTS PM with separate TPs. Notification shall include dates and frequency of conduct but not identity of TPs nor specific nature or quality of CONDUCT unless BP mutually so agree.

III. Duties of Cohabitation

WHEREAS personal presentation is vital to social and commercial success; WHEREAS order and regularity are vital to presentation; and, WHEREAS order and regularity begin with appearance *in personam* and *in domum*;

THEREFORE, EP pledges to keep person and home clean and orderly and to maintain regular co-habits, including but not limited to the following:

A. Duties of BP

In alternating weeks, EP shall NLT OPW T&A (NLT one hour) and NLT OPW C&R (NLT two hours) BPs' entire living space. T&A and C&R shall be separated by NLT 48 hours.

In addition to general duties, specific protocols shall be observed by BP, as follows:

Periodicals—newspapers and magazines shall be removed from periodicals table by respective subscriber before periodical pile reaches the bottom of the bird cage (budgies).

Marshmallow pans—MP agrees that any marshmallow burned on pans by MP shall be scoured off within 24 hours of notification to MP by FP.

Televisions—FP agrees that none of her televisions is to be placed (even temporarily, even with sound off) in such manner that the screen can be seen from any of the bird cages.

Open closets—MP acknowledges that open closets (including drawers and cupboards) are emotionally disturbing to FP, and agrees to shut them *tightly* after each use.

B. Particular Duties of MP

Jacuzzi—MP shall C&R Jacuzzi (including glass-holders and rubber ducks) NLT OPW;

Maintenance & Repair—NLT OPW (NLT one hour) MP shall perform routine home maintenance and repair according to a list prepared by FP, and in the order given.

Bird cages—WHEREAS FP respects MP's pre-existing relationship with and love for his various birds; and WHEREAS MP recognizes that FP is emotionally allergic to bird excreta; THEREFORE, MP will NLT on alternate days remove bulk droppings from all bird cages and NLT OPW *thoroughly* C&R all cages.

Meat & Fowl—MP shall utilize his commercial relationships to procure for BP NLT OPM a supply of meats (varietal, NLT 80% steaks, chops and Stroganoff, no veal unless certified) and fowl (varietal, free range when available, *absolutely no aerial birds*) sufficient for at-home meat or fowl dinners four times PW, including NLT OPW for NMT four guests.

C. Particular Duties of FP

Telephones—FP shall C&R all telephones, with particular attention to mouthpiece hygiene, NLT OPW.

Toiletries—FP shall T&A all toiletries and grooming products NLT OPW.

Toilet/grooming product supplies—FP shall utilize her commercial relationships to procure for BP: facial quality toilet paper; tissues (boutique boxes, bird motif if possible); and hair spray (unscented) of a brand acceptable to MP.

Desserts—FP shall NLT OPW prepare for MP one of the desserts FP made for MP at pre-cohabitation dinners prepared by FP, and procure for MP's consumption on all other nights prepared desserts (dictionary definition) chosen in FP's discretion. but utilizing her dessert imagination.

WRITTEN NOTICE: BP agree that if EP is unable to perform any task in full, he or she is to perform it to the extent possible, and state in writing to OP the reasons why such completion was not possible.

PENALTIES: If EP finds the written explanation of the OP for incomplete performance to be insufficient, the penalty shall consist of an additional equal quantum of performance by the violating party, specific nature of which to be determined by the non-violating party.

IV. Mutual General Fund

Standard-of-Living Fund—EP shall contribute a minimum of $_____ per calendar month, due on the first of each month, to the general fund of BP. Said amounts shall be increased by 15% per annum. If EP fails to make any month's contribution, he or she shall contribute thrice the amount the following month. Failure of EP to meet these requirements shall give OP the right to withdraw from the fund, aside from any other partition, an amount equal to five times the defaulted contributions.

Fund Expenditures—Monies from the fund shall be expended by mutual agreement of BP for the maintenance and improvement of BPs' STANDARD OF LIVING. Expenditures of NMT $1,000 may be authorized by oral agreement of BP; expenditures of NLT $1,000 shall be by signed, written agreement of BP.

V. Entire Agreement

This CONTRACT supersedes all other agreements, oral or written, between BP relating to their NON-NUPTIAL COHABITATION.

This CONTRACT may be amended only by written instrument signed by BP. It may *not* be altered or affected in any way by any promise or declaration made orally, in private, by EP to OP, regardless of any conduct performed by EP for the benefit or pleasure of the OP in exchange or consideration for such promise or declaration.

_____   _____

FEMALE PARTY   MALE PARTY

_____

Oh, and my lawyer's task in all this? Had they, FP wanted to know, left anything out?

No One Special

Although there were several in my law school class older than his thirty-or-so years, William Plimmy's perpetual look of disapprobation managed to earn him—from the few who noticed him at all—the less than affectionate nickname "Plimmy the Elder." During our first semester, I had the misfortune to be assigned a seat in civil procedure class next to Plimmy. It was an hour that always felt like three, the poverty of my interest in the required subject exacerbated by the weight, only inches away, of Plimmy's rancorous concentration. It wasn't that Plimmy evinced a particular appetite or aptitude for civil procedure. Or for anything else, as far as I could determine. Yet in class he never failed to summon a tenacious, unwavering focus, the only visible fuel for which was his resentment against anyone else—meaning nearly everyone else—who had an easier time of it. Every subject was difficult for Plimmy, and he was able to scrape and slog his way through only by the sheer number of hours spent over his books, by the absolute refusal to have anything else on his mind, and by what seemed a desperate sense that for him this was not so much school as a one-and-only chance at salvation.

Attempts to engage Plimmy in conversation disclosed a sympathy for distractions as brutish and short as the range of his interests. Particularly when I proffered remarks in any way disrespectful to the legal maze through which we staggered, Plimmy would respond with a withering expression that could have emanated only from some cold and heavy load of bile. "I have no time for this" would no doubt have been the sentiment he was most fond of expressing—had he been fond of expressing anything at all.

What he expressed to his wife and children I never knew, although I did learn that he considered himself a good husband: that is, he didn't lay a hand on his wife and didn't hit his kids without provocation; didn't drink or stay out late; didn't have any friends; and however many complaints he had, didn't voice them. At eighteen, Plimmy had married the only girl he'd ever kissed, and rather hastily—at least compared to the rest of his life—began to sire children. Thankfully, though, someone (perhaps his wife) eventually clued Plimmy that they didn't *have* to keep procreating, and so after three kids in three years of marriage, he and his wife had no more.

In order to support his new family, Plimmy enlisted in the army but spent the last of his three-year hitch unhappily posted someplace where people stubbornly insisted on speaking a language other than English. So, Plimmy decided to try civilian life. He took a job in his father-in-law's large commercial insurance business. Sales, however, proved no place for the dour Elder, so he was moved into actuarial and risk management tasks. And while the plodding certainties of premiums and payouts were a comfort to him, daily doses of his father-in-law led him to consider other careers. He enrolled in night college mathematics courses but soon realized he had no imagination for math's higher forms and so moved over to engineering. Then a course on the American legal system—What could have prompted it, a "breadth" requirement?—convinced Plimmy that law presented a special kind of equation that engineering did not: in the adversary system, as Plimmy saw it, being right means that someone else has to be wrong. Apparently he found that encouraging, and after six more years of Plimmyesque focus, during which he quit work, took loans from his father-in-law and a degree from a four-year college, Plimmy had hard-won grades good enough to be considered by the better law schools. After graduation he borrowed more from his father-in-law and studied full-time for the Law School Admission Test. With characteristic tenacity, he took the test three times, finally making a score high enough to complement his grades. (Adding to his general state of vexation, however, by the time he got into law school Plimmy knew he'd be in debt to his father-in-law for years to come.)

During our second semester, I again suffered the singular experience of Plimmy's company. But this time he was forced to talk to me: some short cosmic straw had handed me The Elder as my partner for Moot Court, the simulated courtroom argument that is a law student's first taste of litigational blood. To Plimmy's distinct if typically unspoken distaste, our assignment was to argue on behalf of Native American fishing rights, as against the primacy of state statutes and non-Indian property rights. Our preliminary research revealed virtually no direct precedent—that pyramid of prior judicial decisions without the dictates of which, our professors had spent our first year assailing us, civilized life would surely be impossible—in support of the Indians' rights. Plimmy was paralyzed: without specific case law commandments behind them, he considered the Indians' position not only insupportable but unworthy of support—a kind of legal Calvinism. Plimmy and I fell into serious disagreement, which eventually led to his tremulous accusation that I actually cared more about Native rights than for the sanctity of legal precedent. My ready assent that this was true—and that it was due to a curious personal condition that required that blood actually reach my brain—sent Plimmy scurrying to our Moot Court professor. Sensing the depth of Plimmy's crisis, the professor switched him to another case altogether.

It was nine or ten years later that The Elder next spoke to me, then in his capacity as a suburban assistant district attorney. As I recall, his first words were "Didn't know we had any Indians in this county," though my surprise and distress at finding him as prosecutor of my client may have somewhat clouded what I heard.

The fact that Plimmy was a career local D.A., however, made perfect sense. The big-time law firms wouldn't have been interested in his decidedly mediocre law school performance. And while some smaller firms would no doubt have overlooked both his grades and his personality in order to profit from his work habits, Plimmy was the type to feel more comfortable in a bureaucratic setting where he was expected merely to stay within a prefabricated slot rather than to expand a private firm's client list and coffers. That he had chosen a prosecutor's job rather than a behind-the-scenes position with a more anonymous government agency also made sense: Plimmy would find solace in the slam of cell doors, a sound that might convince him that, at least among these unhappy people, he was the one who was free.

I made several phone calls to local criminal defense lawyers to find out what I could about this current version of Plimmy the Elder. I was looking for some angle, some avenue by which I could engage Plimmy and eventually work him around to a softer view of my client. But the lawyers said that Plimmy was rarely seen or heard from outside the D.A.'s office and that apparently his only extramural involvement was as a nominal member of the county's Republican Central Committee, of which his father-in-law was a longtime leading figure. From what I could gather, the Plimmy I had known in law school was still all there was.

My negotiations with Plimmy bore this out. Actually, negotiations is far too expansive a word: my varied efforts to have Plimmy view my client as a human with comprehensible foibles and weaknesses fell on deaf ears. I couldn't even elicit the kind of nostalgic patter one would expect between two people who for an entire year had sat next to each other through the excruciating experience of civil procedure class. All I managed to get out of him were several reprises of that spiritless look—"I have no time for this"—by which The Elder had earned his name.

In court I did what I could to stall the case, hoping that something would happen to turn Plimmy toward my client's better side. Surprisingly, Plimmy did not object to my tactics and allowed the case to lurch along in the miasma of the criminal court calendar.

He was content, it seemed, with the inevitability of the outcome and the equal certainty that when my client and I finally had to face the music, he would be there to enjoy it.

Then a remarkable thing happened—Plimmy was gone. I showed up in court and found a different deputy D.A. handling the case. Plimmy, this new D.A. announced, had just been appointed traffic court commissioner, a kind of junior judge.

I knew that governors frequently tabbed prosecutors to be local judges, both for "law and order" appearances and for the political quiescence promised by intellectual mediocrity and lack of independent will on the bench. What I didn't understand was why such a particular nonentity as Plimmy would get appointed. Simple, a local lawyer explained: traffic court required a full day's boring work, afforded no prestige, and paid considerably less than what lawyers in well-connected law firms hoped to make. It was just that Plimmy had been this small conservative county's only politically active Republican lawyer willing to take the job.

I was delighted not to have to see Plimmy's mug again and gave little thought to his successor. But when I showed up at the new D.A.'s office a few days later to start plea bargaining, I was met by a familiar disgusted expression on a rock-pile face.

"He's an Indian?" the D.A. said quizzically, referring in her file to some cryptic note Plimmy must have made.

"No. As a matter of fact, he's not."

"Well, then, if he's no one special," she barely looked up at me, "let's make it quick. I haven't got much time for this."

What Fortune in Reversals?

M r. Dershowitz, help me out here. I know you've said over and again that you take on someone's defense only for the highest of criminal lawyer principles. It's just that every time you open your mouth—which I'm sure you'd agree is a relentlessly frequent occurrence—a different principle seems to pop out. And truth be told, Mr. D., I'm having a hard time moving from the general to the particular. That is, from principle to practice, when practice has meant cases like Claus von Bulow, Mike Tyson, O.J. Simpson. And, excuse me for bringing her up, Leona ("only 'little people' pay taxes") Helmsley. So, maybe you can understand why I'm having so much trouble.

[Actually, my problem about all this started with Tom. Of course, Harvard professor Alan Dershowitz would no doubt find my old friend pretty suspect: years ago Tom registered to attend a prestigious law school but fled in revulsion after a visit to its desolate bookstore and an

introductory lecture by one of Dershowitz's fellow legal academics who believed he was waxing eloquent about the law's internal beauty but succeeded only in putting Tom to sleep. In fact, I'm certain Dershowitz would consider Tom doubly suspect: not once in the decades since his flight from law school has he ever wished he had stayed.

I had never given any particular thought to Dershowitz and his self-publicized doings until one day Tom calls to say that I've got to see this movie Reversal of Fortune—*I'm gonna love it, he tells me. I ask what he means, but he chuckles and just says for me to get it. Don't worry, he adds, you won't need to watch the whole thing. Then he laughs again and hangs up.*

So, I rented the video. Funny thing is, I did watch the whole thing, in equal measure savoring the nuanced turns in Jeremy Irons's performance as Claus von Bulow—the Old World aristocrat accused of trying to kill his heiress wife—and waiting for the Alan Dershowitz character to deliver a line that didn't sound like it had been filched from the bubble of a bad comic book. Watched it several times, in fact, looking to distill, out of the script's dizzying array of credos, rationales, and rationalizations, that higher lawyer's purpose in which Dershowitz manages to wrap himself in every one of his myriad newspaper columns, TV talk shows, and books. And now in a movie. That thing he drapes around his shoulders, the exact pattern of which always remains just out of sight down his back.]

I thought I was onto something in an early scene in that von Bulow movie of yours, Mr. Dershowitz. It's the scene where your student researchers and apprentice lawyers are gathered in your office. (Lovely scene, by the way: acolytes arrayed amphitheatrically around the desk at which your character stands and expounds, all of it carefully framed to make us see Dershowitz the Teacher *in loco parentis* rather than Dershowitz the Ringmaster in his circus hiring hall.) And in this scene you explain to your band of legal tyros why it is they should sign up with you to defend the seriously wealthy von Bulow—a man who could afford to hire any of a hundred top criminal lawyers—charged with the attempted murder of his far wealthier wife, in a case that seemed to involve no more higher calling than to determine which was more vacuous, medium-old money or deathly old breeding. Telling not just the students, of course, but us, all of us watching the film, why we should join your campaign to . . . . To what?

For the students, you were easily up to the task. But as for me, I'd like to speak to you a bit more on the subject. You'll recall, the students had asked why you were taking the case—other than for the however-many-hundreds of dollars an hour, I mean. And your character replies:

The family hired a private prosecutor. Unacceptable.

Private prosecutor? Apparently you were referring to the fact that to serve their own interests against von Bulow's, the comatose wife's children had taken to their personal lawyer some information potentially inculpatory of von Bulow. Well, Alan (you don't mind the first name liberty, I hope, but it looks like we're in for a long haul here; and after all, von Bulow got to call you Alan, and he wasn't even a lawyer), that one surprised me. I thought an Alan Dershowitz—bulldog advocate ready to chew any legal bone of contention for his clients—would have considered that going to a lawyer was precisely the proper way for people to protect their interests. In the view of someone who seems to love having people come to him, I wondered, what could be wrong with that?

They conducted a private search.

Private search? You mean, the children looked around their own house? And didn't depend on the local cops to do a perfect job of detection? But aren't you the one who contends that the police bungled the forensics in this very same case? And in the O.J. case? And in so many others? Okay, never mind, Dersh. (That's what your students and fellow defense lawyers call you, right? "Dersh." I mean, you like that, right? From those of us on the same side?) Let's grant that this private evidence-gathering could have lengthened the odds for von Bulow. Bad for von Bulow. No question. But *our* question is, What are *we* doing here? Taking this case, that is? Rather than spending so much time and energy and considerable talents elsewhere?

> *Now we let 'em get away with that, rich people won't go to the cops anymore. They're gonna get their own lawyers to collect evidence. And then they are going to choose which evidence they feel like passing on to the D.A. And the next victim isn't going to be rich, like von Bulow, but it's going to be some poor schnook in Detroit who can't afford or who can't find . . . a decent lawyer.*

Rich people won't go to the cops anymore? Now Dersh, it may be that you've spotted the first temblor of a monumental shift in power distribution that has as yet escaped notice by the rest of us, but in my experience as a criminal lawyer, when rich people have been victims of a crime, the cops do the very best of which they are capable. And particularly when "some poor schnook in Detroit"— not terribly subtle code, Dersh; and since all through this movie you're so gratuitously waggling your purported defense of "innocent black kids" at us, why the shyness here?—is accused of committing it. The cold fact is, "poor schnooks" rarely get near enough to the rich to commit crimes against them—that's one of the things being rich and being poor means. And when it does happen, the cops throw all their weight—with considerably heavier hands and boots than Claus von Bulow ever saw—into nabbing the poor schnook. Infinitely more so than when another poor schnook has been the victim. Always have. And until we see some rather extreme political reversals of fortune, always will.

So, can you possibly expect to avoid howls of derision when you spray us with this prattle that rich people won't go to the cops anymore? That rich people will watch how Sonny von Bulow's kids used their wealth to help snatch their mother's fortune from the grasp of *vieux-bourgeois* Claus, and from that will deduce that the cops (and D.A.s and judges) can't be trusted any longer to represent their interests . . . *against the poor*? That the conviction of Claus von Bulow is going to send rich people scurrying to hire posses of lawyer-vigilantes who will specialize in framing "poor schnooks in Detroit" for crimes against the rich? Well, I'm sorry, Dersh, but this, in a word, is horseshit.

[Whoa. Wait a minute, now. We're talking Harvard Law School faculty here. And spokesman for . . . well, as he's said, the highest ideals of the legal profession. So, a little respect, please.

And should we judge the entire tapestry of an advocate's life by a single patch of cheap rhetorical threads? Besides, that was a movie character speaking. Not the real Dersh. We can't hold Dershowitz responsible for his movie character's ham-fisted dialogue ("If I can't save two innocent kids, what's the point? I might as well hang it up." . . . "I am not going to let them execute you! You are not going to die!"). Can we? Never mind that the film was based on the real Dersh's book. And that he sold not only the movie rights but also his cooperation in its making. Or even that his son was the movie's coproducer. True, with his ongoing connections to the film, a court of law might well consider the real Dershowitz's acquiescence in the dialogue to be an "adoptive admission"—if you knowingly allow someone to say things in your name, this legal concept holds, you can't later be heard to complain. Still, a good lawyer might find a way around that. Certainly one as good as Dersh.

So okay, since we don't know which of the movie's lines came out of whose mouth, we'd better go to the source. Reversal of Fortune, the book. His own book. To make certain of what the real Dershowitz has to say.]

Well, Dersh, I took a look at your book on the von Bulow case. To find the reasons you took up the defense, I mean. But I have to admit, I'm still stumped.

In the book's early pages you write that you took the case not because you believed von Bulow innocent—indeed, you admit that at first you assumed him guilty. You go on to say that in general you don't care whether a defendant is guilty or not. Well, that remark sounds like it might have derived from some larger principle, perhaps even from that overarching purpose of yours that I keep scrabbling around for. So, I read on, assuming that eventually you'd reach a bit more depth about why it is you bother to take on these celebrity clients. And I did find several scattered mentions of how this or that case involved a "constitutional principle." Of course, that didn't make much of an impression on me since, like every criminal lawyer, I know that most appeals in criminal cases could include one or another constitutional issue. (But, then, I guess your public pronouncements aren't really aimed at practicing criminal lawyers, are they?) Besides, when these issues are as flimsy as that nonsense in the von Bulow case about rich people's "private prosecutions" threatening to sweep up the "poor schnooks" of Detroit, the mere fact that you manage to hoist the constitutional flag in a case doesn't necessarily send thrills down freedom-loving spines.

So, finally I get all the way through this book of yours, Dersh. And by the end, the only suggestion still standing about the Why of it all is a reference to another of your books, *The Best Defense*. All right, I think. I guess if you've said it there, you shouldn't have to say it again. Fair enough. So, I take a look.

Well, lots of your war stories in this book, Dersh: a separate chapter on each of your "most controversial and dramatic cases." But before you launch into all the juicy particulars, you tell the reader that you will discuss how it is you decide to take a case. Here, I think; here, I'm finally on to something.

You begin by saying that because of your university sinecure, you can be selective about the clients you represent. And in that selectivity you "take on cases from which other lawyers might shy away." Well, you may indeed have taken cases some other experienced lawyers shied away from. But this standard is hardly persuasive when applied to the bulging wallet of a Claus von Bulow, is it? Or to Tyson or Simpson or Helmsley? I mean, how many lawyers would have lined up barefoot in the snow to collect the fees in those cases?

(I also happened to catch one of your however-many TV talk show appearances, Dersh, at a moment when you were plaintively feeding the national audience a version of this same line in regard to representing Mike Tyson: "If I didn't do it, who would?" you turned your rictus smile to the camera. Unfortunately, there were no lawyers waiting on the call-in line who might have personally answered the question. And I guess it must have been an off night for the otherwise trenchantly analytical Larry King, because instead of giving the faintest thought and obvious reply to your remark, he cut to a commercial.)

Another of your proclamations in *The Best Defense* about why you represent the clients you do is that your secure academic position permits you to take "the most challenging, the most difficult" cases. Okay. Von Bulow, Tyson, Simpson, and Helmsley certainly fit that bill. But my problem is that while "most challenging" and "most difficult" may be good lead-ins for a book of heroic courtroom tales, they don't really lead anywhere else. You see, I still can't come up with any principle, any larger purpose, that flows into or out of notions of "challenging" or "difficult." Nothing larger, that is, than the Self.

[Perhaps it's time to engage in some deductive reasoning here. But first, let's take stock. We have been regaled in The Best Defense *with a four-hundred-page feast of Dershowitz's legal derrings-do, yet we're still without nourishment: no* raison de défendre *that seems to matter—at least, to anyone other than Dershowitz—about why the likes of von Bulow, Tyson, Simpson, and Helmsley. In a final chapter, however, Dershowitz gives us a rundown of the kinds of criminal lawyer he disdains, presumably meaning the kinds of criminal lawyer he's not. And so, from what he says he is not, maybe we can winnow what he is.*

Among those on the Dershowitz blacklist are the "media-oriented" defense lawyers who, Dershowitz argues, risk having their own desire for publicity come before the interests of their clients. As example, however, Dershowitz cites only his erstwhile friend F. Lee Bailey's press conferences in the Patty Hearst case. Remarkably conspicuous by its absence is any mention of Dershowitz's own innumerable newspaper forays, television appearances, and highly advertised public "debates." Equally glaring is Dershowitz's focus exclusively on the way cases are conducted, without any reference to a lawyer's decisions about which cases to conduct. Without reference, that is, to the patent media "orientation" inherent in the very act of choosing to represent von Bulows, Tysons, Simpsons, and Helmsleys.

Dershowitz also dismisses—as delusional—the "Perry Mason" lawyers who believe they are "clever strategist(s) subtly weaving a psychological net around the lying prosecution witness." A net that, when tightened over the witness, forces in open court an admission of lies, and results in the defendant's acquittal. Of course, the Professor is right to point out that criminal trials rarely produce such theatrical somersaults. But he does allow that in rare instances such a legal stratagem "really works." Example? Well, he manages to find one. Elsewhere in this very same book. In a case orchestrated by—Are we ready?—Mr. Dershowitz himself.

The Professor unleashes his harshest (if not most coherent) salvo, however, against lawyers who would intrude their own political views as part of a client's defense. Dershowitz frames this most grievous of faults as a willingness to "impose his 'cause' approach on an unwilling client." Dershowitz's only example, however, is William Kunstler's conduct during the "Chicago 7" trial, which arose out of the demonstrations at the 1968 Democratic convention. Now, I realize that contemporary American political amnesia is severe and virtually universal. But for Dershowitz to expect to get away with applying this critique—a lawyer "imposing" politics onto clients—to defendants like Abbie Hoffman and Bobby Seale, he must assume that hardly anyone in this country remembers what was going on in 1968. (Maybe he's right.)

Dershowitz's argument about Kunstler and the Chicago 7 seemed so ludicrous that I read it several more times to see if there was something I had missed. It was obvious that Dershowitz was exercising a considerable personal animus toward Kunstler; I couldn't locate its source and so assumed it must have to do with some private, backstage rivalry. Finally, though, after scratching and scratching, the shadow of an *entirely different accusation began to appear beneath the visible argument's silly surface. Dershowitz's rambling indictment against Kunstler, I sensed, was not actually about the explicit charge of defendant abuse but about a different crime, and different victim, altogether. The real sin in Dershowitz's eyes was not any betrayal of Kunstler's clients, but rather Kunstler's betrayal of his own—and Dershowitz's—prelatic caste. Kunstler becomes anathema to Dershowitz when Kunstler refuses to play the role—the prescribed, delimited, innocent role—assigned to the defense lawyer in the formula courtroom passion play. Instead of speaking his lines as the noble advocate, arguing only the scripted "facts" and "law," Kunstler scandalously "employ(s) the rhetoric of his radical clients." Scandalous precisely because he was willing to be held accountable for the content of what was expressed. Kunstler stood damned before the Professor not as a lawyer who had put his politics before his clients, but as a lawyer who had brazenly put his politics before his place—Dershowitz's own safe and hallowed place—in the Law.]*

I think maybe at last I'm getting the drift of this thing, Dersh. I've watched your movie—well, not exactly *your* movie, I know—a number of times now. And I've read books of yours, too. But it wasn't until I heard what another criminal lawyer had to say that I finally began to piece things together. Things this other lawyer said and wrote that offered a window onto the dynamics of why you take on—and of how you explain—a von Bulow or Helmsley or Tyson case.

Curiously, it began with another movie: Marcel Ophuls's stunning documentary meditation on the nature of remembering and the construction of history, *Hotel Terminus*. Toward the end of this remarkable multilayered film, I was brought up in my seat by the pronouncements of one Jacques Vergès, a Vietnamese-French lawyer as notorious, respected, and reviled in France for his defense of unpopular clients—Algerian FLN fighters accused of "terrorism," members of the French extremist group *Action Directe*, associates of the Baader-Meinhof group, Carlos "the Jackal"—as you are in this country.

But let me back up, Dersh. Bring you along from the beginning. In the film, we first meet Vergès in his office. And the image Vergès scrupulously, almost preposterously, projects is on its surface quite different from your own. While you play scruffy, streetwise Brooklyn for all it is worth, Vergès gives us maximum popinjay Paris: Ophuls waits in a hand-carved chair while Vergès, in tailored silks and a hint of a smirk, sits behind his exquisite Louis-something desk; covering the immense gallery-cum-office floor is a lush Eastern rug; and climbing the wall behind Vergès, a huge tapestry depicting a heavily stylized forest idyll that features in the foreground a preening peacock. Vergès speaks on the intercom: with vowels as opulent and consonants as delicate as the office *objets d'art*, he instructs his secretary to show a waiting film crew—not Ophuls's, but yet another film crew—into the *salon bleu*.

Ophuls asks Vergès why he takes on a monstrously unpopular and difficult case. Vergès's lips move slightly, on the way to a smile that doesn't quite arrive. He waits a beat, then speaks with an insistent delicacy. There are certain defendants, Vergès says, who are not only presumed by everyone to be guilty but are thought to be indefensible. And when such an accused appears, something in Vergès tells him, "Why not take the case and show that, for a lawyer, no case is indefensible . . . . That would be satisfaction enough." And the little smile finally appears.

An immense pleasure lurked behind that smile, Dersh. However complex his emotions, they coalesced in this pleasure at the sheer contrariness of defending the indefensible. A pleasure that immediately suggested consanguinity with someone an ocean and a culture away. You titled one of your books *Chutzpah*, Dersh. And doesn't *chutzpah* mean more than just nerve and a willful disregard for social imperatives? Doesn't *chutzpah* often imply not only a willingness to act but also a certain satisfaction in having acted, in having gone utterly against the grain? And more, a pride—a pleasure—in the pain of being singled out for having done so?

Vergès isn't reticent about the pleasure he takes in his most notorious cases:

*Why deny it? I love the feat, the challenge, to defend
one who is claimed to be indefensible, to cry that the
emperor has no clothes, to probe the idols and to pro-
claim that they are false. . . . If I were a doctor, I
would rather have performed the first heart transplant
than to have cured a thousand cases of flu in Sarcelles
[a nondescript suburb of Paris]. I know well that his
rivals claim that [transplant pioneer] Doctor Barnard
loves publicity, money, and women, but so what?*

Though you are considerably more circumspect in print about
the role your personal version of *chutzpah* plays in your taking of
high-profile cases, it's easy to follow the line that connects Paris and
Brooklyn, Vergès and Dershowitz. And to see along that line the
same overweening lust—for nothing broader, nothing deeper, than
a chance to get in on the action.

But lust for a piece of the action is not at the core of my problem with you, Dersh. Because there are plenty of other experienced
criminal lawyers for whom getting into the rough-and-tumble is
virtually the only reason they continue to put themselves through
the wringer of criminal cases both infamous and anonymous. And
while these lawyers inspire no particular interest or respect, neither
do they necessarily evoke contempt. But you, Dersh. You and
Vergès. With the two of you something else is at work, something
you share that is far more fetid than mere love of the battle and its
tracer fire of notoriety.

I have read and listened to Vergès carefully, Dersh. And once
again have read and listened to you. And finally I think I've found
what rankled me from my very first dose of you. And that is your
smug and perverse reliance—yours and Vergès's—on a certain
unassailable rationale which, as part of its beauty, you rarely have to
utter but on which you nonetheless rely to purify your swim in
whatever swill you choose. Listen up:

The zealous defense attorney is the last bastion of liberty—the final barrier between an overreaching government and its citizens. The job of the defense attorney is to challenge the government; to make those in power justify their conduct in relation to the powerless; to articulate and defend the right of those who lack the ability or resources to defend themselves.

—Dershowitz

I believe that the defense of the individual against any state is the function a defense lawyer must perform . . . . When the establishment, the judicial system, the media, the supposed religious authorities, the so-called humanitarian organizations, are not ashamed to batter away at one lone man, I will always stand with the lone man. —Vergès

Quite right, of course. Both right. Two versions of the reason why *all* defendants, regardless of the crime with which they are charged, must be permitted, or if necessary have provided for them, a vigorous and unfettered defense. But that's not how you and Vergès operate this principle, Dersh. No, the way you and Vergès unblinkingly manipulate the right to a defense turns it on its head. You are able implicitly to back up your participation in a case—any case—with the accused's fundamental right to a defense . . . even though it hasn't got a damn thing to do with why *you* represent that particular client as opposed to innumerable others. In your hands, Mr. Dershowitz, the accused's right to a defense is debased to an immensely powerful if mostly unspoken expedient on which—when your various other self-justifications fall apart—you can always rely . . . in your *own* defense.

Always claiming that you are performing *in response to* this greater good allows you to appear, indeed to revel, in any drama you choose, but without the slightest personal consequence from or shared responsibility in its content. You make pietistic use—cynical or self-deluding?—of the accused's right to a defense, Mr.

Dershowitz, as cover for whatever pleasure it is you get from rolling around in the fields of the rich and infamous. Use it as a free pass to play in von Bulow's suites and Leona Helmsley's castle, in Tyson's ring and Simpson's Hollywood. Use it in these cases, Professor Dershowitz, exactly as Jacques Vergès did in his. As Vergès used it to roam freely in the world of his client, the world of Reichslieutenant Klaus Barbie—Occupation commandant of the Hotel Terminus, Gestapo torturer, deporter to the death camps of the children of Izieu, "Butcher of Lyon."

Collective Noun

In what are self-inflatingly referred to as the professions, people spend most of their time, both on and technically off the job, with others who do the same work. No exception are trial lawyers, who are surrounded by their partners and associates; by other lawyers to and from whom cases are referred; by cocounsel in multiple litigant cases; and by lawyers with whom research, expertise, and inside information is shared. But while their parallel struggles give rise to a certain collegiality, there is also jealousy, backbiting, and a fierce competitiveness: Who gets the credit? Who gets the blame? Who's mentioned in the paper, whose face on TV? And of greatest concern to most, Who gets the next big case with the nice fat fee? Played out with the cunning and aggressiveness litigators develop to perform the job itself, these internecine battles often turn what might otherwise be comradely relationships into major sources of stress and insecurity.

And those are your friends. But if you are one of that special breed of trial lawyer known as the criminal defense attorney, you also spend many of your long days and nights with a varied cast of other characters, almost all of whom harbor some secret dream that involves you dangling by a thread off the roof of a very tall building, the images differing only in the thickness of the thread and the part of your body to which it is attached. Prominent among these characters are your antinomic counterparts, the prosecutors, so many of whom would like to take out on your clients all their barely suppressed hatreds of the underclasses and the underraces, of swarthy foreign enemies and uppity foreign allies, of their own fathers, mothers, spouses, and lovers, of their third-grade bully and their untouchable high school crush. Prosecutors—who are not among the highest regarded within the legal profession, and know it; are not among the highest paid of the legal profession, and know it; are resentful of the money they presume you make, even if you don't; are contemptuous of the moral ground they think you claim, even if you've slipped far off it; who no longer believe they represent the forces of righteousness, though every day they pretend they do; who are overworked cogs in a law enforcement machine advertised as the last bulwark against chaos and savagery but which they know to be, instead, merely another layer of chaos and savagery; and who are, of course, lawyers.

And then there are the judges, many of whom are former prosecutors and all of whom engaged in enough political sycophancy to get appointed to the bench; some of whom upon their advent assume the wounded mien and inclement disposition of a mid-level aristocrat charged with the distasteful task of sifting through the sordid quotidian problems of the serfs; others of whom shoulder the cross of the beleaguered bureaucrat, lips always formed around the word "No" as shield against an endless stream of tall stories, shaggy dog stories, and almost always sad stories, and against the flock of fractious lawyers bleating about why their story is truly something different; and who are themselves, of course, lawyers.

Then there are the cops, who do not distinguish in any meaningful way among those who commit crimes, those who look to them like they commit crimes, and those who defend either.

Plus the probation officers who, even more than the prosecutors, are overworked and underpaid; who, through their presentence reports, often seal the fate of your client without your being able to do anything but beg, wheedle, and cajole, much more of which than you can stomach you've already done and will have to do more of with the cops, the prosecutor, and the judge; who have heard it all before; and who never quite come to grips with the fact that you're a lawyer and they aren't.

And, of course, there are your clients, many of whom—at least for non-talkshow criminal lawyers—are poor, yet by whom you want to be paid with money for which you must repeatedly entreat them and about which they repeatedly reply that they do not have but will pay you anyway; whose trust during this convoluted dialogue you are trying to inspire so that they will fully tell you what happened even though much of it you might be in calmer conscience and therefore stauncher defending posture not knowing, and which even if you are told, you can never really know because no matter what your experience with the world from which your clients come, you are never them; who might wind up sort of trusting you and sort of paying you because they have nowhere else to go; for whom much of the time you can do very little because you see them only after they have done what they have done; many of whom are, when you meet them, at the lowest point of their lives; many of whose long-bred implacability scorns whatever minor consolations your efforts are sometimes able to obtain; and many of whom, despite whatever mitigation you can manage of what the State would otherwise do to them, are likely to sink again soon into the mire of poverty and hopelessness that dragged them to the jailhouse in the first place.

And, too, the family and friends of these clients—who are often just as poor; who may be victims of the clients as well as their sole support; who are certainly victims of the same mean streets; whom you must shepherd through the long and maddening undulations of the criminal court system; whom you feel compelled to comfort even though there is little with which to do so; who, like the clients, remain unmoved by the minutiae of your legal stratagems; and on whom, despite all this, you must rely for the witnesses and information upon which may depend your ability to do for your clients what they rightly doubt you can.

Then there are the monied defendants, the "good cases," over whom lawyers scratch and claw; the supramoral fat cats who, like most people with money, assume that by having spent any of it on you they will receive both your deference and exactly the product they want, regardless of any other considerations (such as their having been caught red-handed embezzling, defrauding, or otherwise stuffing their coffers more obviously or unconscionably than normal; or their having assaulted, shot, or "had done" someone whom they believe their money or status should have allowed them to abuse with impunity); who, in any event, resent having paid you at all; who, because of pressure and fear, are even more obnoxious than usual; whose cadres and toadies treat you with a disdain for the hired hand and with a shrill presumption that you are one of the multitudes trying "unfairly" to separate their master from his lucre; who are often professional criminals of one sort or another—dope dealers, con artists, brokers, real estate investors—guilty not only of the charges against which you defend them but probably much more besides; about whom you can't find the energy to care whether you prevail in the case or not . . . and may secretly wish you don't.

And finally, there are the clients of every type and class about whom once upon a time you might have been able to care but who have now passed so far into venality or thugdom that nothing can overcome your revulsion at their insensate deeds and their withered, uninhabited souls.

To care about the fate of *any* criminal client, though, is so often to be left deeply dispirited. Hope continually slams against the vast imbalance of the (nonwealthy) individual against the State. And in those moments when you have managed to gain an advantage or win a reprieve, rare is the client who has room to appreciate your work or your sense of relief. Meanwhile, each maneuver that fails takes another strip off your hide. And even when you free from the jailhouse an "innocent man," you know that merely by having been wrung through the process the client has lost inestimably. You also know that after an hour or a day or if you're lucky a weekend there will be yet another cartload of sleepless nights dropped on your doorstep; and that despite all your work, your stress, your emotional tumult, none of it, finally, is about you.

Of course, to some criminal lawyers their clients' lives are simply not involving. There are many lawyers, for example, for whom the only grail is the rush of a personal victory or the glamour of a headline. Other criminal lawyers are former prosecutors who became defenders only because they wanted a shot at more money. And there are lawyers for whom the rough trade of criminal cases is simply an alternative to the deadly boredom of estate planning, tax, or corporate law. For all of these, the criminal case is predominantly an intramural contest of wits among cops, lawyers, and judges, with the clients just passive pieces in the game.

Also common, though, are the lawyers who originally entered criminal practice with some sense of choosing the underdog's side but who, after a time, find themselves reeling from battle. And who eventually retreat behind the glass of professionalism: still they take the client's side, but only from a considerable distance; still they stand and are counted, but for the defense more than the defendant; still they fight the cases hard, but with egos and fees in place of heart.

It wasn't long after law school that I had my first exposure to this latter type, this carapaced pro. But since I didn't know then how different from my own imaginings criminal law had become for them, I naively read their closed-down spirits as a remarkable and enviable capacity for equanimity in the face of extremely high stakes. Carl Bigelow, an old hand at the criminal law wars, was co-counsel with me in one of my first heavy cases after I left the public defenders' office. One afternoon only a few days before trial, we had sat through an excruciating meeting in which our two clients had spilled an extremely potent fact in their case, a fact previously unknown to us and which would make it extremely difficult to keep them out of prison. I had received the news with undisguised distress and had come out of the meeting drained and drawn. Carl, though, had remained unfazed, and he was soon tugging me into one of his favorite watering holes, joking with the waiter, then hooting his way through the tale of a crusty judge whose name had recently turned up in the police report of a raid on a local peep-show joint. When the first gulp of scotch had warmed my temples, I asked him just how he was able to maintain such aplomb when it suddenly seemed likely that our young clients, to whom I thought we had both become quite attached, would be going down for the count.

Carl looked at me strangely, his bushy eyebrows pinning together for an instant then slowly easing apart, like two furry caterpillars in a purely instinctual but nonetheless satisfying act of union.

"You see . . . . Well, okay. Let me tell you 'bout this guy I know." Carl spoke slowly, watching me with the long-practiced eye of a man ready at any moment to change direction. He leaned back in the red leather booth and rubbed at the stubble on his throat. "His name is Jack . . . and Jack is back in New York, see . . . and he's at this party. Cocktail party, in one of those Manhattan high-rises. Way up there, you know? Thirty-fifth floor or something. So, he gets to talking with this guy, and somehow it comes up that the guy raises bees. Well, it's kinda unusual and all, so Jack asks the guy some more about it.

"'Oh, yeah, lovely creature, the bee,' the guy tells him. 'But so misunderstood. Only stings when provoked. Really a gentle creature, *Apis mellifera*. Beautiful creature. And very gentle. Once you get to know them. A shame the way people act, so rude, swatting at them and all. Gets them so distressed; it's so unnecessary. And, there's the honey, of course.'

"'Your bees, you get honey from them?' Jack asks.

"'Oh, yes,' the guy says. 'Wonderful honey. Delicious. Not always, of course. Conditions and all. Sometimes they disappoint. But when they do produce, it's lovely. Just open it up and scrape it off.'

"'Huh. Sounds great. So, where is it you keep these bees? Upstate somewhere?'

"'No. Right here in Manhattan.'

"'In Manhattan? You keep bees in Manhattan?'

"'Sure. That way I can watch them closely. Delicate business, bees. Besides, I can enjoy them more. Beautiful creatures, you know.'

"'Oh. Well, in Manhattan. But where can you . . . ?'

"'In the building, actually. I live here.'

"'In this building? The bees?'

"'Oh, yes. In my apartment. Forty-first floor.'

"'In your apartment? You keep bees in your apartment? But . . .
I mean . . . . Well, how many bees do you have?'

"'Oh, twenty thousand . . . . Give or take.'

"'Twenty thousand bees! In an apartment!?'

"'Well, you need a good number. For the honey.'

"'My God! I can't . . . . In an apartment? But where . . . ?'

"'The bedroom.'

"'Twenty thousand . . . in a bedroom?'

"'In the closet, actually.'

"'The closet? Twenty thousand bees in a closet!? But how do
you . . . ? I mean, in some special . . . ?'

"'A cigar box.'

"'What!? Twenty thousand bees? A cigar box!? But they must be
crushed. Suffocated . . . . That's . . . I can't believe it. That's . . . horrible! I mean, how can you *do* that!?'

"And the guy, he just looks at Jack, calm as you please. '*Do* that?'
he says. 'Fuck 'em, they're bees.'"

Carl let the story sink in, then smiled benevolently at me.

I took a gulp of scotch, tried to form a careful question, then
gave up and spoke without masking my incredulity. "Your clients,
Carl? Your clients?"

He seemed startled that I had anything else to say on the subject. His smile disappeared.

"Well, no, of course," he sputtered. "Not exactly. I mean . . . not
all of them."

The Last Word

It can be a matter of extreme irritation to a Parisian of a certain sort—admittedly, an easily exercised type—if one ventures to mention the English language on anything approaching equal terms with the French. And if, despite such effrontery, the discussion is deigned to continue, the Parisian is likely to lapse into sputtering dismissal followed by petulant silence when one further suggests that English's mongrel American version may be markedly more fertile than purebred French, if for no other reason than it contains some five times as many words as does the *Académie française*'s hermetic tongue. (Samuel Beckett, one could fill the uncomfortable silence by pointing out, switched from English to French not to enrich the language of his writing but, in his own description, to "impoverish" it.)

But more than merely offering the pleasure of pointing out such lexical disparities, the expanse of the English language provides an immense and liberating richness to its speakers, and particularly to its writers. Its enormous variety and malleability permit attentive practitioners of American English to illuminate reality in ways simultaneously resonant and forceful, nuanced and precise. Out of the mouths of lawyers, however, English all too often becomes instead an instrument of torture both to common sense and to the sinew and song of language itself. For centuries, lawyers have been broadening their grip on both public and private life, abetted by a cryptic pseudolanguage in which they cloak the rules and laws, decisions and documents, by which the rest of us are supposed to abide. Because by creating such an inaccessible tongue, the lawyers establish an endless need for translating services . . . which only they can provide.

Government lawyers and their minions are bloated with an especially bilious version of this stuff. When confronted with the dread civilian, these lawyer-bureaucrats are apt to pump out vast amounts of inflated language in an attempt to hoist even the most pedestrian of their doings onto the flatulent balloon of authority:

> *Officer, please iterate for the court what occasioned post-alightment from your Department-issue service unit.*

> *You mean, what happened when I got out of my car?*

In addition to this sort of crypto-speak, there is a vast legal glossary of sort-of-Latin lingo, chunks of which are strewn through juridical discourse like so many boulders in the path of civilian accessibility: *exceptio in rem; jus gentium; animus quo, animus furandi.* And, of course, almost anyone who has had to spend time around lawyers is familiar with the phenomenon of barristerial bombast—most lawyers love to hear themselves talk and will do so ceaselessly until they think they have found something to say.

The most insidious shredding and flattening of the language, however, is caused not by shards of legal lingo nor blasts of lawyerly wind, but by the gears of the basic machinery within which legal disputes are processed: the adversary system, which seeks to determine what is just or true by dropping disputants into a legal ring and seeing which one emerges victorious. It seems tellingly anomalous that it is this vaunted fundament of American jurisprudence that prompts legal scholars to be as rapturous as legal scholars are able ("I see a princess mightier than she who once wrought at Bayeaux . . ."), at the same time it serves as the protective lard with which judges slather their most shabbily mendacious rulings ("Although the police withheld significant exculpatory evidence, defense counsel's opportunity to cross-examine witnesses rendered such misconduct harmless.")

Popular myth notwithstanding, the adversary process appears almost never in the form of the steely-eyed trial lawyer dissecting some loathsome character until he breaks down on the witness stand and blubbers out a confession of his slimy misdeeds. Rather, the adversary system takes charge of lawyers and their clients from the first moment a legal matter peeks over the horizon—often even before there is an adversary. More than a process, the adversary system is a frame of mind, a one-lane, no-exit highway of contentiousness entered as soon as a lawyer begins to think on a client's behalf. Most of a lawyer's everyday tasks—writing an opinion letter, interpreting a statute or regulation, drafting a contract—consist of seeking to counter in advance all arguments about what is and is not covered by the legal blanket woven for, or scurried under by, the client. Because every lawyer knows that no matter how simple or obvious the client's rights may seem, no matter how clear or encompassing the applicable rule or authority, somewhere out there is the adversary, that Other Lawyer, who may someday prance and pettifog and peck away in the hope of spotting even the smallest crack in the legal armor. And if such a crack does appear, that Other Lawyer will drive in a wedge and pound and pound until the crack becomes an opening into which an argument—any argument—can be forced, therein to weaken the first client's rights and perhaps even bore to their very vitals and eviscerate them.

The Other Lawyer, that other self, is forever lurking in the shadows with a fearsome weapon: not logic, nor precedent, nor principles of jurisprudence, but language itself—mother of doubt and tireless subverter of clarity and finality. It is words, those slippery shifting eels, that wake the lawyer in the middle of the night. And before sleep can come again, each terrible twisting term must be pinned down and captured, paraded single-file and naked into transparent numbered boxes, and held there, exposed, neutered of its capacity to suggest and inspire.

For the one lawyer, then, language is the fount of a client's security. For the Other, it is the river of evasion and the bottomless well of rebuttal. And in the struggles between these lawyers, language is the field of battle. But to a lover of language, what dreadful and dreary little battles they are. For example, consider a writer friend of mine, who had a contract drawn up with an independent television producer to turn one of the writer's stories into a script. This assumedly simple two-person agreement wound up running almost twenty single-spaced pages, each filled to the margins with paragraphs like the one reproduced below.

So, you want to be a lawyer? Writing paragraphs like this, and trying to sort out the ones written by other lawyers, is how you spend a distressing number of your days:

> *A. Ownership: Without limiting the generality or inclusiveness of the foregoing, Writer expressly acknowledges and agrees that all inferences are to be drawn in favor of the express terms herein, to the effect that Producer is, and will in perpetuity unless waived in writing by Producer, his successors or assigns, remain, the owner of all now or hereafter existing rights of any and every kind and character whatsoever throughout the universe, whether or not such rights are now known, recognized, contemplated, understood or otherwise extant, and the complete, unconditional, undiluted and unencumbered title throughout the universe in and to the following:*
>
> *Writer's services as described herein and pursuant hereto, and any and all results and proceeds thereof including but not limited to any and all literary,*

*dramatic, docudramatic, comedic and musical mate-
rial, incidents, plots, dialogue, characters, actions,
gags, routines, ideas, concepts, inventions, moments
and events, whether or not based upon real or historical persons, moments, events or ideas; and such other
and further material written, composed, improvised,
interpolated, invented, imagined or otherwise
authored by Writer hereunder; and the complete,
unconditional, undiluted, unencumbered, exclusive
and perpetual right throughout the universe to
exhibit, record, reproduce, broadcast, televise, trans-
mit, publish, copy, print, reprint, vend, hypothecate,
distribute, perform and/or use for any purpose, in
any manner, by any means, in any venue, whether or
not now known, invented, used or contemplated, all
or any part of the matters and things referred to in
this section.*

*Producer shall also have the exclusive right to add to,
subtract from, arrange, rearrange, revise, adapt,
amend, append, bowdlerize and/or eliminate altogether all such materials in any manner.*

*As the term is commonly understood and to the full
extent it is alleged to exist within the community of
writers, Writer hereby waives any and all elements
and aspects of 'the moral rights of authors.'*

Although this was the final version of the contract, it wasn't the
last word. The producer paid the 10 percent advance and the writer
spent the next six months trying to fashion a script that fit within
the insipid Hollywood paradigm without doing too much damage
to his original story. As happens so often in Hollywood, though,
the writer's script didn't "work" for the producer, who insisted on
some changes before it would be "acceptable" (though neither that
term, nor any obligation to rewrite, appeared in the contract). And

no extra pay for this extra work, the producer said, since the changes were necessary to turn the script into something "make-able." In other words, the producer huffed, he was doing the writer a favor. Anyway, the producer added, the changes would be simple: just make the protagonist a cop instead of a teacher, add a female reporter, a grizzled sidekick, and an oleaginous police commissioner, then gruesomely kill off as many of them as possible.

The writer balked, so the producer refused to pay the remaining 90 percent of the contract fee. For a few days phone calls and faxes went back and forth in an attempt to salvage the deal, but within a week the producer had become so twitchingly tumescent over some new concept for a game show that he lost all interest in the writer's script and no longer returned his calls. Fearing the dread Hollywood blackball, the writer did nothing more to collect his fee and bitterly wrote off the experience as just another Hollywood screwing.

There the matter lay until at a party two years later the writer happened to mention his original story to a different producer who immediately—that is, before actually reading the thing—wanted to put together a deal for the writer to develop it into a script. The writer told the new producer about his earlier experience. No problem, the new producer said, and went to phone his lawyer. This second producer's Other Lawyer combed the old contract's thick verbal underbrush for an opening, for some weakly-worded provision that would permit the new producer to sidestep the old contract entirely and commission his own script. The Other Lawyer even went so far as to consider a direct assault on the contract's purported waiver of the author's "moral rights," but backed off when he realized that a victory might mean he wouldn't be able to use similar clauses in the contracts he drew up for his own producer-clients.

Finally, after weeks of research (by his assistants, meters running), meetings with other lawyers (meter running, plus consultation fees), and conversations with various behind-the-scenes veterans in the entertainment industry (over lengthy and expensive meals, meter running, vintage wines included), the Other Lawyer came up with a plan of attack based on a single word repeated throughout the original contract but nowhere therein defined: Writer. The Writer who wrote the first script, the Other Lawyer's argument went, was not in a legal sense the same as the Writer of the original story. That is, if a second script were to be the product solely of the original story and not a derivative of the first script, the first producer would have no legal claim against any movie made from the second script since it would have been written by a different Writer. In a carefully crafted letter, the Other Lawyer bolstered this "different Writer" argument with the assertion that the intervening years inevitably had changed the original Writer as a writer, and thus—follow closely—any work the writer now produced must be considered as authored by a different Writer than the Writer who had performed under the original contract. "Artists," the Other Lawyer's letter concluded, "are forever shedding their skins."

Of course, Hollywood odds make it extremely unlikely that either of these scripts will ever actually be filmed. But should that second script somehow get made as even the lowest-budget movie-for-TV and find its way onto the most obscure local late-night cable channel, the two producers are likely to wind up in court. And there, the first lawyer and the Other Lawyer will play out this particular turn of the adversary wheel, lawyers arguing to the finish about the meaning of a word, about what really is a writer.

Before, During, and After

The miracle of performance. Not just the trial lawyer's ability to summon so many selves, but the ceaseless wrenching and leaping from one to another. Emotional gymnastics: to inhabit one persona so thoroughly and convincingly, then quickly and as confidently a different one, then another, and still another, all in the course of a day. Most every day. From comforting counselor to fee-hustling knave, cunning tactician to wheedler and needler, sophist and trickster to righteous protector or thick-fingered brute. And then . . . home at last. This final transformation the greatest feat. Day for night. Once again the civilian, the human, the real—at least, approximately.

Take, for example, a criminal lawyer named Roger. In the courtroom as brilliant an advocate as any around: an uncanny ability to find the animating pith of a witness, D.A., or judge; a remarkable sense of timing—the capacity to summon just the right look, the telling phrase; and an infectious charm with which he could sell a jury on almost any defense. But outside the courtroom, somewhat less brilliant. Loving the action and always ready to believe, he would take on a case at a whimper and a promise, and so was forever swamped with work but stiffed on fees. As devout about commitments as he was profligate with time, he found himself forever suspended in a desperate purgatory of the overdue and the underdone.

And with loved ones, too, a leaky boat. Giving so much of himself to stitch and salve his clients' lives, Roger was able to muster neither energy nor focus for his own: yet another meal skipped, plan canceled, or tryst interrupted (the phone, the phone, always the phone). "Hopelessly scattered," "maddeningly distracted," "insufferably self-absorbed" were phrases with which Roger heard himself described, usually by a spouse (one) or lover (several, though one at a time) as she headed out the door. The latest had accused him of arranging his life so as to completely escape the consequences of introspection; Roger was puzzled, but at that moment didn't have time to sort out what she meant . . . .

Roger eventually understood enough of her point, though, to sense that some changes had to be made. His first response was to engage a bookkeeper to hover over his accounts; his second, to cut back his street crime cases and handle more white collar criminals—a calmer practice with reasonably regular hours, retainers up front, hourly fees, and monthly billing.

One of Roger's new commercial fraud cases led him to seek out some technical assistance from a business law firm recommended by an acquaintance. Roger was startled by the hourly rate these lawyers were to charge him, but his friend assured him they were worth it. So, Roger set up an appointment and found himself face to face with a handsome, self-assured, and articulate female attorney. Roger was attracted to Jane and was immediately certain that she was at least pleased by his presence. When he found out Jane was single, Roger thought that his recently modulated lifestyle might support a new stab at the riddles of romance. He was professional enough not to broach the social ramble while they were still engaged in work, but once Roger had all the help he needed, he called Jane and asked her to lunch.

She was friendly on the phone, though she did put him on hold while she took another call, and then said that yes, they could meet for lunch; she had an hour free a week from Tuesday. The lunch went well enough, if quickly—Jane had a 1:30 deposition, had to be back in the office by 1:00 to prepare. She was smiling and animated, though when Roger veered conversation toward the personal, she would turn it back to the case about which he had previously consulted her.

The next week he called again. Jane wondered whether Roger had encountered some problem with her advice, since during their lunch he hadn't said so. Roger assured her he was completely satisfied, but asked if they might have lunch again anyway—an investment of time, he said, that might prove fruitful. Jane was momentarily silent, then agreed to meet Roger the following week.

The second lunch came and went much as the first, Jane voluble if a bit stiff, talking about Roger's case, and Roger about anything but, Jane checking her watch and finally hurrying back to the office. Roger waited a week, then called to say he had business in Jane's building the following Wednesday and asked if she would like to have lunch, or maybe a drink. Jane checked her calendar, determined she had time for neither, gave no hint whether the idea interested her, and made no suggestion of an alternate plan. In fact, she said nothing at all, apparently waiting for Roger to speak next. Goodbye is what Roger said next, and decided right then to give it up: though he thought Jane had initially enjoyed seeing him, she was so consumed by her work that she appeared to have room for nothing else, and finally seemed to Roger a real bore.

It wasn't until three months later that Roger again gave Jane any thought. Roger's bookkeeper had prepared a summary of his previous six months' accounts, and as part of Roger's new resolve he actually sat down to look it over. His eye was caught by scattered debits to Jane's law firm, particularly several amounting to almost a thousand dollars but identified only by the unilluminating billing category of "file review & follow-up."

Roger sent a note to Jane, inquiring about these billing entries, in terms as cordial and unassuming as he could manage. He was careful to point out that he had paid the bill in full and was merely seeking a clarification for his own files.

Jane responded by letter that records regarding files closed more than sixty days prior were in storage and that Roger would need to advance them a fee for "retrieval and assessment." Roger wrote back, politely, that the "assessment" was occasioned by Jane's firm's failure to state clearly what work these hours represented. Jane's next note stated that if Roger had questions about the billing, he should have raised them before paying, and that he could not now hold their firm accountable for his own lack of organization.

"Lack of organization." That one hurt. Roger had taken such pains to pull his life and practice together, and here was that old bugaboo again. Besides, what did she mean "lack of organization"? Hell, it was *his* organization that had spotted these sloppy billing records. And Jane should have understood that; after all, she had gotten to know him, well, personally.

Roger called Jane's number. She kept him on hold for quite some time and then answered in an icy voice. Roger made a pitch for her to respond to the billing in a manner congruent with their "friendship" but Jane remained conspicuously silent at Roger's use of the word and was curt in the extreme when Roger finished his spiel: she would make an exception, she said, waiving the "retrieval and assessment" fees and sending him a further explanation of the bill. This would, she concluded, perforce terminate their professional relationship. "Terminate their professional relationship?" That was finished months ago. Roger stared at the phone, mumbled, "Thank you," and hung up.

True to her word, in the following week's mail came an explanation of the bill from Jane's office. There, next to two entries of one-hour-twelve-minutes and one-hour-eighteen-minutes was the description "Prepare for and lunch meeting with client"; in the weeks before these lunches, there were entries of six minutes, twelve minutes, and twelve minutes for "telephone client conference"; and finally, a last six-minute entry—minimum billing time for even a few seconds' exertion—next to another "telephone client conference" that Roger realized must refer to their last phone call, which had consisted of Jane turning him down for a drink. The final insult was new charges of nine hundred dollars, described as "billing review"; next to them was stamped "Waived—client courtesy."

Despite this last outrage, Roger decided against further reply: he wanted no more of the inexorably productive Jane. However, he did think that the lawyer who had referred him to Jane's office ought to hear about Roger's experiences before deciding to refer anyone else there. So, in what he considered an evenhanded telling, Roger sent a note to this lawyer praising the quality of Jane's legal work but describing the firm's billing practices and asking rhetorically whether such practices were up to the "standard of the profession." As an afterthought—perhaps in the spirit of fair play, perhaps not—Roger sent a copy of the note to Jane.

Three days later Roger got a letter from another lawyer in Jane's firm demanding a retraction and a formal written apology to Jane and the firm. Otherwise, the lawyer threatened, they would "have no recourse" but to sue Roger for libel, "forthwith."

Or, consider the travails of Hector, another criminal lawyer. Though he was no more than an acquaintance and our meetings usually consisted of only the few minutes between a chance arrival in the same courtroom and the judge's appearance on the bench, for some reason Hector felt an affinity for me, which always led him immediately to launch into a monologue about whatever was "really going on" with him. And what was going on with Hector unfailingly consisted of a litany of miseries arising from his criminal lawyer life: too much work and not enough money; too much responsibility but not enough control; cases too depressing, clients too bizarre; high expectations, no appreciation. And Hector's tales of woe always wound up with his personal life, in which—after a divorce and two failed live-togethers in just three years—a large number of unsatisfactory encounters was made possible, given the time demands of his cases, only by their unvarying brevity.

"My ex-wife called last week to tell me I was having a midlife crisis," Hector reported one day. "Shows what she knows: I've had the same damn crisis since my first day in practice."

Then there were Hector's complaints about the legal world's intellectual strictures. Before a shrinking academic job market and two kids had made law school seem a financially prudent idea, Hector had been a graduate student in English and was still in love with literature, though he rarely had time to read. He chafed terribly at the narrow scope of legal argument and the narrow minds of its practitioners. "Nothing but lawyers," Hector would moan, gesturing around the courtrooms of our occasional encounters.

Whenever I was bored or distracted enough to respond with what seemed the obvious question about why he didn't quit the law and return to some kind of literary endeavor, Hector had a ready if perfunctory set of answers. The ex-spouse, the kids—teenagers now—and, well, he could admit it to me, he did like the money, nice things, eating well. And there's the respect, he would remind me; being a "professional," having people need you—he liked those things, too. "Anyway," he would end with a sigh, the unremitting strain of trial work tugging at his sagging face, "it's no better out there. People just don't speak my language."

One morning I was sitting in the cafeteria of the criminal courts building when in dragged Hector, looking even more forlorn than usual. He made his way through the coteries of cops and the huddled families of defendants, and slumped down in a chair across from me.

"Hiya," he said, barely moving his lips. "Got a minute?"

Having taken only one bite of my breakfast—scrambled eggs served, like everything else, with fried won tons, the cafeteria kitchen giving a dyspeptic literalism to the notion of the urban melting pot—I couldn't very well say no.

"Gotta tell you. You understand these things."

It was unclear to me why, exactly, he thought I understood "these things." But understanding being relative, I suppose just my willingness to listen put me up near the top of his list.

"I got this motorcycle, see. Nothing big. For weekends, you know? Just get out of town for a day, clear my head."

'Day-out *ex machina*,' I thought, but an undercooked won ton kept my mouth occupied.

"So last weekend I go for a ride, way up past Clear Lake. Really beautiful. Saturday night in a little motel up there, and I'm all relaxed, all peaceful like . . . and then wham! I wake up, it's still dark and I'm sitting there in this motel room, and my neck's all tight and my cases are flying around in my head, and it's all just gone. Every ounce of peace gone. Even before I'm awake, I'm back in the middle of it, right back in the shit. One day, that's all I get. One fucking day . . . ."

Hector shook his head, then let it drop to his chest. I stopped a forkful of food halfway to my mouth, wondering if he expected me to say something. We sat there for a few moments, Hector with his head down and me with the scrambled egg in the air and thinking how the cafeteria had won again, fulfilling its solemn secret promise to serve every plate of food at a temperature deceptively warm at first bite but precisely calibrated to go stone cold before an average person could eat more than a third of it. finally, Hector looked up again. I put the scrambled egg in my mouth—air-cooled scrambled egg.

"So, I start back. And on the way, I stop at one of those country roadside places, you know, with the thick pancakes, and the real fresh eggs from the chickens out back . . . . Oh. How's your breakfast? Looks, ah . . . good."

"Mm." I waved the fork, then took three stabs at a won ton.

"Anyway, I stop at this little café next to the state park up there, and there are these three motorcyles out front. All big traveling bikes, but none of that chrome or pipes or that other biker-fetish bullshit. And one of the bikes has this saddlebags thing, open at the top . . . and it's full of books."

He looked at me with eyes wide in recollected wonder.

"Books," I repeated, not knowing what I was supposed to say.

"Yah, but on a bike, see. A big bike. And then I see her, sitting against a tree: this curly-haired woman, about thirty, thirty-five, and she's wearing leathers, but not all biker-looking. Just kind of . . . together, you know? And this red bandanna holding her hair up, legs sticking out in front of her into the sun . . . and bare feet. On a biker. With her boots standing up next to her, waiting like an old dog or something. And what's she doing, this woman? Reading a book. And you'll never guess what it is . . ."

I doubt Hector really expected me to guess, but he seemed to think a dramatic pause was called for.

". . . *Middlemarch*. I mean, *Middlemarch*. You can imagine how I felt, what with me and George Eliot . . . ."

The allusion escaped me, but rather than invite another whole subplot, I just nodded again. Maybe that's why Hector always thought I understood him?

"So I'm standing there, staring at this woman, but she doesn't even notice me, which makes sense, of course, while you're reading George Eliot. Then after a minute she sort of looks up at me and, well, she . . . smiles."

Hector smiled, perhaps in approximation of the smile from the woman with *Middlemarch*. The power of this particular expression escaped me, however; from Hector it seemed just a smarmy bit of emoting. I wondered what juries thought of him.

"Now, you gotta understand," Hector went on, "a smile is not the first thing you expect from a black-leather biker. But then neither is George Eliot, right? And not just a smile, you understand, but, well, I dunno, really . . . intelligent."

Hector was beginning to lose me, in part because of his feeble descriptive powers but also because over his shoulder four thick-necked cops were engaged in a circle of squad-room sniggering that could only be at the expense of someone I was likely to be grinding my molars to defend.

"And then out of the café comes this couple, in motorcycle gear. Real calm people, no biker attitude or anything like that, and not saying anything, but eyes that seem to take everything in. And they kinda glide by me, all quiet and easy-like, and the woman under the tree, she sort of gives 'em a little wave. And they give her a little wave back, and the woman gets herself up and puts on her boots, and the three of them get their gear together, and they're not saying a word, see, but just all moving like . . . in harmony. You know what I mean?"

At some other time I might have tried to know what Hector meant, but at that moment outside the cafeteria door a man in handcuffs was being dragged into the bowels of the courthouse.

"So I'm just standing there, watching this woman pack up her *Middlemarch,* and then the three of them get on their bikes and pull away, real smooth and peaceful. Almost slow-motion, like. And you'll never guess what happened . . . ."

"Okay."

"Well, the woman with the *Middlemarch?* She turns and kinda waves her hand around, like almost, you know . . . inviting me along. And smiles again. And then off they go, up this dirt road and into the park."

Hector stopped, and I thought perhaps this was the end, a poignant enough moment for Hector, perhaps, but difficult for me to comprehend as the source of his even greater than usual distress. But he was just gathering strength to go on. Quickly I speared my last bites of egg and won ton.

"So I head back to the city. But I can't get this woman out of my mind. It just seemed like everything about her was . . . right, you know? A real person. Making it work. And George Eliot, for God's sake."

"Mm."

"And her hand, signaling me. Plus, I mean, *Middlemarch.* I kept going back to *Middlemarch,* you see, with Dorothea clinging to that property instead of going off with whatsisname. And Lydgate, giving up on his projects and letting his life just slip away. And I'm thinking this is me, it's me, I got to get out, like Dorothea, get out . . . ."

"But then I remembered my clients, and the money, and well, you know, it isn't easy. But I couldn't get that smile out of my mind. A big bike, with big books. And I just knew . . . that woman . . . I knew . . . we speak the same language."

I looked at Hector's eyes, and the emotion there seemed to run far deeper than his wobbly words could convey.

"So I do it. I get home, pack some stuff, call my partner Alex— you know Alex, right?—and tell him it's all his, the whole thing.

And before dawn I'm on the road again, back up to that park, and the woman in the red bandanna."

I looked at the briefcase on the floor next to Hector, at his blue suit and tie.

"And I get up there, see, and I try all these trails. And finally there she is . . . . I come over this hill and there they are, the three of them, in a little meadow down below, sitting together near a couple of tents, all peaceful, and quiet. And I stop, 'cause I don't want to go charging in there, and I want to think about my first words, the first thing I say to her, that'll be just right, you know, the first lines in the novel. So I'm standing there, thinking about what we'll say to each other, and, well . . . that's when I notice . . . the quiet."

"Quiet?"

"Yeah. Real, real quiet. And the guy, I see him gesturing, like. But he doesn't say anything. And the curly-haired woman, she gestures back, you know, with her hands. And doesn't say anything either. So I watch, and all three are doing that, with their hands. And, well, that's when I realized . . . ."

"You mean . . . ?"

"Signing, yeah. All that quiet. She spoke *my* language; I'm sure of it. But, well . . . turns out, I didn't speak hers."

Or take, for example, another criminal lawyer, Hank. As a public defender passionate, dedicated, clever, bold. Could have made a bundle in private practice but public defending suited him: random clients with losing hands, an endless sea of trouble, and never a moment's rest. The camaraderie, too: Hank loved the overcrowded raft, hauling each other up from the deep. Regardless of how heavy his cases—and he handled the most difficult of trials—he always had time for someone else in the office, always a hand to prop someone up.

He was a bit less successful at home. Hank's wife had left him a year before, and as Hank said himself, it took him awhile to notice that his life was any different. But now there was someone new.

She was great, he said, but very sensitive; he had to go easy. Hank was telling me about her as we sat in the office lunchroom where we often wound down with a beer at the end of a long day. His day today had been grueling, the last part of it taken up with a hearing on whether his client, the young girlfriend of a heavy thug, should get local jail time and probation or be sent to state prison, for being caught up in her boyfriend's drug scheme. The prosecutor had brought out the clear bags full of cocaine and had left them sitting in the judge's view—and only inches from Hank—throughout the hearing. In the end, the judge had rejected all of Hank's arguments and had given her the max: four years in prison.

Hank was exhausted and distraught, but also edgy with anticipation at seeing his new love. It was late already, almost seven. Hank was to pick her up at eight but he couldn't get himself together to go home. He was so full of his client's tearful, terrified young face as they took her away that he couldn't bring himself to step outside the office. When I reminded him of the time, he asked if I'd come with him. Just to his house, steady him while he got ready for his date. And to show me his special present for her, find out what I thought.

I followed Hank home, where he set down on the coffee table a small package wrapped in plain brown paper. A long day in the jails and courts leaves a nearly indelible stink, and in any event Hank's shiny suit was not likely to impress out in the wider world, so he left me with the mysterious package and its swatch of colorful stamps from Hong Kong while he grabbed a quick shower. When he emerged, I didn't have the heart to tell him that his flowered silk shirt was not much improvement over the suit.

Hank plopped down on the sofa and drew from the package an unmarked cardboard box, inside of which was something wrapped in Chinese newspaper. Hank carefully folded back the newspaper to reveal a plastic bag about the size of a grapefruit and full of a fine, off-white powder.

I sat up straight and sputtered that he was crazy. After a moment's puzzlement, he laughed and said, "Ginseng," realizing that I had thought we were sitting with a kilo of something else altogether. Ginseng, he repeated, finest you can buy. Ordered it weeks ago, day after I met her.

Chinese, he said. Hadn't he told me? His new girlfriend was Chinese American. He'd seen ginseng in her kitchen. And this stuff was the very best. He knew she'd be pleased.

I asked what she did with ginseng and Hank realized he didn't know. Tea, he guessed, or soup. The plastic bag was closed with a simple twist-tie, and Hank opened it as if getting closer could somehow tell us how it was used. We sniffed at the opening and a pungent tickle shot up the nostrils.

Hank stared into the bag. Beautiful, he finally said softly. Look how fine. He put ink-stained fingers into the powder and sifted with his thumb. Acting on their own, the fingers moved to his tongue. Very interesting, he said, tasting. You know . . . it's so pure. I mean, seems like tea might be a real waste . . . .

The texture and luminous white of the powder fascinated me as well, and I watched transfixed as he carefully poured a bit onto the table. Oughta have a dip, Hank said, don't you think? With a post-card he divided the powder on the table into four three-inch sections each a half-inch wide. He found two relatively crisp bills in his wallet, handed me one, and we rolled them up. I glanced at him to see if maybe we would think better of this, but he didn't return my look.

I was a few seconds behind him as we put the rolled bills to our nostrils and onto the thick lines of powder. I was a bit skittish and inhaled accordingly, but Hank snorted in proportion to the abundant lines he had formed.

Hank's deep sucking noises were followed after a few moments by a deep moan of pain and regret. After another couple of seconds I was aware of Hank thrashing about on the floor, but a heat searing my sinuses and flaming towards my pineal gland had me paralyzed on the couch, no help to him.

During the seemingly endless writhing torment that followed, I came to the empirical understanding that there is no orifice through which human fingers can reach the upper nasal cavities.

Unfair, I thought: Where is nature's balance? Isn't the god who invented ginseng the same one who created nostrils?

But while I was questioning the mercy of Heaven, Hank was struggling directly with Hell. He was still on the floor, rolling around in his flowered silk shirt, alternately raking his face and pounding his head. His howls had now taken on the character of a final expiation: not so much in pain as in hope that a Greater Being would take pity and release him from the fires.

I knelt down next to him but didn't know what to do. I tried to stop him battering himself, but I couldn't manage to grab hold of his wrists. The phone was nearby and I thought to dial 911, but the looming bag on the table stopped me. Sure, Hank had said it was ginseng, but what if it wasn't? What kind of Hell would we be in then?

I staggered into the kitchen and for lack of any other idea got some water. I poured some into Hank but he only choked and spit it back up. Then I got the idea that the water should go where the ginseng was, so I dribbled some into his nose. This created manifold convulsions including choking, sneezing, and a short left hook to my head which, despite his clear lack of intent, dissuaded me for the time being from further attempts at first aid.

Some of the water, though, seemed to find its mark. Hank's twitching and howling slowly abated, he stopped clawing at his face, and after a few minutes we both lay still and panting on the floor. The phone rang. Many rings. Neither of us moved.

I sat up and looked over at Hank. Even our clients accused of resisting arrest don't usually look that bad: his face was red and swollen, marked by scratches and welts; all I could see of his eyes were wildly dilated pupils; and the flowered shirt had taken on an entirely new abstract motif.

By the time we got him cleaned up, it was after nine o'clock and the phone that had twice rung long and hard had now fallen silent. Hank asked if I would call his date and make some excuse about his being held up in jail, but I had no desire to get mixed up in that mess and begged off. Hank nodded in understanding and I left with him staring across the room at the phone.

Hank missed work for a couple of days and when he returned I heard nothing more from him about the new girlfriend. Not long after our ginseng affair, I left the Public Defender's office and lost touch with Hank. I heard that he also left the office soon after and moved to somewhere in the mountains where he intended to set up practice doing wills for retirees. I wondered whether anyone had moved up to the country with him, but people said that, as far as they knew, he was still alone.

Meaningful
Relationships

My old friend Michael used to joke that it didn't matter what sort of foolishness he got into when he was out with me because he just happened to have his lawyer along. He still makes the remark on rare occasion, but now it's with a different, private understanding.

Another Friday, a long, miserable day in court after a long miserable week, and here's Michael turning up at my office, wants to haul me out to dinner. Bottle of wine . . . and I'm asleep in my pasta. But an espresso, and another, Michael's pouring them into me and . . . . What? . . . A party? We're going to some party? I can't remember the last time. A party . . . .

So, now we're out of the party, it's 3:00 A.M., and Jesus, I've got all this work tomorrow—the weekend just a chance to catch up for the week to come. But no, I'm not ready; just not ready to go home. The ocean, Michael says. The ocean? Michael's driving us out there, and I'm stripping off my court clothes, diving in . . . .

Back in my clothes—God, I hate 'em, these suits—and I'm wet, sandy, freezing. But for a minute, at least for a minute, I'm free from the tightness in my throat, the all day, every day pounding in my head, the pounding of other people's lives . . . .

On the way home, now, passing a neighborhood park. Michael slows, stops the car.

"Huh. Still there."

"What is?"

"That pile. Over by the walkway."

A new path, in the park; inset with flagstones. And to the side, a few leftover stones.

"I saw them putting it in last week. Be great for my mud, those stones. Match the ones in front of my door."

Michael's bungalow originally a rear garage. Low rent, but the upkeep is Michael's, and winter rains turn the unpaved portion of his dirt-and-gravel walkway into a moat.

"Guess they didn't need 'em all." Michael's eyeing me. "Not easy to find, pieces just like that."

Taste of salt on my lips . . . and a blue suit, necktie bulging in the pocket. Whose clothes are these?

"Okay, let's go," I say, and I'm out of the car. We haul some flagstones over, pile them on the curb, start loading the trunk . . . .

Studies of black boxes, which record the final sounds of pilots whose planes crash, show that 90-some percent blurt exactly the same last words: "Oh, shit!" And I'm no different: It's a patrol car, creeping around the corner; we've got half the stones in the trunk, half still on the ground. "Oh, shit!"

Police car stops. I'm in some bushes, just took a piss. Cop's headlights catch Michael and the trunk, but I'm still in the shadows. Whoa, searchlight fires on. Nails Michael to the spot, now slow-mo's around: the flagstones, Michael, the trunk, back to Michael. Fucking *busted*, we are.

My lawyer future passing before my eyes: Okay, whadda we got here? . . . Penal Code section 488: petty theft . . . . Nah, worse—public park, that's theft of government property. Government Code section, ah . . . . What the hell's that section? Whatever, it's a theft: "crime of moral turpitude" . . . . Christ, that's State Bar stuff; might mean I get suspended . . . . Okay, gotta be a way to beat it.

Come on, think . . . "Abandonment." . . . Yeah, abandoned property, no criminal intent: "Theft requires a specific intent to permanently deprive another . . . ." Yeah, that's it, abandoned property.

Abandoned . . . but the work site not cleared away yet? No criminal intent . . . but three o'clock in the morning? Nah, no way they buy it. Shit.

But hey, this cop still doesn't see me. If I slip away through the park . . . . Of course, if he spots me, it's "flight": "Evidence of flight admissible to show guilt."

He's moving on Michael now, watching him close.

"This your car?"

"Yes it is."

All right, Michael's copped to his car . . . . So, I'm clear of "possessory interest" . . . . Cop never saw me loading, so no eyewitness—circumstantial evidence all they got. No *prima facie* case against me; not even aiding and abetting. I make a motion to dismiss, they got to throw it out . . . . Michael'll just have to ride it without me . . . Unless he says something stupid, makes me an accomplice . . . . Okay, so he does, I make a motion to sever—separate trial. They got to give it to me. And wouldn't be worth it to try me separate, so they dismiss against me, just nail the perpetrator . . . . Perpetrator? For Chrissakes, this is Michael I'm talking about here.

"Evening, Officer." I casual my way around the car.

Cop gives me a quizzical look ("What's the guy in the suit doing here?") that quickly turns to chagrin ("Holy Mary, why didn't I spot this guy before?").

"Step into the light."

Not easy to smile. And that flashlight on my face, holding it a long time. What, something strange about me? But . . . yeah, something about him, too.

"You two together? . . . I know you, don't I?"

'Suspicion of crime focused on particular suspect. Suspect has the right to remain silent.'

"Yes, that's right, Officer . . . Phillips, isn't it?"

"Philbert. Where do I know you from?"

"Ahhh, I'm not sure. I guess we must have been on the same case or something. See, I'm . . . ."

"Oh, yeah. That's right. The paper cup . . . ."

It had been about a year before. Late one night, Officer Philbert had stopped my scruffy soon-to-be client for a minor traffic violation. Another cop named Mattel arrived as backup and tore the car apart looking for drugs. In his report, Mattel had justified his search-and-destroy by claiming that from outside the car he had been able to see directly into a paper cup holding marijuana seeds, sitting on the passenger-side floor. Mattel had found no other drugs, but they had arrested my guy for possession of the seeds and charged him with a felony.

My client told me that the top of the paper cup had been folded over and taped shut, apparently inside his roommate's rucksack under the seat. There was no way Mattel could have seen the cup, let alone into it, and he'd only found it while illegally ransacking the car. So when the prosecutor produced the seed-filled cup—open at the top but with ineradicable fold marks—at the preliminary hearing, I decided to engage in a little physics experiment. The first to testify was Officer Philbert, and I encouraged him to justify his initial stop of the car by describing the speeding turns and sudden starts of my client's driving. Then I placed the open paper cup on the counsel table and asked how it could possibly have remained open and standing on the passenger floorboard during all this without tipping and spilling. As Philbert began some mealy response, I turned and brushed my sleeve against the cup, knocking it over and sending the seeds clattering over the counsel table and onto the floor.

The cop stopped answering, the court reporter stopped reporting, and the deputy D.A. smashed his knee as he leaped out of his chair. I was immediately down on my hands and knees collecting the seeds, muttering apologies, and sneaking a look at the judge, who was not amused. When finally I had put all the seeds back in the cup and stood it upright again on the counsel table, the attention of the courtroom was considerably more focused on the issue than it had been moments before.

"I'm sorry, now what were you saying, Officer?" I resumed my questions while shuffling papers perilously close to the cup. Officer Philbert mumbled something about "having to speculate" and I cut him off with "Well, I'm sure none of us wants you to do that. No more questions, Officer. Thank you."

I knew I had made my point with the judge, but I also knew I hadn't yet won him over. Now it was Officer Mattel's turn. After perfunctorily giving his story, he was mine to cross-examine and I led him laboriously through each step of his arrival as a backup unit and his approach to my client's car before he supposedly saw the cup. By now the slow repetition of uneventful details had numbed the judge and district attorney again, and the spill was all but forgotten. I handed the cup to Mattel and asked if it had been in that condition when he had found it. Mattel looked at the wide-open mouth and said that it had. Then I asked him to describe its position on the floor of the car. His only possible answer was "Standing upright," after which I asked him to demonstrate by putting it on the corner of the judge's bench "just as it had been that night." At my request, Mattel had remained outside the court-room during Philbert's testimony and so hadn't seen my "accidental" spill. And what the judge and district attorney hadn't seen was that while putting the seeds back in the cup and again while handling it before giving it to Mattel, I had exaggerated a crease in its base which had been started by the original folds. Standing this cup upright was now extremely problematic. And when Officer Mattel heedlessly put the cup on the corner of the bench, it tipped over and spilled seeds across the judge's papers and into his robes.

Philbert had stayed in the courtroom after his own testimony was finished and had seen the whole show, including the judge's grudging dismissal of charges because of Mattel's now obviously illegal search. It was not something Philbert was likely to have forgotten, even after a year.

"Right," Philbert says. "The paper cup . . . . And this here, Counsel? What is it we have here?"

"Well, you see, Officer, my friend here's been putting down these paving stones around his house . . ."

Poor Michael, look at him—he thinks I'm giving us up.

". . . and he wound up with all these extras. Then he saw they were using stones like these in the park here, so, well, he just decided to leave them here for the park people, you know, to add to the walkway."

"You mean, the gardeners, park maintenance?"

"That's right. A donation."

Jesus, Michael, close your mouth. And would you mind backing me up a little, here? At least nod your head, or something.

"Donation, huh. Kind of a strange time for it, isn't it?"

"Oh, it was just that, see, this way I could help him out. 'Cause we were going to this party near here . . . but we waited until afterwards, 'cause of the dirt and stuff."

He's on the edge, Philbert is; I can see it. Doesn't want the hassle. But can't quite swallow it yet.

"Besides, you know what it's like trying to deal with the City. Even to give something away. Forms to fill out. Probably want somebody to inspect the stupid things. Ridiculous. And we're trying to do them a favor. I mean, there's never enough money for the parks, right?"

"Well . . ."

"I mean, think what it's like when you drive your own car to a training or something, and later you just try to get your mileage reimbursed. You know, they make you feel . . . well, like you're stealing."

"Yeah . . . ."

"Look, we're almost through. Just these last few."

"Well . . . ."

My God, he's buying it. He's actually buying it.

"Come on, Mikey. You unload, I'll carry 'em over."

Hey, maybe I should ask Philbert to help. Nah, don't push it. Come on, Michael, hurry up . . . . Uh, oh—another patrol car.

Keep driving; please, just keep driving. Ohhh . . . . Oh, Jesus. It can't be! Oh, shit! . . .

"Ho, what've you got here?"

"Nothing much, Mattel . . . . You gentlemen just hold it right there for a minute, all right?"

Mattel. I can't believe it. He's listening to Philbert but he's staring at me. Please God, Philbert, don't remind him.

"What the hell was that paper cup stuff?" Michael whispers, but I don't take my eyes off Mattel. And Mattel's looking at me. Looking ugly . . . . Uh, oh. Here it comes.

"Nice to see you again, Officer."

"That so?"

"No hard feelings?"

"No, no. 'Course not. Just doing your job, weren't you . . . . But mine's protecting the public. Like this here park."

Right. It's over. Who am I gonna call for bail?

"Listen, Officer . . . ."

"No, save it, mister. You can just forget about this Good Samaritan shit. I'm going to enjoy writing this citation."

"Citation?"

"Hey, I thought you were the smart lawyer. 'Illegal dumping,' mister. That happens to be a crime. Only an infraction, but I'll take what I can get."

"Dumping?"

"You heard me. Now start loading it up."

"You mean, back in the . . . ?"

"That's right. You and the dummy here managed to get 'em out of that trunk. So you oughta be able to get 'em back in."

Heart to Heart

It turned out to be a watershed day. It was a Friday. In the latter days of my full-time practice. And it was my birthday.

I hated a fuss on my birthday. If asked by a friend or acquaintance, I would provide a false and faraway birth date. And if by chance the person remembered when this randomly chosen day rolled around, I would simply change the date, claiming the other's mistake if challenged on the point. It wasn't the getting older I minded; I simply didn't want the attention. More precisely, I didn't want to be forced to receive attention graciously. An emotion with more than one component, no doubt, but in large part it was a function of my desire to stay angry. I did not merely defend people accused of crimes, but believed in—cared about—defending people accused of crimes. And the part of me that believed in being a criminal lawyer believed as well that my passion about it, my wrath— about the way, and against whom, the criminal legal system was wielded—sustained me in the work. The words of C.L.R. James were tacked above my office desk: "A man who could get uncompromisingly angry is one of the most effective works of God."

It was only grudgingly, then, that I acceded to Janice's plans for a birthday dinner with four of our friends. We had been seeing each other for half a year, Janice and I; and the others were good friends. But that wasn't the point. In many ways, I could be completely myself with these friends. But regarding the burning place inside that required the most of me, they didn't have a clue. No matter my repeated assurances that it had nothing to do with them, people couldn't help being upset by deep anger; even at a distance, they were uncomfortable just being in sight of it. Well, that was okay with me. I could understand that. It was all right with me if they didn't stick around . . . .

Knowing this birthday dinner would be waiting for me did not make my day go any more smoothly. And this was a day that would have tested far sunnier souls than mine. Over the weekend, the young cousin codefendant of one of my clients had been gunned down by a rival Chinatown gang. I had begun the morning in court requesting a postponement of my client's imminent trial because the murder had made it impossible, for the time being, to locate and speak with witnesses. I further argued for a continuance because my client now could not help prepare his own defense: he feared for his life, and for his younger brother who had nearly been hit by the same gunfire that had killed the cousin and who had now gone into hiding. The presiding judge—known around the courthouse as the Snake—had not only denied the continuance but had announced that since the defendant's ability to prepare for trial was now in jeopardy, the judge knew a place where he would have no more distractions. Without further ado, the Snake had ordered bail revoked and my client immediately taken into custody. And just to rub it in, the Snake had stated for the record that it had been *my* comments that had raised the possibility of the defendant fleeing the jurisdiction, thereby justifying the bail revocation. I had tried to control what I said to the Snake, so as not also to get thrown in jail, then did my best to commiserate with my client, who had been yanked into the courtroom holding cell. I spent the rest of the morning putting together emergency appeal papers for a higher court to postpone the trial and to release my client.

In the afternoon, I had to switch cases, to the third day of a pre-liminary hearing—the trial-like examination of witnesses upon which a judge decides if there is enough evidence to make a felony defendant stand trial. This particular case involved a massive baton-wielding police charge into a Latino community center where a Saturday night fiesta had gone on beyond its dance permit curfew time. The police tactics had provoked an angry response from many of those present, which in turn had led the cops to reply to the "increasingly hostile atmosphere" with "preventive measures" (read: preemptive baton strikes). The resulting brawl had left four dance patrons with split heads, one with a baton-broken hand, at least three others treated for injuries from being trampled on, plus one cop with a bruise where a fist had struck the base of his helmet, just above his armored vest. It had also resulted in the arrest of four young men: two of the four split heads, the broken hand, and one of the trampled bodies. They were each charged with assaulting a police officer and, as always, resisting arrest.

I was handling the case alongside my old friend and fellow defense attorney, Mario, who each long day of the hearing fought through excruciating pain, refusing to take his medication for a degenerative back condition because he feared the drug would dull his cross-examining skills. Mario's sea of pain never swamped his marvelous capacity for inventiveness, however. To "assist" the police officer witnesses in illuminating their versions of the events, Mario and I had made a diagram of the community hall. During the first officer's testimony, we had him indicate his path of move-ment by marking on the diagram with a brightly-colored felt pen. And at each point where he indicated some moment of conse-quence, we had him mark with his initials his position and that of a defendant, or of anyone else—invariably a "UHM" (unknown Hispanic male)—supposedly involved.

After the first of these markings, Mario rose painfully and sham-bled over to the diagram. To keep the officer's position separate from those of the UHMs, Mario said, it would help to indicate more clearly the spot where the officer had been. Mario then pulled from an envelope an inch-high cut-out picture of a cop, waved it at us all as if he were a low-rent magician showing a playing card, and with a piece of tape on the back, stuck the mini-photo over the cop's initials on the diagram. Never looking up, Mario moved gingerly back to his seat. Although I didn't know what Mario was up to, I quickly resumed my cross-examination before the D.A. or judge could think of some reason to complain.

I now had the cop mark another sequence on the diagram, and as the officer returned to the witness box, Mario again rose and, as if it were a long-accepted part of the proceedings, attached to the spot another of the tiny cut-out policemen. The mini-pictures seemed generic and innocent enough, and to move past a moment's hesitation, I asked the cop another question.

A second officer took the stand and was asked to mark the diagram with a different color pen. As this officer made his marks, Mario handed me the envelope of tiny policeman cut-outs, and I attached one to each newly marked spot. Close up, I now noticed that the cut-out seemed to be from a grainy photo of yore. But it wasn't until a break in the proceedings that Mario admitted to me, with a little smile through pain-clenched teeth, that indeed the picture was not of a local cop but of an *Ausländerpolizei*—a 1930s German "foreigner police."

The hearing was now in its third day—the Friday afternoon of my birthday. The first two days' witnesses had described our clients as having been among the many fiesta-goers who had loudly objected to the police raid, but they had failed to identify any of the defendants as having actually delivered a blow to any police officer. Mario and I had quietly led the cops through their inconclusive testimony without so much as hinting at this essential weakness in the prosecution's case. But with the final witness—the officer "in charge" that night and on whose written report the D.A.'s office had based its accusations—Mario and I hammered away at the complete dearth of evidence that any of our clients had assaulted anyone. The charges against these accused depended solely on circumstantial evidence of their movements and positions before and after officers had supposedly been struck, Mario and I argued. And they had been arrested only because they had been so brazen in their complaints about the police invasion. Turning finally to the diagram, Mario demanded that the commanding officer point to one spot, any spot, where he could testify that any defendant had struck a cop that night.

By this time, of course, the diagram resembled some sort of abstract expressionist collage: scores of criss-crossing multicolored lines blotted by hordes of identical tiny (German) policemen. The maze of lines and cut-out pictures made it virtually impossible for this witness to find his way in the diagram. And the cumulative impression of the cut-outs—particularly absent any pictures of non-police—was of nothing so much as an occupying army, which supported our contention that it had been the overweening police invasion of a peaceful community hall that had caused the brawl in the first place. When the prosecutor complained that the diagram was a muddle, I reminded the judge that it was the officers, not the defendants, who had drawn the lines and marked the spots.

After discrediting the police report and pointing again and again to the hopeless mess of the diagram, Mario and I managed to force even our crusty curmudgeon of a judge to concede, unhappily, that there was insufficient evidence to send these defendants to trial for assault. *But* . . . time stopped for our clients, Mario, and me . . . the judge contended that the evidence *did* show a criminal conspiracy to obstruct the police in the lawful exercise of their duty. And if the prosecutor chose now to ask the court's permission to add such a conspiracy charge, the judge would grant it. Despite having lost his enthusiasm for the case, the prosecutor immediately obliged. So, instead of having their case thrown out, our clients suddenly found themselves ordered to return to court in a week for the setting of a felony conspiracy trial.

I watched Mario's tortured face of pain disappear into a cab, then spent a half-hour with our young clients trying to suppress my own rage sufficiently to convey some sense of hope about their fate in this crudely loaded legal system, despite what they had just seen of overwhelming empirical evidence to the contrary. Then I went to the jail to pay a quick visit to my client from the Chinatown case, to make sure he knew he hadn't been abandoned. By the time I left the jail, I was running very late. And I still had to go back to my office before going home to change clothes and then crossing the bridge to get to the birthday dinner Janice had arranged at our friend's place. It was pitch dark now and pouring rain, the streets awash and traffic barely moving. It took me almost thirty minutes to get back to my office, a trip that usually took ten.

The birthday dinner was for seven o'clock and it was already quarter to, so before making work calls that could not wait, I phoned Janice to tell her I'd be late. No answer. I phoned my friend's, where the dinner would be. Busy. So, I began making my other calls: to the mother of that morning's client, to explain why her son hadn't made it home from court; to the client's little brother in hiding; to several witnesses, hoping they'd still come out to testify. By the time I hung up from the sixth or seventh attempt that day to explain the grotesquely covinous workings of the criminal legal system, I was seething. And later still for dinner.

I called my friend's house but again got a busy signal, slammed down the phone, and decided to skip going home to change: they would just have to take me in my courthouse garb, unwashed and unalloyed. I threw together the appeal papers I would need to work on all weekend, got the friend's busy signal one more time, and dove out into the rain.

As a traveling companion had once said, staring across the vast blue Montana sky at a gathering storm a hundred miles away, "Weather is large." Well, the weather this night was huge: streets flooded, bridges snarled, cars barely crawling in any direction. Though normally this hour would see only the latest of rush hour traffic, on this night the earliest, middle, and latest were all still crushed together—windows fogging, motors and tempers steaming—on the nearly impassable streets.

After half an hour and only six blocks, I decided to give it up, return to my office, call in my apologies, and skip the whole damn dinner. I soon discovered, however, that moving back was impossible, turning was impossible, just seeing out the window was impossible. The whole fucking day was impossible. I fumed and ranted at the rain and at the clock, at my overheating engine and my overbearing friends. By the time I reached my friend's house, that beast within me—the one I daily summoned to fight the ever-uphill battles—had by now raged far too long out of control and had devoured completely all my mechanisms of restraint. What's more, I was two hours late.

Setting my jaw, I climbed the stairs. Janice opened the door—likely no one else was up to the task of greeting me.

"The rain. The bridge," I growled. "Unbelievable."

"We figured that was it. We heard on the radio." Janice's face was drawn tight, but I did not look closely enough to see whether it was more angry or worried.

"Hey, I tried to call . . . . You weren't home." I went to the living room, Janice trailing behind. My friends had waited dinner for me but were on their third bottle of wine.

"Sorry. I'm sorry." I stopped and spoke from just inside the door, as if the quality of my friends' reply would determine whether I'd come any closer. For a moment no one spoke, and I realized that the force of my seething was holding their responses at bay. I went in and sat down. "Damn, I could use some of that." I poured myself a glass of wine.

"Really that bad out there?" my friend Rick said.

"What do you mean, 'really'?"

"What do I mean?" Rick replied, puzzled.

I saw that Janice had moved over behind the others and remained standing.

"Well, you asked whether it was 'really' that bad? Does that mean it 'really' might not have been?"

"It doesn't mean anything."

"Well, you're the one who said it."

"Listen, no offense. It was just a word. All right?"

"Yeah, yeah. Sorry, just . . . what a nightmare." I took a gulp of wine, leaned back, and blew out some air. Janice sat down across from me.

"We have that great baked garlic," she said unconvincingly. "It'll take awhile, though. We didn't know when to put it in."

"I said I called you. And you weren't home."

"No, I was here. Cooking the dinner. Remember?"

"Well, I called here, too. But the phone was busy."

"Okay."

"Six. Six-thirty. Seven. I could never get through."

"All right."

"Come on," Rick's wife, Leticia, said. "It's your birthday, right?"

"Yeah, had most of the day off." I gulped some wine and tried to smile. "Didn't stay at the office much past seven."

"A-hah," my old college friend, Brian, joked, looking at his watch. "Late getting on the road, then. Bit of an admission there, eh?"

"Admission?" I snapped. "What?"

"No, well . . . ." Brian backtracked, still with good humor.

"That's not an admission." I leaned forward.

"I didn't mean . . . ."

"An admission is a statement against a defendant's interest."

"Listen . . . ."

"So, point one: I didn't know I was a defendant here . . . ."

"You're not . . ."

"And point two: How is it that busting my ass for my clients is against my interest?"

"I only . . . ."

"Against this dinner's interests, maybe," I looked around the room. "But not *mine*."

"Look," Janice said. "The dinner is for you. And we've been sitting here for two hours waiting, not knowing when you were coming, whether you were coming at all. We didn't know where you were and we didn't hear from you. It so happens we were worried. *Mea* bloody *culpa*."

"Yeah, well, first of all, I didn't need a birthday party right now, did I? And I told you so . . . . And second, I *did* call, when I could. But someone was on the line, weren't they? And I had other things to do, you know, besides checking in here. . . . And third, what kept you from calling *me*?"

"We did call. But you weren't home and you weren't picking up the office line, so all we got was the answering service."

"You know I don't pick up the office line after hours, or I'd never get out of there, would I? But there *is* another line, isn't there?"

"Ah. The hallowed 'inside line'?"

"Yeah, that's right, the inside line. A number you have, if I'm not mistaken."

"Look, Joseph, you've told me . . . ."

"Wait. First things first: Do you have the inside number or don't you?"

"Yes, of course I have the number, but you've made it very clear . . . ."

"And did you try calling that number?"

"Look . . . ."

"Did you try the number or didn't you?"

"No, I didn't try the number, and you know . . . ."

"So, you were all so worried about me, and you had a way of getting in touch, but you chose not to, right?"

"You told me the inside line is for when people have been busted, trials, emergencies. And I happen to know what you're like when you've been in court all day."

"But you were the one who chose not to use it, right?"

"Joseph, don't . . . ."

"Right. And did I ever tell you not to use it in an emergency?"

"Joseph . . . ."

"Well, did I ever tell you not to use it?"

"Please . . . ."

"And did I ever tell you what constituted an emergency?"

"Stop it, please . . . ."

"No, I didn't, did I. So you decided for yourself whether you wanted to call, didn't you? Whether you *really* wanted to call?"

"Joseph, stop . . . ."

"You sit here and accuse me, but all you had to do was pick up the phone, didn't you?"

"Stop it!"

"So, did you or didn't you?"

"Stop, Joseph . . .!"
"Answer the question . . . ."
"Stop! . . . ."
". . . did you or didn't you!"
". . . for godssake, stop!"

Acknowledgments

My great appreciation goes out to several courtroom lawyers, not only for their conversations with me about themes in this work but for their example as the best of what trial lawyers can be—dedicated, compassionate, imaginative, thoughtful, persevering: Juliana Drous, Richard Duane, Paul Harris, Richard Hodge, Joel Kirshenbaum, Meriel Lindley, and the late Stuart Buckley.

A number of friends and colleagues were generous with their time and extremely helpful with their comments on earlier versions of pieces that appear here. For their critically supportive and supportively critical remarks, I am most grateful to Iain Boal, Robbie Butler, Tim Clark, Tony Dubovsky, Tom Farber, Bill Goodman, Stephen Kessler, and Rita Rosenkranz.

Thanks, too, go to Chelsea Vaughn for the insight, care, and respect with which she edited this book, and for the grace with which she moved us both through the process.

And finally, special thanks to Maria Teeuw, Kiek Bak, Sameer Mehendale, and Jolle Demmers, who kept me humored, fed, and mostly sane while I worked on the early drafts of these pieces in an attic in Amsterdam. And, of course, to Sanjyot, who has both put up with and encouraged it all.

About the Author

Born in Boston and educated in California, Joseph Matthews graduated in 1971 from Boalt Hall, the law school of the University of California at Berkeley. He practiced criminal defense and civil litigation in San Francisco and environs, and has taught at the University of California, Berkeley. He is the author of four books for Nolo Press and the novel *Shades of Resistance* (Creative Arts/Headlands).